ORDINARY ABORTION

# ORDINARY ABORTION

## Reproductive Choice in Twenty-First-Century Women's Writing

Mary Thompson

THE OHIO STATE UNIVERSITY PRESS
COLUMBUS

Library of Congress Cataloging-in-Publication Data Names: Thompson, Mary (Women's literature specialist), author.

Title: Ordinary abortion : reproductive choice in twenty-first-century women's writing / Mary Thompson.

Description: Columbus : The Ohio State University Press, [2026] | Includes bibliographical references and index. | Summary: "Analyzes abortion as an undramatic feature of everyday life in the literature of the Roe v. Wade era, contrary to public discourse. Writers under discussion include Sharon Olds, Cheryl Strayed, Jennifer Haigh, Lois-Ann Yamanaka, Joyce Carol Oates, Ayelet Waldman, Terry Tempest Williams, Alison Bechdel, and Celeste Ng, among others"—Provided by publisher.

Identifiers: LCCN 2026011423 | ISBN 9780814216170 (hardback) | ISBN 081421617X (hardback) | ISBN 9780814284971 (ebook) | ISBN 0814284973 (ebook)

Subjects: LCSH: Abortion—United States—21st century. | Abortion—Social aspects—United States. | Abortion in literature. | Reproductive rights—United States—21st century.

Classification: LCC HQ767.5.U5 T58 2026

LC record available at https://lccn.loc.gov/2026011423

Other identifiers: ISBN 9780814259870 (paperback) | ISBN 0814259871 (paperback)

Cover design by Susan Zucker
Text design by Juliet Williams
Type set in Adobe Minion Pro

∞ The paper used in this publication meets the minimum requirements of the American National Standard for Information Sciences—Permanence of Paper for Printed Library Materials. ANSI Z39.48-1992.

# CONTENTS

INTRODUCTION

# The Epistemology of Abortion

A common feature of most defenses of abortion is a call for more narratives about ending a pregnancy to combat the silencing power of stigma, misinformation, and stereotypes (Joffe, *Dispatches*; *Shout*; Watson). The argument in this book is that while more narratives are needed, twenty-first-century women's writing is infused with an epistemology of abortion and that by changing how we read, we can better appreciate its ordinary appearance in literature. *Ordinary Abortion* considers the undramatic reality of abortion in the US and how it has shaped the cultural imaginary and, specifically, twenty-first-century women's writing. This book contends that many twenty-first-century texts by women depict abortion thematically as a commonplace decision that is ordinarily entwined with health, education, career, sexuality, family-making, relationships, and motherhood. In addition to thematic portrayals, this book also examines how legalized abortion has influenced the rhetoric, periodization, settings, and genres of literary expression. It attends to how ideas about abortion circulate to shape literature and how literature in turn has repro-political designs on audiences. It reveals that much of twenty-first-century American women's writing is aligned with Katha Pollitt's belief in *Pro: Reclaiming Abortion Rights*: "We need to talk about ending a pregnancy as a common, even normal, event in the reproductive lives of women" (15).

*Dobbs v. Jackson Women's Health Organization*, the 2022 Supreme Court decision that ended constitutional protection for abortion, undeniably redramatized abortion access for Americans. This book does not dispute that abortion access was and continues to be politicized, stigmatized, and dramatized in public debates and many cultural productions. The decision to terminate a pregnancy is dramatized, for example, in many twenty-first-century films, such as *Juno* (2007), *Revolutionary Road* (2008), *Obvious Child* (2014), and *Grandma* (2015). The drama of deciding to have an abortion is present in some of the twenty-first-century texts discussed in *Ordinary Abortion,* but greater attention is given in this work to portrayals that do not make a termination the central narrative conflict or poetic situation. Instead, this study considers the influence that legalized abortion access has had across several registers of the American cultural imaginary. An alternative title for this project was *Abortion Is Ordinary,* a direct reference to Raymond Williams's "Culture Is Ordinary," which called for studying culture not only through elite forms but also by examining the everyday circulation of values, beliefs, and practices across all social registers. In response to Williams's call, this book argues that abortion is better understood by looking not only at policy debates but also at the commonplace and nuanced ways that mainstream literature reflects the effects of almost five decades of legalized access. This study understands abortion to be *ordinary* in at least four ways: the frequency of occurrences, the breadth of national support, the professionalization of abortion services and advocacy, and the emergence of a vernacular rhetoric arising from an epistemology of abortion.

One way of thinking about abortion as ordinary is to acknowledge its frequency in American life. In her excellent book, *Scarlet A: The Ethics, Law, and Politics of Ordinary Abortion,* Katie Watson describes a "prevalence paradox" in the US, in which abortion "is both common and clandestine" (19). Since 1973, over thirty million American women have had abortions, while one in five American pregnancies is terminated (17). Watson's observation is confirmed by the Guttmacher Institute, the leading research and policy organization committed to advancing sexual and reproductive health and rights in the US and globally, which reports that despite decreasing rates of unplanned pregnancy and birth rates overall, over one million abortions were provided in 2024, and one in four US women will have abortions before the age of forty-five ("Abortion in the United States"). The frequency of abortion is linked to the CDC-reported fact that just over 40 percent of US pregnancies are unplanned (a rate that is falling) ("Updated" 15), of which 34 percent are terminated according to a Guttmacher factsheet ("Unintended Pregnancy and Abortion"). Watson notes how despite this frequency, *ordinary* abortion is rendered "clandestine" by both sides of the abortion policy debate (pro-life and pro-choice) who draw on emotional stories about *extraordinary* cases:

> Ordinary abortion is the 74% of women ending pregnancies who say having a baby would dramatically change their life, interfering with work, school, or their ability to care for dependents; the 48% who say they don't want to

> be a single parent or they are having problems with their husband or partner; the 73% who say they cannot afford another child. (20)

My point in identifying abortion as ordinary is not to diminish the (sometimes dramatic) importance of an individual exercising control over reproduction. Nor is my intention to diminish how individuals struggle extraordinarily to access abortion, while advocates scramble to assist them, and other professionals labor to navigate the legal, medical, and ethical chaos brought about by *Dobbs*. My point is that abortion is integral to ordinary, everyday women's healthcare, a fact that is made evident by *Dobbs*'s disruption to the fabric of American life.

In addition to frequency, the safety of abortion is another way in which it plays an ordinary role in US women's lives. Diana Greene Foster's groundbreaking work in *The Turnaway Study* reveals the overwhelmingly safe and positive outcomes of abortion, disproving decades of antiabortion claims to the contrary. Citing available CDC data, she challenges the mistaken belief that abortion poses extraordinary threats to women's health compared to the "natural" act of childbearing by noting that only 1 in 160,000 women dies from abortion compared to 1 in 11,300 from childbirth: "A woman in the United States is 14 times more likely to die from carrying a pregnancy to term than from having an abortion" (142). For her study on abortion patients' mental health, which took place over two years in more than thirty clinics in twenty-one different states, Foster interviewed women with unwanted pregnancies who were either able to obtain abortions or turned away due to gestational limits. The study determined conclusively that abortion does not hurt women, and that there are "many ways in which women were hurt by carrying an unwanted pregnancy" (21). Jessica Valenti, the author of a long-running newsletter that tracks developments in abortion-providing as well as antiabortion policy, similarly affirms that Americans ordinarily benefit from safe, legal abortion. Contrary to antiabortion messages claiming abortion poses an insurmountable loss to individual women, Valenti contends that legalizing abortion not only beneficially acknowledges women's humanity, but it also advances their well-being by "creating lives": "Abortion is often framed as the end of something—even prochoicers say someone 'terminated' or 'ended' a pregnancy. But often it's very much the opposite. For many, abortion has been the start of something" (4). Valenti also confirms the widely researched and established safety of abortion medications, which have been maligned recently by antiabortion groups: "American women have been using them to end pregnancies for decades, and credible studies find them safer than Tylenol or Viagra" (10).

Additionally, abortion is ordinarily supported by a majority of people in the US. Six out of ten Americans support legalized abortion access ("Public Opinion"). Valenti observes that "Voters have overwhelmingly supported abortion rights for decades, support that's only grown since *Roe* was overturned." She goes on to report, "Eighty-five percent of voters say abortion should be legal in some or all circumstances, more than 70 percent want abortion medication to be legal, and over 80 percent believe abortion should be unregulated by law, that it should be a decision solely between patient and doctor" (16–17). Further evidence of widespread support for abortion can be seen in the millions of Americans who marched in its support at coalitional events like the 2004 March for Women's Lives and 2017 Women's March on Washington and its sister marches across the country. Moreover, the 2022 midterm elections following the decision in *Dobbs,* for which a Republican sweep was predicted, instead produced only a minor loss in the House and a strengthening in the Senate for Democrats, an outcome that polling analysis attributes to support for abortion (Kann et al.). Presumably some of this support arises from the frequency of abortion: According to the Pew Research Center, "most Americans (59%) say they personally know someone who has had an abortion, such as a close friend or family member, or themselves" ("How"). The broad backing for abortion rights arises, Watson speculates, from what she identifies as a "web of abortion beneficiaries," those people who "didn't terminate a pregnancy themselves, but are glad someone else did" (26). This web also includes people who may never have a direct connection to abortion:

> All the unmarried and married couples who never had an accidental pregnancy, but have been able to enjoy their sex life because they weren't constantly afraid contraceptive failure would upend their lives, are beneficiaries. And some women and couples who become accidentally pregnant consider abortion before committing to parenthood, making their pregnancy experience and parenting relationship a product of their own affirmative choice rather than something the government forced on them. (27)

Watson admits that some people may lack awareness that a particular woman is in their life only because she had a safe termination, but her work reveals that most Americans only need to scratch the surface of our reproductive lives to see the beneficial impact of legalized abortion. While the web of beneficiaries illuminated by Watson's work is neglected in policy debates and under-researched by scholars, its presence helps explain the widespread support for abortion rights in the US.

**FIGURE 1.** Detail from *The Last Safe Abortion,* Bemiss Center for Contemporary Art, 2025. Used with permission from Carmen Winant.

An additional aspect to abortion's ordinariness is the number of Americans who work and serve in abortion-providing professionally. While this labor is seldom visible and often misrepresented in antiabortion rhetoric, many Americans volunteer or are employed as advocates, escorts, and medical providers at clinics. They work in abortion advocacy at organizations like Reproductive Freedom for All, the National Abortion Federation (NAF), SisterSong, and at national, state, and local abortion funds. Carmen Winant's photography, for example, is remarkable for highlighting this labor. *The Last Safe Abortion,* her large-scale installation of assembled photos of clinic workers, captures not just a sense of the number of people working in abortion-providing but also the ordinary labor taking place in these settings. Individual photos reflect the day-to-day business of clinic employees who perform office work, answer phones, clean procedure rooms and instruments, educate and advocate for patients, celebrate each other, and build community inside and outside of clinics. The assemblages of these photos provide a sense of the scale and scope of abortion-providing. Together the individual photos and assemblages serve to humanize and destigmatize abortion workers. Importantly, Winant's photography highlights clinic work as *work,* a kind of professional labor that, like abortion itself, is ordinary but clandestine (see figure 1).

As a result of the ordinary work of abortion-providing since 1973, an ordinary or vernacular rhetoric of abortion-providing has arisen. While the pro-choice and pro-life sides of the polarized policy debates have carved out their ideological territory through carefully deployed and policed language, the rhetoric on the ground that is used in clinics and by many supporters reflects an epistemology of abortion that borrows language and ideas from both camps. By *epistemology of abortion* I mean the intimate knowledge that is produced through having one, supporting someone who has one, benefitting from someone else having one, working as a provider, and/or working in defense of abortion. This knowledge has changed the vernacular rhetoric for defending abortion. *Abortion Under Attack: Women on the Challenges Facing Choice,* edited by Krista Jacob, is one of the first works to capture this shift to what Jacob calls "the new language of abortion" (13), which, in addition to supporting abortion rights, seeks to express and explore areas that are more difficult to convey in traditional pro-choice rhetoric. Some of these taboo feelings and topics include grief, remorse, loss of control, concern for the fetus, religion, and motherhood. As Jacob notes, the new language originates in and reflects evolutions in abortion praxis, such as when clinics provide patients with the opportunity to look at fetal tissue. Providers observe that during these moments, patients will refer to the fetus as "a baby," pray, grieve, and identify themselves as "mothers" (Joffe, *Dispatches*; Ludlow, "It's a Boy!" and "Love"; Schoen; Thompson, "Believing"). Abortion defenders contend that this vernacular rhetoric reclaims the fetus, grief, spirituality, and motherhood from antiabortion rhetoric (Jacob). The vernacular defense of abortion is another aspect of what is meant by *ordinary abortion* in this book.

It is literature's ability to depict the elements of ordinary abortion that interests me in this project. Countless scholarly articles and books from across a range of disciplines have scrutinized the topic of abortion in the *Roe v. Wade* era. Since 1973, feminist scholars and writers have analyzed the origins of the abortion debate (Ginsburg; Solinger, *Abortion Wars*), the history of abortion access and stigma (Joffe, *Dispatches*; Luker, *Abortion*; Solinger, *Pregnancy*), the history of abortion (Fissell; Reagan), body politics and abortion (Bordo), abortion law and policy (Petchesky; Ziegler, *Abortion*), the decision-making process (Gilligan), the fetus and its visual rhetoric (Balsamo; Hartouni; Hurst; Morgan and Michaels), depictions in popular culture ("Abortion Onscreen"; Boudreau and Maloy; Hess; Hurst; Melendez), the antiabortion movement (Saletan), and abortion care work (Hume; Rankin; Simonds)—to name just a few topics—while more recently, many authors have written against the *Dobbs* decision (Bell et al.; Fried and Ross; Littlejohn and Solinger; Valenti). Twenty-first-century literature about abortion demands our attention, I argue, because these depictions supplement the more dramatic narratives that are deployed in policy debates and provide a more complete and ordinary picture of abortion's role in the American cultural imaginary. This book responds to a need for the study of four areas in which literature contributes to the abortion picture: combatting stigma and misinformation by building a community through literature; the evolution of proabortion vernacular rhetoric; the emergence of new forms and genres; and the creation of a space for nuanced storytelling.

First, proabortion myths, stereotypes, and stigma, as Carole Joffe and others have shown, continue to affect women's access, while the everyday reality of abortion in women's lives remains distorted, poorly understood, and "clandestine." These myths include the beliefs that a majority of Americans oppose abortion; that it is a dangerous procedure posing threats to women's reproductive and mental health; that providers are motivated by profit and are indifferent to their patients' well-being; and that women who have abortions are careless, antifamily, child-hating, and lacking religious beliefs (Diaz et al.). These myths prevent American culture from openly acknowledging how ordinary abortion is. This book explores how the epistemology of abortion in twenty-first-century writing by women debunks stereotypes and stigma, offers compassion for patients and providers, and importantly builds a community of compassion and support for abortion.

"Books make communities" (17) Sara Ahmed writes in *Living a Feminist Life,* in which she describes feminist praxis as one that includes being surrounded by literature. Books have the power to share experience, to inform readers, and to challenge misconceptions, and they also, Ahmed points out, combat the isolating experience of living with and resisting oppression. Such "companion texts," Ahmed reminds readers, provide the encouragement "to travel on a path less trodden" (16). In terms of frequency, abortion could be described as a well-trodden path but one whose defense is complicated by myths and misinformation sustained by dominant power structures, and so defending abortion requires a community. Thus, reading and writing about abortion is community-building; it is, as Ahmed notes, "how we pick each other up" (1).

Literature about abortion can educate readers who lack direct and indirect experience (or believe they do) and thereby effect social change. In *The Palgrave Handbook of Reproductive Justice and Literature,* Beth Widmaier Capo and Laura Lazzari suggest that by unmuting stories about abortion, literature "allows a space for reflection" and a "space for previously unheard voices" (5). Literature, they contend, impacts all readers—not just those who have had abortions—by serving as a corrective to myths: "Fiction and film can create counter-narratives to dominant narratives and place these stories in the imagination, enabling recognition and engagement" (6). It exposes readers "to conflicts and issues they do not have first-hand experience with, creating empathy" (5), and can "aid in understanding current events" (6). Rachel Hurst similarly observes in *Representing Abortion* that abortion narrative is a site of political struggle to (re)tell the story of abortion, to debunk and discredit antiabortion misinformation and stigma (3). Knowing someone who has had an abortion increases one's support of abortion access (Swernoff), and by providing this knowledge by proxy, literature is a corrective to antiabortion mythology.

Literature also builds community for people who feel isolated by the experiences of having, providing, and defending abortion. Capo and Lazzari assert that literature can "engage with social debates and shape cultural attitudes" (6), not only through reeducating but also by uplifting readers who have had abortions and empowering them to speak. In *Choice Words: Writers on Abortion,* an excellent collection of literary representations of abortion spanning genres, editor Annie Finch recounts having an abortion years ago and looking for literature to navigate her experience only to discover that depictions of ending a pregnancy had never been collected. This lacunae inspired her volume. The need to process the experience and reach others despite taboos and years of silence is evident in abortion testimonies like Annie Ernaux's *Happening,* Honor Moore's *A Termination,* and Irene Vilar's *Impossible Motherhood: Testimony of an Abortion Addict.* When these stories are told, an embodied community is created: "To share a memory is to put a body into words" (Ahmed 23). Furthermore, literature allows activists to voice personal and collective rage at antiabortion policies. In the introduction to *Fighting Mad: Resisting the End of "Roe v. Wade,"* Rickie Solinger explains how this edited work—a timely and impressive collection of writings by activists and scholars responding to the post-*Dobbs* landscape—provided an outlet for herself and her coeditor, Krystale Littlejohn, noting that assembling the volume "felt like both a service to readers and a therapeutic respite for ourselves" (Littlejohn and Solinger 6). A proabortion community is built through the stories that are told by writers.

Secondly, there is a need to study the literature of abortion because, as noted earlier, a "new language" has arisen during the five decades of legalized access. Vilar's exploration of the metaphor of addiction mentioned above in *Impossible Motherhood,* for example, reveals an author reaching for vernacular language and metaphors for understanding her experience of having repeat abortions (Thompson, "Impossible Motherhood"). Sometimes the search for new language is a struggle against taboos that were put in place by both antiabortion and pro-choice camps. Pro-choice advocates in the twentieth century, for example, resisted calling the fetus a baby out of concern that this bestowed it and the pregnant woman with equal value. *Baby* is commonly used by patients in clinics, however, to the point that providers have stopped trying to correct them (Joffe, "Politicization"). Additionally, some pro-choice advocates avoided identifying abortion as a mothering decision to resist the way that women are reduced to the maternal role in antiabortion rhetoric specifically and society normatively. Providers, however, recognize that six out of ten women having abortions are already mothers ("Induced Abortion"), an identity that strongly informs how they make decisions about unplanned pregnancies and that is reflected in their language. The language of both antiabortion and pro-choice positions is appropriated, revised, and rejected within the dynamic epistemology of abortion. Literature, I argue, captures this subversive, vernacular rhetoric.

An example of how literature can incubate a proabortion rhetoric that is different from the pro-choice rhetoric of policy debates is a trope that I name *the aborted woman.* Not to be confused with the antiabortion idea of aborted mothers (women who allegedly lost out on motherhood by having an abortion), this figure is the counterfactual woman who might have existed had she not had children. This figure appears in vernacular arguments and scholarship anytime someone wonders about a mother's possible alternative life as a nonmother (Doan and Erlich; O'Reilly, "Out of Bounds"; Tierce). It presents a disquieting challenge to the taboo on expressing maternal regret, but this figure is invoked to counter antiabortion assertions of fetal primacy. Antiabortion arguments, for example, sometimes contend that aborted fetuses are future Einsteins and Beethovens. The aborted woman asks instead, What if a future genius is lost to coerced childbearing? To be clear, this figure is a just trope: No one identifies as an aborted woman (although increasingly it is possible to discuss maternal regret). The emergence of this rhetorical figure suggests that rhetoric evolves over time and across different registers of culture, all of which is reflected in literature.

A third reason for exploring twenty-first-century literature is to expand what is meant by *abortion literature* and the forms that have been relied on to illustrate it. When defining this genre, a good place to start is with narratives about terminating an unplanned pregnancy, but only considering this plot structure forecloses an appreciation of how pervasive the influence of legalized abortion has been on literary expression. Depictions of abortion are not limited to plot. In fact, women's writing reflects how periodization, setting, and genre have been influenced. For example, the year 1973 (when *Roe v. Wade* was enacted) serves as an important temporal reference point in nonfiction biography and autobiography by women. Biographical accounts of women who may never have had an abortion nevertheless reference 1973 to identify as being part of the "web of beneficiaries." They recount enjoying heterosexual sex and the opportunity to plan families alongside educations and careers with confidence that their plans will not be disrupted by childbearing. In addition to temporal settings, the physical setting of the abortion clinic—as a space of liberation, violence, and work—has appeared in twenty-first-century thrillers. Genre conventions also have been impacted by almost fifty years of legalized abortion. Not only has the genre of the thriller adapted to depict antiabortion violence, but the pronatalist, confessional genre of the mommy memoir has provided an unexpected space for depicting abortion alongside accounts of in vitro fertilization (IVF) and fetal genetic testing. Finally, the paratopia, a new type of dystopian fiction that is set in the near present rather than the distant future, has emerged as a vehicle for representing threats to abortion and reproductive freedom generally.

Expanding the genre of abortion literature contributes to the defense of abortion by including the stories of providers and "beneficiaries." Testimonies about having an abortion are vital to its defense, but they should not and cannot be the only form. In the past, the strategy of having large numbers of women testify about their abortions has been effective in moving abortion out of the shadows. The "Manifesto of the 343 Sluts" in *Le Nouvel Observateur* in 1971 (de Beauvoir), and an issue of *Ms.* in 1972 (*Ms.* editors), for example, in which prominent women identified as having had abortions, were models for challenging stigma and defending reproductive freedom. However, expecting abortion patients alone to defend abortion exploits people whose situations may already be precarious. As a result, the alternative to the personal stories of patients has been the testimony of providers, but this also has limitations. Watson observes that providers are uniquely positioned to witness the reasons for needing pregnancy terminations, but when they become the storytellers, "we ask those who provide something millions of women and families want and need to also shoulder most of the burden of its defense" (6). Moreover, providers are no more likely than patients to publicly discuss abortion due to the stigmatization of being labeled "dangerous, deviant, or illegitimate" (74). Expanding the definition of abortion literature beyond testimony and plot to include other literary forms and stylistic elements removes the expectation that patients and providers do the heavy lifting of defending abortion through their testimony. Defending abortion is everyone's job, and this task begins by recognizing its ordinary presence in our lives, which becomes possible in literature when focus is shifted away from plot and onto other elements.

Finally, an appreciation for the aesthetical nuance of stories about ordinary abortions is a fourth reason motivating this book's study of twenty-first-century literature. Numerous scholars and activists have made the call to defend abortion by telling more subtle stories (Capo and Lazzari; Foster; Joffe, *Dispatches*; Watson) that counterbalance the abundance of extraordinary stories circulating in polarized policy debates. In *Representing Abortion,* Rachel Hurst praises literature for its ability "to tease out the excess meaning in dominant representations, to resist dominant understandings of abortion that intend to be totalising, and, through this work, to inspire more complex conversations about abortion as an experience and as a central element of healthcare" (3). In *Choice Words,* Annie Finch similarly highlights the complexity of literary representation, noting that abortion, as "a physical, psychological, moral, spiritual, political, and cultural reality that navigates questions of life and death, . . . should be one of the great themes of literature" (1). Literature should and can reflect all aspects of human experience, including ending a pregnancy, and these accounts can be beautiful. The aesthetic appreciation of literary expression is enhanced by considering the nuances of abortion's representations, something that has been eclipsed by a focus on the politics of abortion.

While the political importance of this literature cannot be understated, the defense of abortion depends on nuanced stories about reproductive politics and family-making that account for intersecting systems of oppression and critiques of neoliberal biopolitics. The defense of abortion is strengthened, for example, when defenders recognize the shortcomings of *Roe v. Wade* rather than getting mired in mourning its loss. *Roe v. Wade* never fully protected the reproductive freedom of all women, as was demonstrated by the passage of the Hyde Amendment (1976), which prevents federal funding for abortion and thereby blocks access for women on Medicaid. In contemporary accounts, *Dobbs* is often described as a shocking reversal of women's reproductive freedoms ("Dobbs Got It Wrong"), as if prior to the decision, reproductive equity had been achieved for all women. For many poor communities and communities of color in the US, though, *Dobbs* reflects only a continuation of reproductive injustices that originate in histories of enslavement, colonialism, eugenics, and anti-immigration sentiment. A more nuanced, long view is reflected in how the Black activist-scholar Loretta Ross responds to the description of the post-*Dobbs* era as "these troubled times": "Which troubled times?" Ross asks, paraphrasing Dr. Willie Parker's observation: "It's at times like these we must remember it's always been times like these" (Ross et al. 12). The decision in *Dobbs* represents a renewed formal constraint on women's freedom, but from this perspective, it was hardly a surprise. In an interview about reproductive dystopian fiction, Native American author Louise Erdrich similarly observes:

"Indigenous people in the Americas are descended of relatives who survived the dystopia of genocide. To us, dystopia is recent history. (For many, it is the present.)" (Coleman). Erdrich and Ross offer reminders that defining reproductive freedom solely in terms of abortion access prevents a more nuanced, intersectional understanding of reproductive injustice. Literature, including Erdrich's dystopian *The Future Home of the Living God,* in which a pregnant Native American woman seeks to evade a government that asserts claims on her genetically unique baby—echoing the removal of Native children from their families—is capable of capturing nuanced legacies of inequality. Dolen Perkins-Valdez's historical novel *Take My Hand* similarly weaves the story of the African American Relf sisters, who were coercively sterilized in 1973, into a fictional narrative about an African American nurse who, protected by class privilege, is able to secure an abortion for herself, but who unwittingly participates in the eugenicist program that mistreats the sisters. Both novels contextualize reproductive choices within intersectional histories and systems of reproductive injustice that, when recognized, call for new strategies for achieving reproductive justice.

Novels like those by Erdrich and Perkins-Valdez reflect the nuanced tenets of the reproductive justice movement that Ross helped to found as a member of SisterSong, a multiethnic healthcare collective founded in 1997. The reproductive justice movement responded to what Ross and others termed the "dehumanizing status quo" of reproductive politics characterized by the pro-choice versus pro-life debate (Ross et al. 11). Reproductive justice theory, as Ross defines it, centers the needs of communities of color rather than the reproductive needs of white Americans and brings to bear race- and class-based historical perspectives to the analysis of childbearing, birth control/abortion, and mothering (Ross et al.; Ross and Solinger; Silliman et al.). These reproductive needs include the right to abortion but also the right to have children and to raise them in safety and with dignity (Ross et al.). At its core, reproductive justice theory exposes "stratified reproduction," the way that the reproductive and family-making decisions of some women (white, middle class) are socially valued and enabled by the state over the decisions of other women (young, poor, nonwhite, immigrant) whose family-making is devalued and discouraged.

In addition to reproductive injustice, twenty-first-century writings by women offer intricate critiques of the impact of neoliberalism on not just abortion but reproductive freedom generally. As an economic and political philosophy, neoliberalism fosters deregulation and the dismantling of social welfare nets, while emphasizing markets, personal responsibility, and self-reliance. As numerous feminist scholars have argued, American women are encouraged to identify themselves as beneficiaries of expanded choices, but they make their decisions about educations, careers, and family-making in the absence of affordable educations and healthcare, well-paying jobs and careers, and available child- and eldercare (Briggs; W. Brown, *Undoing*; Duggan; Fraser; McRobbie; Oaks; Roy and Thompson). The division of women into categories of good choice-makers and bad choice-makers (to borrow Rickie Solinger's terms in *Beggars and Choosers*) reflects their relative *responsibilization,* a process by which subjects assume self-responsibility for navigating the increasingly impossible demands of family-making and careers without programs and policies that offer protection and access to opportunities. Neoliberalism frames the choices of more privileged women as good choices that reflect proper responsibilization, while less privileged and underresourced women are condemned for their seeming inability to be self-reliant.

Many of the texts explored in *Ordinary Abortion* reflect the nuanced role of responsibilization and biopolitics, or the way that social power comes to bear in women's family-making and reproductive freedom. Several texts chafe at women's alleged "freedom to choose," instead pointing to how responsibilization requires women to make choices in the absence of the freedom not to choose. This dilemma arises visibly in texts that explore prenatal genetic testing and how the results compel women (as the ones to whom the responsibility falls) to make "free" choices about terminating or continuing pregnancies with anomalies. These writings expose what Rottenberg calls "neoliberal feminism." Unlike liberal feminism, which makes claims for equality based on shared humanity, neoliberal feminism, according to Rottenberg, aligns itself with the demands of market philosophy and the emphasis on individualism and self-reliance. Collective action, a hallmark of liberal feminism, is perceived by neoliberalism as anathema to the individual's success and survival, resulting in a disarticulation of women's solidarity. Many of the texts analyzed in *Ordinary Abortion* can be defined as proabortion, but their political identification with feminism is complicated by this disarticulation, while other texts provide new visions of solidarity and activism on behalf of reproductive rights.

Finally, literature by women in the twenty-first century reflects the nuanced relationship between abortion and mothers, mothering, and motherhood. As noted earlier, six out of ten women having abortions are mothers, a fact that is explored by Heather Jackson and Jessica Shaw in *Abortion and Mothering: Research, Stories, and Artistic Expressions.* In their introduction, the editors argue that abortion is a mothering decision as much for women who want to care for the children they already have as it is for women who are not prepared to be the mothers they intend to be. While much twenty-first-century literature still depicts abortion as a service sought by women who want to be child-free, others, such as Leila Mottley's novel, *The Girls Who Grew Big,* are beginning to tell this more common experience of maternal abortions after having children. The mommy memoir, a type of life-writing about motherhood, for example, is an unexpected space for accounts by women who have abortions before, during, and after having their other children.

Although its focus on twenty-first-century literature is timely, *Ordinary Abortion* is not unique in arguing for the importance of studying abortion and literature. Several scholarly monographs have traced a literary tradition of abortion in the twentieth century. According to Karen Weingarten in *Abortion in the American Imagination: Before Life and Choice, 1880–1940,* for example, literature of the modern era reveals the role that economic, eugenic, and immigration ideologies played in abortion rhetoric. Her analysis of abortion in modern cultural representations reveals a rhetoric that both created and reflected the division of women into groups of desirable and undesirable reproduction. The subsequent rhetoric of liberalism in the late twentieth century that defends abortion in terms of choice, individualism, and morality continues to obscure the state's persistent interest in regulating reproduction based on class, race, and immigration. Similarly, Heather Latimer's *Reproductive Acts: Sexual Politics in North American Fiction and Film* examines how cultural forms in the 1980s to the early 2000s were shaped by and helped to shape reproductive politics and were more nuanced than the stalemated pro-choice and pro-life debate. Similar to Weingarten's purpose, Latimer's project identifies literature's value as an alternative cultural space for thinking about abortion: "Fictional representations of reproduction offer a chance to examine reproductive politics outside the cyclical frames concerned with rights and choices" (5). Judith Wilt's *Abortion, Choice, and Contemporary Fiction: The Armageddon of the Maternal Instinct* focuses on abortion as a plot device in mid- to late twentieth-century fiction. Drawing on twentieth-century feminist critiques of essentialized mothers, mothering, and motherhood, Wilt contends that these depictions of abortion in literature worked to denaturalize motherhood, exposing it as a social construct. The works by Weingarten, Latimer, and Wilt are reminders of literature's role in cultural discourse.

Following in the footsteps of the work by Wilt, Latimer, and Weingarten, this study explores the literariness of twenty-first-century depictions of abortion. *Ordinary Abortion* combines feminist literary/cultural studies, the interdisciplinary academic field of motherhood studies, and the activist-academic theories of the reproductive justice movement. Drawing from the genres of US poetry, fiction (including novels, dystopias, and thrillers), and nonfiction (including bio-autographies and mommy memoirs), this book points to evolutions in literary representations of the biopolitics of abortion. *Ordinary Abortion* identifies new or renewed thematic takes on the relationships between abortion and motherhood and mother-loss, birth control, unplanned pregnancy, family-making, neoliberalism, stratified reproduction, masculinity, violence, care work, and disability. Rather than focusing on the plot of abortion narratives, *Ordinary Abortion* examines the sometimes unexpected appearance of abortion in twenty-first-century literature.

*Ordinary Abortion* is not an exhaustive survey of every reference to abortion in twenty-first-century texts, nor does it consider the antiabortion fiction and nonfiction that has emerged during the *Roe v. Wade* era—including polemics, activist memoirs, young adult novels, and romances. Antiabortion works contribute to the circulation of negative stigma and all-too-familiar stereotypes, which the works in this study seek to disrupt. This book is attentive to the need to defend abortion access using new strategies, and it examines the evolving literary devices and themes that normalize abortion and combat antiabortion myths. These strategies refute the primacy of the fetus, reveal the realities of clinical settings and the violence directed at them, and expose the injustices of stratified reproduction as well as the shortcomings of the rhetoric of choice.

A note about language in this book. The movement for transgender rights encourages the adoption of gender-neutral language, such as *pregnant people*, to erase a gender binary that obscures the pregnancies (and abortions) of trans men and nonbinary people. The most recent data from the Guttmacher Institute in 2021–2022 shows that gender nonbinary or transgender individuals constituted more than 1 percent of people having abortions last year ("As Many"). The language of women and mothers that is used in this book—rather than pregnant people—reflects how the texts refer to characters and speakers and how authors identify themselves. It is beyond the scope of my project to read the trans politics of these texts, but my work is concerned with challenging socially constructed gender norms and the biopolitics of policies that are enacted to reinforce gender roles. Many—but not all—of the texts I examine are heterocritical or queer in regard to how they depict heteronormative roles and family-making. They understand motherhood and gender to be socially maintained categories that support systems of oppression and that therefore should be challenged.

Additionally, *Ordinary Abortion* unapologetically uses the term *proabortion* rather than the term *pro-choice*. The critical approach to the texts in this project uses "choice" but also understands it to be an attenuated concept under neoliberalism. As discussed above, both the reproductive justice movement and critiques of neoliberal feminism have exposed the weakness of representing, let alone defending, abortion using the rhetoric of choice when it so easily conceals some women's lack of choices. In *No Choice: The Destruction of "Roe v. Wade" and the Fight to Protect a Fundamental American Right,* Becca Andrews, for example, has become the latest voice to call for reclaiming the word *abortion* for advocacy purposes. My project uses *antiabortion* rather than *pro-life* to describe those individuals and groups opposed to abortion access because the former term more accurately describes their position.

Chapter 1, "Flipping the Script and the Aborted Woman: Revisiting Johnson's 'Apostrophe, Animation, and Abortion,'" is a reexamination of Barbara Johnson's well-known essay in which she analyzes rhetorical strategies of address in twentieth-century women's lyric poetry. Johnson argues that rhetoric reflects regimes of gender, such that maternal lyric speakers apostrophizing unborn children cannot help but appear to affirm the antiabortion rhetoric of fetal primacy. While Johnson's essay, from *A World of Difference* (1988), does not consider what proabortion rhetoric might look like, this chapter examines how twenty-first-century women poets and writers engage in feminist strategies of flipping the script and using the rhetoric of uchronia to develop proabortion strategies to resist the primacy of the fetus. Drawing on and contributing to the epistemology of abortion that has evolved during the *Roe* era, the works examined in this chapter flip the antiabortion script that focuses on the fetus's potential and instead refocus on the lives of women, children, and families. Examining the poetry of Judith Arcana and Sharon Olds, this chapter considers alternative structures of address for depicting abortion before considering the rhetorical trope of the aborted woman as a counterfactual figure haunting the nonfiction writings of Diana Huet de Guerville and Merritt Tierce.

In chapter 2, "Women's Time in Feminist Bio-Autography: The Abortions Their Mothers Did Not Have," I build upon the trope of the aborted woman to examine the reproductive politics in three "bio-autographies," a term borrowed from Janet Beizer's work to describe life-writing that blends memoir and the biography of another figure: Cheryl Strayed's *Wild: From Lost to Found on the Pacific Crest Trail,* Terry Tempest Williams's *When Women Were Birds: Fifty-Four Meditations on Voice,* and Alison Bechdel's *Are You My Mother? A Comic Drama.* These three memoirs intertwine the reproductive stories of pre-*Roe* mothers and their post-*Roe* daughters across decades of feminist resistance to heteronormative patriarchy. Their texts establish the year 1973 as a temporal marker distinguishing the lives of white, middle-class mothers from the coming of age of their daughters, who each aspired to and achieved a life characterized by the pursuit of writing and art. Although not thematic, abortion provocatively occupies the structural center of these memoirs. The temptation to follow a simple story of generational progress is resisted, however, by the texts' refusal to adopt a pre-*Roe* versus post-*Roe* periodization of feminist advancement, privileging instead stories of women's agency across generations.

Chapter 3, "'How Can You Work There?': Violence and Care Work in Twenty-First-Century Abortion Clinic Thrillers," shows how twenty-first-century thrillers challenge the stigmatization of abortion providers by exposing violence against clinics, patients, and healthcare workers. To date, four abortion-providing doctors have been murdered in the US, and according to the National Abortion Federation, providers have suffered hundreds of threats, attempted murders, woundings, assaults, and kidnappings. Abortion clinics have been the sites of threats, acid attacks, invasions, bombings, and anthrax exposures and scares, while social media has provided another setting for the harassment of providers. While the social sciences have studied clinics (Joffe, *Dispatches*; Simonds; Rankin), literary scholarship has overlooked these sites as narrative settings, which this chapter seeks to correct by examining Elisabeth Hyde's *The Abortionist's Daughter,* Joyce Carol Oates's *A Book of American Martyrs,* Jodi Picoult's *A Spark of Light,* and Jennifer Haigh's *Mercy Street.* These twenty-first-century thrillers critique the violence of toxic masculinity (Kimmel; Miller-Idriss) and provide proabortion arguments through denaturalizing motherhood, humanizing abortion providers, and destigmatizing the clinic space. Through elements of literary realism, these novels depict providers' professionalism and concern for patients, the safety of abortion, and day-to-day clinic operations, as well as the resources and labor that go into countering antiabortion threats of violence.

Chapter 4, "Resisting Responsibilization: Abortion and Disability in Twenty-First-Century Mommy Memoirs and Fiction," considers how twenty-first-century narratives negotiate the biopolitics of abortion and disability. This chapter examines two memoirs and a novel that make calls for more nuanced reflection on the relationships between abortion and disability. Martha Beck's *Expecting Adam: A True Story of Birth, Rebirth, and Everyday Magic* and Ayelet Waldman's *Bad Mother: A Chronicle of Maternal Crimes, Minor Calamities, and Occasional Moments of Grace* are both mommy memoirs that rely on the warm, pronatalist approbation for this genre to authorize their potentially disruptive discussions of abortion. The mommy memoir, a twenty-first-century form of life-writing, conventionally recounts maternal experiences of conceiving, pregnancy, childbirth, and child-rearing. Unexpectedly, perhaps, the genre reveals the normal but undramatic role of abortion in many women's family-making histories. Rebecca Walker's mommy memoir, *Baby Love: Choosing Motherhood After a Lifetime of Ambivalence,* for example, acknowledges that discussing abortion has become a convention of these texts: "Oh, that it were possible to write about having a baby in America without writing about not having a baby" (99). Beck's and Waldman's texts introduce the dilemma of prenatal genetic testing and depict mothers who arrive at different decisions about how to proceed after receiving a diagnosis of fetal anomaly: Waldman has an abortion when an amniocentesis reveals that her fetus has a trisomy disorder, while Beck, after a similar discovery, decides to continue her pregnancy. For many decades, pro-choice rhetoric has drawn on disability as a justification for legalized abortion. In the twenty-first century, this defense has been challenged by disability rights groups (Hubbard; Jarman; Saxton; Weingarten, "It's"). These memoirs illustrate the need for a feminist disability rights discourse on abortion (Piepmeier; Weingarten, "It's"; Ziegler "Disability"). One response to this need may be found in Lois-Ann Yamanaka's *Father of the Four Passages*. Yamanaka's novel tells the story of Sonia and her autistic son, Sonny Boy, through her process of healing from childhood trauma and her previous abortions. Sonia gradually embraces her son's diagnosis after mourning her previous pregnancies and reclaiming her identity. Despite differences in genre, these texts reflect the tensions created at the discursive intersection of fetal testing, motherhood, selective abortion, disability, and feminism under the pressures of neoliberalism.

Chapter 5, "Choice Without Justice: Reproductive Dystopias, Neoliberal Feminism, and Stratified Reproduction," examines recent revisions to the popular dystopian form. Increasingly, twenty-first-century reproductive dystopias tell stories that are set in locations and times that are not distant. Instead they are what Leni Zumas, the author of *Red Clocks*, has called "paratopias," or stories that are set close to the near-present moment in recognizable worlds. In these settings, reproduction is constrained in familiar yet new ways, rendering the bodies of the powerless vulnerable to the reproductive needs of the elite. This chapter considers three recent paratopias that connect abortion, adoption, surrogacy, and IVF as related sites of reproductive injustice: Leni Zumas's *Red Clocks* (2018), Celeste Ng's *Little Fires Everywhere* (2017), and Joanne Ramos's *The Farm* (2019). The narrative structures of these novels adopt multiple, shifting narrative perspectives that not only build empathy for a diverse cast of female characters but also reveal how their glancing encounters have bearing on one another in a challenge to the disarticulation of women under neoliberalism. Each character is revealed in her social location of relative inequality and shows how her choices can depend upon another woman's choicelessness. The simultaneous isolation and connectedness of these characters exposes how neoliberal self-reliance makes collective organizing impossible even as it promises empowerment through a charade of free choice. In this way, these novels are able to expose stratified reproduction and the false promise of neoliberal feminism.

*Ordinary Abortion* argues for looking at alternatives to plot and dramatized abortion decision-making to define more broadly what might be considered abortion literature. A narrow focus on plots can serve to redramatize abortion. *Ordinary Abortion* argues that twenty-first-century women's writing often reflects less dramatic and more widespread normalization of abortion in the American cultural imaginary. Attending to the common, ordinary ways that abortion appears in twenty-first-century women's writing is at least as important to defending reproductive freedom as dramatic stories about extraordinary abortions.

CHAPTER 1

# Flipping the Script and the Aborted Woman

## Revisiting Johnson's "Apostrophe, Animation, and Abortion"

Barbara Johnson's "Apostrophe, Animation, and Abortion" in *A World of Difference* remains one of the best-known works of literary scholarship about abortion. In this chapter on lyric poetry, Johnson argues that women speakers who apostrophize the fetus invoke a rhetorical strategy of address that incidentally favors antiabortion politics. During the 1980s, when Johnson published her work, antiabortion rhetoric grew to dominate the cultural landscape, while proabortion rhetoric was largely reactionary.[1] In this chapter I argue that the rhetoric for defending abortion has evolved since the publication of Johnson's essay, a shift that has been produced by the epistemology of ordinary abortion—the knowledge garnered by patients, defenders, and providers over the decades since *Roe v. Wade*. As a result, twenty-first-century women writers draw on the rhetorical strategies of flipping the script and uchronia to reframe and resist fetal primacy. These strategies foreground the material present moment, normalize abortion decision-making, and refocus on the figures whom Katie Watson names "the web of abortion beneficiaries"

1. In this chapter, I will use the term *proabortion* rather than *pro-choice* to identify support for abortion rights. The term *proabortion* claims abortion as an essential part of healthcare, gender equality, and the protection of human rights. This term is a move away from the much-criticized call made by Hilary Clinton twenty-five years ago to keep abortion "safe, legal, and rare" (Flanagan; Sherman; Weitz), which critics labelled apologetic and weakly supportive of the human right to abortion. Similarly, this chapter forgoes *pro-choice* as a euphemism for abortion rights because I share the skepticism voiced by twenty-first-century advocates for reproductive justice, who challenge the ways that structures of power and privilege shape access to choices (Solinger, *Beggars*; Ross and Solinger). *Proabortion* more directly and unapologetically identifies abortion as a human right, not just a choice.

(27). This chapter examines the poetry of Judith Arcana and Sharon Olds as well as essays by Diana Huet de Guerville and Merritt Tierce to identify twenty-first-century strategies of address that reflect a rhetoric of ordinary abortion. The texts by these women writers minimize—while not erasing—the fetus's role in the discussion of abortion. In shifting attention from the anthropomorphized fetus, these writers invite readers to identify with the lives of pregnant people, women, and mothers.

In "Apostrophe, Animation, and Abortion," Johnson compares the apostrophizing of a deceased child in lyric poetry by men to poems about abortion by Gwendolyn Brooks, Lucille Clifton, and Adrienne Rich. She identifies how the speaker of Brooks's poem "The Mother," poignantly represents the uncertainty that abortion produces when the speaker struggles to identify her loss and her role in it. After the speaker observes that she has heard the "voices of my dim killed children," she shifts to address these children in a series of equivocations that, Johnson claims, animates them: "you are dead. / Or rather, or instead / You were never made." Johnson notes that if the speaker's status is unknowable in the poem (is she a mother if she did not give birth?), it is no more uncertain than the status of the fetus (was it a life or not?). She concludes that the speaker's "attempt to absolve herself of guilt depends on never forgetting, never breaking the ventriloquism of an apostrophe through which she cannot define her identity other than as the mother eaten alive by the children she has never fed. Who, in the final analysis, exists by addressing whom?" (192).

Johnson concludes: "It is clear that a great many poetic effects may be colored according to expectations articulated through the gender of the poetic speaker" (198). In these poems, maternal speakers convey complex feelings and experiences, but, Johnson argues, "a taboo is being violated" when a woman/mother describes the death of a child as anything less than "pure loss." This taboo is produced through an identification with the "discursive position" of the child (199) that begins with the original verbal demand/address from the infant for "Mama!" and subsequently determines "the entire verbal universe" (198) of the reader. In other words, poems with maternal speakers that relate the death of a child—like Brooks's "The Mother" or Clifton's "the lost baby poem"—rely on rhetoric that incidentally provokes identification with the child. The ambivalent maternal speaker who does not perform "pure loss" becomes "monstrous," reflecting a "disturbing" or "sinister" tone (197). The poem "blur[s] the boundary between life and death" (194) through language that refuses to identify when life begins, an "undecidability" (193) that Johnson nevertheless anticipates being overruled in favor of identification with the fetus and antiabortion ideology. The challenge in defending abortion, Johnson hypothesizes, is "in the attempt to achieve a full elaboration of any discursive position other than that of child" (199).

Johnson and numerous critics—feminists and otherwise—have described how antiabortion groups successfully built campaigns around the discursive and visual rhetoric of the fetus following the legalization of abortion in 1973, resulting in an ideology of fetal primacy (e.g., Balsamo; Dubow; Ginsburg; Holland; Hurst; Petchesky; Poovey). These campaigns not only conjured the fetus's personhood but constructed it as a "super-subject" with greater rights than its maternal host (Bordo). The deployment of images created by ultrasound technology could diminish the presence of the pregnant woman's body or malign it as a potentially hostile site (Balsamo; Bordo; Kumeh). Additionally, antiabortion groups produced the documentary *The Silent Scream* (1984) to depict abortion from the fetus's perspective.[2] In related street tactics, antiabortion activists wielded signs, circulated pamphlets, and sponsored ads on billboards that featured gruesome, distorted images of fetal tissue linking abortion with murder and genocide. Protestors also personified the fetus in front of clinics by taunting entering patients with ventriloquized pleas of "Don't kill me, Mommy" (Phelan; Stabile). These messages existed concurrently with dire threats about women's well-being should they have abortions. So-called aborted mothers were women who suffered from postabortion regret for their actions and grief for this lost child. Antiabortion rhetoric elevated this grief fictitiously with the title "postabortion syndrome." To reflect and affirm the anthropomorphization of the fetus, antiabortion groups developed terms like *unborn child* and *pro-life* to construct a platform from which to argue for fetal rights that would equal or surpass women's interests and rights. As a human-like figure, the fetus has rights, desires to be born, and feels pain. In these representations, the fetus becomes like the figure of the Child in Lee Edelman's critique of reproductive futurity: an unquestioned emblem of progress entitled to present-day, hegemonic sacrifice.

In this context, it's no wonder, really, that Johnson thought Brooks's and Clifton's poems encourage antiabortion interpretations. The dominance of antiabortion imagery and rhetoric along with the absence of a proabortion rhetoric that could address the fetus, grief, and motherhood made any discussion of those issues fraught. When antiabortion groups leaned into the visual and discursive rhetoric of the fetus's personhood, for example, abortion defenders asserted that the fetus was an insentient blob of cells. Amid proliferating ultrasound images that anthropomorphized the fetus, abortion advocates

2. Later, the antiabortion feature film *October Baby* (2011) depicted the story of Gianna Jessen, whose birth—during a failed saline abortion—seemingly gave embodiment and a voice to the fetus.

countered with the chilling images of Gerri Twerdy Santoro, a woman who died in 1967 from an illegal abortion, or the menacing shape of a coat hanger. While antiabortion groups claimed that women suffered postabortion syndrome, abortion defenders promoted the rhetoric of choices and freedom. Abortion defenders avoided the term *mother,* arguing that normative ideas of motherhood were preventing wider support for abortion access. Ultimately, even the term *abortion* was buried in favor of the euphemistic term *choice.*

There is a nervous concern in "Apostrophe, Animation, and Abortion" that poems in which women speakers parse the meaning of abortions, grief, babies, and mothers reinforce twentieth-century antiabortion ideology. Not only do these speakers remember and grieve abortions, but they also give value to the fetus and claim the title of mother—gestures that align closely with antiabortion rhetoric of the twentieth century. We might ask, though, if a twenty-first-century reader—someone who reads these poems in an era of ordinary abortion—automatically interprets the poems about abortion, grief, maternal uncertainty, and fetal value the same way as a twentieth-century reader.

## Abortion Beneficiaries and Flipping the Script on Fetal Primacy

Krista Jacob's important volume *Abortion Under Attack: Women on the Challenges Facing Choice* reveals that by the beginning of the twenty-first century, important criticism from within the pro-choice movement was creating a change in rhetoric and strategies for defending abortion. Many of these criticisms were first voiced by members of two proabortion organizations: the Abortion Conversation Projects, formed in 2000, which merged with the National Coalition for Abortion Providers in 2008 to form the Abortion Care Network. The Network has fought for two decades to destigmatize abortion and to promote postabortion emotional health ("Our History"). The authors in Jacob's volume observe how abortion patients, providers, and supporters—sensing the futility of continually reacting to antiabortion rhetoric—used their voices, experience, and knowledge of abortion to tell a different story to a mainstream audience. The epistemology of abortion in this volume breaks many pro-choice taboos on how to discuss unplanned pregnancies, motherhood, fetuses, grief, and terminations: "It was time to explore some of the new ideas that had emerged—such as making room for exploring the notion of fetal pain and women's grief after abortion experience—even though these ideas challenge the platform the pro-choice movement had fought so hard to develop and maintain" (Jacob, *Abortion* 13). The authors reflect a subjugated epistemology (muted by both antiabortion and pro-choice factions) that affirms the emotional experiences of abortion patients and their supporters, including grief, concern for the fetus/baby, and maternal identity. Acknowledging these feelings, Jacob and her authors contend, does not mean patients will be dissuaded or harmed. Contributors to Jacob's volume discuss the importance of grief and healing postabortion, the role of supportive clergy and religious faith in that healing as well as in the decision-making process. The essays call repeatedly for pro-choice rhetoric to stop "shielding abortion patients from their feelings" and to stop reducing abortion to simple, popular, or defensible stories like those of the young, unmarried women who are pregnant for the first time and who have plans for family-making after education and career: "We can't paint all abortion experiences in one stroke" (16).[3]

A number of scholars observe a shift in abortion advocates' rhetoric in the twenty-first century, arguing that when abortion providers are honest about the feelings and uncertainties involved with abortion, it not only makes for better patient care, it also makes for a better proabortion movement. Jeannie Ludlow ("Sometimes") and Carole Joffe ("Politicization"), for example, have observed that abortion-providing has changed to "meet patients where they are at" (Joffe, "Politicization" 122). Noting that abortion patients often described the fetus in ways that made providers uncomfortable (using the term *baby* or worrying about what happens to its soul), they go on to observe how these patient perceptions do not make patients any less confident in their decisions. Joffe describes how providers were pushed by such patient reactions to develop supportive strategies—such as using the term *baby* themselves when counseling patients (rather than correcting them) or creating ways for patients to mourn its loss ("Politicization"). The strategies also tackle head-on the fact that some abortion patients come to clinics not knowing how they feel but with the expectation that they *should* feel regret. Having open conversations about real and expected feelings, these scholars point out, improves abortion-providing. According to Ludlow, this development in abortion rhetoric reflects trust, love, and respect for women and an appreciation for the emotional complexity of abortion ("Love").

---

3. Essays in *Abortion Under Attack* describe new ways advocates support people seeking abortion, including "How to Talk (Really Talk) About Abortion" by Caroline De Robertis, one of the cofounders of EXHALE, the first proabortion, postabortion counseling service; "Abortion Clinic Days," by two providers who created a blog to discuss their experiences working in abortion clinics; and "I'm Not Sorry," a proabortion call to remove stigma modeled on the website ImNotSorry.net. The new tactics described in these essays embrace Peg Johnston's call to "stop fixating on the next awful thing the anti-abortion forces think up, and use our energy for a more proactive agenda" (77).

An appreciation for this evolving proabortion rhetoric informs not only the literature being produced in the twenty-first century but also how readers approach texts that were published earlier. In a recent query on *WMST-L*, the national listserv for feminist academics, for example, a member sought recommendations of literature that could be used to discuss *Dobbs* in feminist classrooms (August 22, 2022), prompting recommendations for Brooks's "The Mother" and Clifton's "the lost baby poem." Additionally, Annie Finch includes these poems in her edited volume of abortion literature, *Choice Words*, describing them as "courageous, iconic texts that speak out ahead of their time" (2). Her volume, she notes, includes works that "invoke grief, defiance, fear, shame, desperation, love, awe, tenderness, sorrow, regret, compassion, hope, despair, resolve, rage, triumph, relief, and peace" (1), without concern that these emotions might serve to reinforce antiabortion ideas of maternal regret and fetal primacy. These endorsements suggest that the depictions of uncertainty, loss, motherhood, and grief in these poems are important to the defense of abortion and provide a reminder that rhetoric can change: What the fetus signified rhetorically in the 1980s was arguably different from its meaning at the time of these poems' publication, which is also different from its twenty-first-century meanings.

In what follows I consider how the evolving rhetoric of ordinary abortion foregrounds the beneficiaries of abortion and flips the script on fetal primacy. The beneficiaries of abortion are those people who, according to medical bioethicist Katie Watson, "didn't terminate a pregnancy themselves, but are glad someone else did" (26). In *Scarlet A*, her analysis of abortion storytelling that argues for the importance of telling more numerous and varied stories about having abortions, Watson provides a subtle shift in perspective that allows for a new proabortion rhetoric. Leaning into the vast numbers of people who, post-*Roe*, have benefited from abortion—women who had safe abortions, who didn't become mothers when they didn't want to, families that did not add to their numbers when they didn't want to, and heterosexuals who enjoyed nonreproductive sex—Watson reveals a powerful framework for defending abortion access. She points out that Americans have been "voting with their feet" in favor of abortion even as the political discourse remains deadlocked.

*Flipping the script* is colloquially understood to mean reversing a situation by exchanging the roles of the participants or doing something unexpected or looking at something from a different perspective. The now-popularized expression originates in hip-hop music and culture, although some commentators attribute it to graffiti culture wherein a writer replicates a rival's tag upside down and backward as a sign of disrespect. I use this term with care for its African American hip-hop origins and in solidarity with the intent to disrupt and expose systems of domination. I see this rhetorical strategy aligning with the long history of feminist satire as a means of exposing the injustices of sexism;[4] they share resistant strategies that are both creative and playful. Flipping the script on fetal primacy entails decentralizing the hypothetical fetus's life, pronatalism, reproductive futurity, and patriarchal norms and revaluing the temporal present, material circumstances, and people impacted by unplanned pregnancy.

To flip the patriarchal, pronatalist script on whose potential is valued (the woman's or the fetus's), one must disidentify with interpellation into what Lee Edelman has termed "reproductive futurity." In *No Future: Queer Theory and the Death Drive,* Edelman contends that political subjects sacrifice on behalf of a deferred future that is represented through the Child. Edelman's queer critique contends that this investment comes at the cost of our collective present selves, and he urges replacing reproductive futurity with a revaluation of the present and jouissance. This reassigning of value is a political gesture for Edelman: The always diminishing horizon of the reproductive future is, in fact, a conservative project "that returns to the Child as the image of the future that it intends" (3). The resulting political order defines itself through a future horizon that needs ongoing protection from "anti-sociality" or "those not fighting for the child" (3). Thus nonreproductive sex—represented by queer sexuality and abortion—figures as the antisocial Other of reproductive futurity threatening the continuance of a way of life that is assumed to have existed in the past. Like feminist critics before him, Edelman points to the regulation of bodies, desire, and pleasures as being the end product of investment in the Child and that which must be resisted. Along with other feminist critics, I find Edelman's theorization of abortion, pregnant bodies, reproductive labor, and motherhood to be inadequate,[5] but the figure of the

4. College introductions to gender studies routinely supply students, for example, with Gloria Steinem's classic satire, "What If Men Could Menstruate"; "The Heterosexual Questionnaire" attributed to Martin Rochlin; and Peggy McIntosh's antiracist exposure of whiteness, "White Privilege."

5. Anca Parvulescu, for example, takes Edelman's work to task for failing to consider reproductive labor beyond heteroreproductive labor, which signals his lack of attention to motherhood, materialism, and "women's work." Jennifer Doyle questions Edelman's use of abortion politics and his failure to consider pregnant bodies, motherhood, and prior feminist theories, some of which point out that the child's perspective is culturally valued over the silencing of the voice of the mother (this is seen, for example, in antiabortion rhetoric but also in psychoanalytic theory). This leads Doyle to observe that Edelman himself comes close to sounding "like a child" in his inability to consider the mother's perspective when discussing reproductive futurity (35). Although not expressly feminist, the critiques of Edelman's work for not considering how some children are not socially perceived as having futures (Muñoz) adds to the sense that *No Future* does not adequately engage with

"child-hating" sinthomosexual (one who is not literally child-hating but who opposes reproductive futurity) is useful in considering how contemporary poetry by Judith Arcana and Sharon Olds challenges heteroreproductivity in support of abortion rights and valuing women's lives. This poetry destabilizes the politics of reproductive futurity by suggesting that lives of people in the temporal, material present have a definite value compared to the subjective and indeterminate value of the (future) fetus/Child of Edelman's argument. It shifts the perspective away from the fetus/Child and onto the individuals who are impacted by unplanned pregnancy and who may benefit from abortion: women, mothers, fathers, siblings, and daughters.

Judith Arcana, a member of the pre-*Roe,* underground abortion service Jane (1968–73), is also an educator, activist, and author of fiction, nonfiction, and poetry. "What If Your Mother," the eponymous poem from her 2005 collection, provides an example of flipping the script on fetal primacy through a direct attack on antiabortion rhetoric. In this poem addressed to an assumed sympathetic listener, the speaker describes confrontations with antiabortion activists: "Sometimes when you talk to them . . . / they say, What if your mother had an abortion?" (7). In the first line, the structure of address—the absence of "I" and presence of "you"—collapses the speaker and addressee into an alliance and a shared alienation from "them," a third party with antiabortion views. In the second line, the speaker assumes the identity of an adult child, to whom "they" pose their unnervingly hostile question. The structure of this address differs from the ones considered by Johnson in that the speaker is a(n) (adult) child. This speaker can consider abortion simultaneously from the perspectives of someone who might need an abortion as well as from the perspective of the child. This bifocal vantage point serves to flip the script on readerly identification with the fetus. The unflappable speaker reports that their mother did have an abortion, "only / that wasn't me," an admission that nevertheless refuses "their" insistence that the speaker identify with the fetus, causing two disruptions to expectations. First, it disproves the myth that mothers don't terminate pregnancies, and secondly, the speaker disrupts the questioner's authority by asserting that "nobody / but my mother ever knew that baby."

---

reproductive politics. Penelope Deutscher, in her work analyzing reproductive politics, argues that, while Edelman's work fails to consider gender politics when thinking about reproductive politics, his model for attending to reproductive "Othering" may be useful for rethinking reproductive choice arguments that are based upon distinctions being made between "good" and "bad" choice-makers. Mairead Sullivan critiques Edelman's conceptualization of the sinthomosexual in solely masculine terms and failing to consider more completely the female sinthomosexual as represented by radical lesbian feminism.

The speaker's cheeky tone counteracts the threatening tone of the question: "But they / mean me, the people who say it, mean / what if she aborted me." The question, the speaker knows, is rhetorically provocative—What if you never existed?—and intended to produce silence. The speaker counters it not only by breaking the silence but by diminishing the questioner's motives and authority. The repetition of the word *mean* suggests the questioner is being mean-spirited in wishing or conjuring the absence/death of the very-much-present speaker. The indignant speaker undermines the questioner's authority by announcing, "like that's hard / to answer" and then responding, "Then everything / would be different." The speaker predicts they would not be angry at their mother simply because they wouldn't exist. The speaker concludes that the questioners need to "[g]et real," an assertion of the material and temporal present that flips the script on antiabortion rhetoric. The speaker's gesture of solidarity with their mother rejects identification with the fetus and asserts the voice of the living, already-here (adult) child and mother. Arcana's poem reflects the epistemology of abortion, first by revealing that mothers have abortions, and second, by showing that Johnson's claim that readers identify with the discursive position of "the child" may be disrupted.

Flipping the script on fetal primacy without diminishing the value of the fetus is also well exemplified in the work of Sharon Olds, the Pulitzer Prize–winning author of twelve books of poetry. "The Foetus in the Voting Booth" (from *The Unswept Room,* 2002) is an address by a woman who enters a voting booth only to be confronted by antiabortion propaganda: a sticker depicting a fetus "like a flat cocoon spun above the levers" (35). The privacy of the voting booth (and its violation) evokes the privacy of the abortion decision (the legalization of which, in *Roe v. Wade,* was based in a right to privacy). The speaker registers the violation, saying, "as if I were not the only living / thing in there." This subjunctive statement too contains a double meaning: both that the sticker's image asserts the fetus's life—possibly over her own negated being—or that she sees herself as the only living being in the booth. The speaker also sees the beauty of the cocoon/fetal image, but when she contemplates making others accept this "God," the beauty of the image is undermined by sinister diction: "archaic," "a Pandora sphinx," or "a death's-head moth." She animates the cocoon/fetus by noting that its gaze "seemed to be following me," but she undermines this animation by emphasizing its fiction compared to her embodied materiality: "I was supposed to be / alone in the booth, the way a woman / is supposed to be alone with her body."

This speaker does not claim any relationship to the fetus/cocoon; she does not identify as mother, daughter, or sister. Instead, she identifies as a would-be beneficiary of modern progress, linking her observation that "A man has

. . . walked on the moon" (an image that invokes Armstrong's androcentric proclamation, "One small step for man, one giant leap for mankind") with another observation: "A woman has gone / up the passage of her body to the rosy / attic of the womb, with her whisk broom." In these lines, legalized abortion is described in cozy, domestic terms of the private sphere but is nevertheless counted alongside and analogously with the twentieth-century public achievement of walking on the moon. Olds's work acknowledges the fetus and its value, but that value is fluid and subjective. As this broom-wielding woman cleans out "larvum," web, or "chrysalis," she may be either "weeping or singing," and yet, the speaker asserts, "she decides." The certainty in the poem is that abortion access means progress even if not every abortion results in joy.

Both Arcana's and Olds's poems flip the script on the antiabortion tactic of granting primacy to the fetus. Both poems also assert the primacy of the material present, and both destabilize received and romanticized ideas about motherhood and reproduction. In her essay in Jacob's volume, Frances Kissling, the former president of Catholics for Choice, argues that when abortion defenders stop engaging in the fight about when life begins, they can reclaim discussions about the value of life—fetal, maternal, and more. Olds's poetry frequently depicts women's reproductive lives—Adam Kirsch describes her treatment of the personal, the body, and sexuality as "blasphemy" (272)—to assert the primacy of the material present and women's bodily sovereignty. "Diaphragm Aria" from *The Unswept Room*, for example, is about the act of removing a diaphragm, a barrier-method contraception. The female speaker addresses a male partner, unapologetically imagining children who were not conceived or born.[6] She collapses the distinction between abortion and other forms of birth control by implicating the diaphragm in disallowing her "not-children." "Diaphragm Aria" rejects privileging unborn life over the needs of the living. The poem begins with a series of observations about the postcoitus contents of the diaphragm. They are described as "sweet" and "curious" and compared to the items of a "treasure hunt," or findings on a woodland floor, or the "dregs" of a teacup. This last image leads the speaker to prognosticate about "our daughter" and "our son," whom she also identifies as "not-children." The speaker goes on to animate these unborn children who had a "finicky way" or "somersaulted." Olds's word choice, "not-children," reflects how language blurs the line between life and inanimate figure (44).

6. Olds explores a similar theme in an earlier work, "The Unborn," from *Satan Says* (1980).

In the last twelve lines of the poem, the speaker adopts another metaphor for the diaphragm, noting, "When I have reached / into myself, and glistened out the dome, / I search its planetarium sky." In this aria—a moment of postcoital thoughts—the speaker reminds the reader of her agency and her pleasure. She constructs the image of the diaphragm as a boundary between spaces and entities. On the one side are bodies, matter, density, activity, and earth, and on the other side are heavens and inaction. On the earthly side of this dualism are "grateful bodies" engaged in pleasure, while on the other side of the barrier there is a seeming waiting room for potential life, whom the speaker salutes: "I bless the lollers who / stay in that other sphere as we come / like surf on the shore of it." The double entendre contributes to a sense of wonder, sexual gratification, and relief that there are no unwanted consequences (i.e., pregnancy), even as she seeks protection and divine favor for these "lollers."

"Diaphragm Aria" reflects an epistemology of abortion in numerous ways. First it provokes an unorthodox spirituality that supports women's sexual pleasure and reproductive choices. In this poem, material bodies, pleasures, and sexuality are privileged over immaterial, future children. The "mattery paradise" of the lovers destabilizes the line between heaven and earth and diminishes the power and promise of a heavenly paradise. Pleasure is enjoyed and the "not children" wait indolently in their own heavenly "sphere" while their absences are acknowledged but not regretted. This image flips the script on the antiabortion idea that every child wants to be born and that heaven is the reward of the living solely. Additionally, despite the collapse of earthly and divine, the poem asserts the primacy of the material and the temporal present. Materiality is also emphasized through the speaker's bodily agency—"reach[ing] into [herself]"—in an almost godlike way to defer the future (pregnancy). The poem flips the script on the fetus's primacy and reproductive futurism, and instead privileges nonreproductive sex.

The poem also is interesting for its reference to "*our* not-children" (emphasis mine), an indirect invocation and implication of a male partner. Other poems by Olds make similar acknowledgments of the roles of both men and women in reproduction, even as her poetry favors women speakers.[7] The reminder of men's reproductive role and the impact of unplanned pregnancy on their lives is increasingly part of the conversation that makes up the epistemology of abortion,[8] signaling shared responsibility and how pregnant people take male partners into consideration when making decisions about

7. "The End," from *The Dead and the Living* (1984), for example.

8. This way of including of men in conversations about abortion does not privilege their role or voice over the pregnant person's—as some antiabortion men's rights groups seek to do.

contraception and abortion. In *Scarlet A,* Watson further identifies abortion beneficiaries as "all the men and women who never had an accidental pregnancy, but have been able to enjoy sex as part of their romances and marriages because they weren't constantly afraid of contraceptive failure" (65). Olds's poetry foregrounds these beneficiaries, and in doing so, flips the script on fetal primacy.

Olds returns to the theme of gratitude to the unborn in "The Tending"—also from *The Unswept Room*—this time from the beneficiary perspective of a sibling. In this poem, the speaker walks in an otherworldly woods, remarking that "My parents did not consider it, for me," before claiming an identification with "the aborted" (113), the inhabitants of this forest. The "for me" punctuated by commas sets her apart from these strange but familiar siblings. The speaker's identification with the inhabitants is both mournful and disturbing: "the air is ashen as if from funeral-home / chimneys," and there are images of stunted, humanlike plants populating a grim garden. Imagining herself to be "one of the gardeners here," the speaker cares for children who are described using images from Romantic poetry and nursery rhymes but who have become blighted figures. She interrupts this description with the assertion, "yet this is / a Holy woods," and an explanation for her presence there. The speaker is motivated by grim memories of her childhood home and the awareness that these siblings would have been harmed or would have done harm there, such that, "I wonder if some, here, have done, / by their early deaths, a boon of absence / to someone in the world." The unnamed horrors of the speaker's childhood home remain terrifying for being unspeakable, but the poem hints darkly at a familial situation where the absence of additional children made a bad situation better. The speaker's description of the dismal surroundings turns into an appreciation for noble sacrifice and an awareness that her life is not better than the not-lives of those she tends. Instead, this speaker identifies with them but does not address them: "I am / among the sung who will not sing, / the harmed who will not harm." Their shared inability or choice to not "sing" promises that although they were harmed by being conceived, they will not do similar harm themselves; a violent cycle has been interrupted. The speaker acknowledges the "boon of absence" that her aborted siblings gave her, and she repays it not by animating them—she refuses to "sing to them—their lullaby complete"—but instead by tending them through this poem. Like the speaker in "What If Your Mother," Olds's speaker instead leaves the assignment of fetal value to parents, as is implied by her concluding description of this dreamscape as "a kind of home / a mothers' and fathers' place."

"The Tending," like Arcana's "What If Your Mother," exhibits an epistemology of abortion in its understanding that decisions to have abortions sometimes happen in complicated family circumstances, where an additional child poses potential harm to existing children. Olds's poem flips the script on the fetal primacy rhetoric that argues all children want to be born by suggesting that parents may do worse things to children than not having them. The mixture of sweet images from nursery rhymes and macabre dreamscapes again asserts the (difficult) temporal present and real over the romantic and ideal. Parents and families choose abortion under conditions that sometimes make the decision feel like it isn't a choice. Families and homes are sometimes places where no child would want to be born. Ultimately, though, the speaker who occupies the present and reality is privileged over the unborn. Unlike Arcana's speaker, who rejects any connection to the sibling that only her mother "ever knew," the speaker of "The Tending" imagines a close identification with her sibling and extends to them a tenderness that maybe she herself never received.

So far I have considered Olds's poems about the value of not-being-born from the perspective of would-be mothers or siblings. Now I want to consider poems that use a child's voice to speculate on their mothers' counterfactual, child-free lives. This strategy of address is first displayed in her earlier poems in *The Gold Cell* that draw on her childhood experience coming of age in an abusive family. In "I Go Back to May 1937," a speaker imagines their parents' first meeting with prescient horror, knowing the cruelties they will enact on their children. Should the speaker, burdened with future knowledge, prevent this union? "I want to go up to them and say Stop, / don't do it," proposing their own "abortion" or nonbeing. The intervention will prevent future pain, but the poem pivots, and the speaker instead asserts her desire not only to live but also to create: "I say / Do what you are going to do, and I will tell about it." The calamity of the parents' family-making becomes the speaker's choice as she animates them through her art, and her art becomes the reason for wanting to be born. This speaker animates her unborn self to challenge reproductive futurism and to testify against the atrocity of domestic violence and child abuse.

Although the poetry of Arcana and Olds disrupts the fantasy that children wish to be born and parents never regret reproducing, Johnson was not the only critic in the 1980s and 1990s for whom antiabortion rhetoric seemed totalizing. Judith Wilt, in her 1990 volume, *Abortion, Choice, and Contemporary Fiction: The Armageddon of the Maternal Instinct*, considers the abortion narrative in American literature to be a site of "profound anxiety" for the teller and also for the listener,

> who must encounter in this story the specter of his or her own potential not having been. If the pregnancy narrative ends before birth, even by accident

> but especially by choice, it leaves two ghosts in its wake: the ghost of the child that might have been and the ghost of the self that might have borne and parented that child. And for a moment, the hearer may experience, in the confrontation with these imaginable but not real beings, the radical contingency of his or her own consoling "reality." (5)

Wilt's characterization assumes the abortion narrative is always told first-person by someone who had one, and the listener is someone whose mother avoided a regrettable choice. Her account fails to consider how something might be lost when a woman becomes a mother or how adult children might ponder with equanimity their own mothers' abortions. Wilt's argument fails to consider that the "hearer" and "teller" of the abortion narrative might occupy the same rhetorical position, that an adult child telling the story of abortion might also have—radically—contemplated being aborted and might be more interested in their ghostly counterfactual, child-free mother. In subsequent decades, however, authors like Olds have asserted the "radical contingency" of birth to disrupt the "consoling realities" of reproductive futurism.

The figure of the critically reflective daughter, in particular, presents a rhetorically powerful challenge to the idea that all children want and need to be born. Diana Huet de Guerville, for example, explores fully this taboo in her essay "Birth Is Not Always Best: Confessions of an Unwanted Child" in *Abortion Under Attack*. Huet de Guerville's story directly confronts the antiabortion story of the activist Gianna Jessen, a woman who was born alive during a saline abortion in the 1970s. Jessen has made a career of arguing against abortion rights by seeming to give voice and body to the fetus's perspective of abortion. Huet de Guerville, on the other hand, uses her voice as a daughter to flip the script on fetal primacy and to defend abortion against ideologies of pronatalism and the heteronormative family. She begins her essay with the observation, "My mother wanted me; my father did not. Nor did he want the second child they would bring into the world three years later," before recounting her regret that her parents had children:

> I first learned about abortion as a teenager, and began wondering if my parents had debated that option. I imagined an impassioned dialogue between their younger selves, with my father making rational arguments for terminating the pregnancy, and my mother making an emotional plea to have me. If they did have such an argument, she, as always, got her way. Yet I was convinced that she had made a mistake by dragging me into a world where I didn't belong. (112–13)

In this personal essay, Huet de Guerville acknowledges that after a difficult teenage period during which she suffered enormously from the emotional abuse of knowing that her father did not want her, she arrived at a place in her thinking and relationships where she is "glad to be alive" (113). However, she makes this claim with a caveat: "Unlike those who opposed abortion from a sense of relief that their own lives were spared, my painful experience convinced me early on that it's not always in the best interest of the child to be born" (113). She rejects Wilt's "consoling reality" as cold comfort to present a more stark, less romantic, reality: "I believe my mother made a selfish choice by deciding to have and keep me. I'm sure she hoped that my dad would grow to love me, and she couldn't have known that he would be so cruel" (115). Huet de Guerville's essay flips the script on dominant ideas of fetal primacy, pronatalism, and heteronormative family structures. Like Olds's speaker, she regrets the unnecessary suffering that is a product of these ideas.

## The Aborted Woman as Counterfactual

In texts in which the speaker/narrator is an adult child who questions their parents' decision to become parents, the script is flipped on fetal primacy and reproductive futurism. Arcana, Olds, and Huet de Guerville all share a strategy of refocusing on women's lives instead of their children's lives. This strategy invokes the rhetorical trope of what I am calling the aborted woman. This figure should not be confused with the antiabortion aborted mother who is denied existence when a woman has an abortion. Rather, the aborted woman is a rhetorical figure who is conjured by—as in the case of Arcana, Olds, and Huet de Guerville—a daughter, a neutral observer, or even a maternal speaker, and is a spectral figure representing the woman who is lost when a child is born. As a reminder that there are costs to childbearing—that something might be lost when a woman becomes a mother—this figure contributes to proabortion discourse. In what follows I delineate this rhetorical figure's queer relationship to loss, regret, and reproductive futurity.

The aborted woman represents the losses produced by heteronormativity and reproductive futurity. Antiabortion rhetoric asks, What if the unborn is the next Beethoven? or the doctor who cures cancer? The figure of the aborted woman asks, What if the woman seeking an abortion is the next Beethoven? Or the doctor who cures cancer? If most Americans are unaware to varying levels of the beneficiaries of abortion, they are blind to the losses produced by reproductive futurity. In *Living a Feminist Life*, Sara Ahmed offers the metaphor of "being directed" to illuminate the almost irresistible power behind sexual and reproductive norms, and the disorienting experience of becoming aware of how one's life has been directed by them. She writes,

> Perhaps feminist consciousness also means becoming aware of one's life as a marvel or even marvelous. Being estranged from one's own life can be how a world reappears, becoming odd. You might become conscious of a possibility once it has receded. In Mrs. Dalloway's consciousness, other people, other possibilities, flicker as memory. To become conscious of possibility can involve mourning for its loss. You can feel the sadness of what could have been, but was not to be. Maybe we realize it would have been possible to live one's life in another way. We can mourn because we didn't even realize that we gave something up. The shape of a life can feel like a past tense; something we sense only after it has been acquired. (47)

Awareness of the losses produced by childbearing challenges the foundation of compulsory heteronormativity and reproductive futurism. In pronatalist culture, pregnancy and motherhood grant women legibility: What is a woman without a child? This received knowledge is contradicted by the idea that something is lost when a woman has a child. The rhetorical aborted woman is a liminal figure—both here and not here—a counterfactual product of memory and imagination. The mother is here, but her other possible self has been lost to a(nother) child, thereby becoming a site of potential mourning. The aborted woman reflects what Pauline Boss named "ambiguous loss," a kind of grief that lacks closure or understanding, and a socially contested "grievable loss" (Butler), one that lacks social recognition but that is experienced nevertheless.

A feminist, lesbian, mother of three sons, theorist, and writer, Adrienne Rich explored analogies between abortion and queer politics before Edelman and returned often in her poetry and essays to the threat of women's lost potential. Her writings on motherhood reflect an interest in recovering the lost voices and reproductive experiences of women and mothers under heteropatriarchy,[9] and her concern for mothers as writers and social actors

9. In *Of Woman Born: Motherhood as Experience and Institution* (1976), Rich identifies patriarchal motherhood as an institution that is deeply interwoven with regimes of gender, sexuality, race, nationhood, and citizenship. While the experience of mothering cannot happen outside the institution, Rich also reflects on how it is not wholly or even mostly determined by normative motherhood, leaving hope for the potential relationship to mothering that women might have beyond the restrictive norm (*Of Woman* 13). Rich saw the institution of motherhood as something the woman (artist) must survive, but she left open the possibility for women's diverse experiences of mothering, such as her own, as journeys of self-discovery and agency.

is evident in "To a Poet," from *The Dream of a Common Language,* another text that Barbara Johnson considered in her analysis of gendered structures of address. In it, the speaker addresses a fellow woman writer in acknowledgment of and solidarity with her struggles to write while caring for young children. Rich's speaker frets that the addressee will give up "before your pen has gleaned your teeming brain"—a line that not only likens the addressee's abilities to Keats's canonical (male) abilities but also compares Keats's terminal illness to motherhood as fatal threats to poetic expression. That someone's life is at stake is certain in the poem—"you are not a suicide / but no one calls this murder"—but less certain is the cause of the fatality/crime. For Johnson, this poetic situation set up art and motherhood in conflict. She notes that while death was the mother of Keats's poem on mortality, motherhood "is precisely the death of poetry" (196). Johnson observes that the poem reflects "a kind of competition . . . between artistic creation and procreation" (196) that is different from the writing about children by male poets, who may mourn lost children but not selves lost due to fatherhood. The last stanza of the poem, however, adds another layer to the poem's purpose. The speaker pivots from her address to another woman writer to announce that the poem is intended "for" another woman:

> dumb
> with loneliness     dust     seeping plastic bags
> with children     in a house
> where language floats and spins
> abortion     in
> the bowl (15)

The speaker shifts attention away from her addressee, "you," to dedicate the poem "for" another woman, who does not write and whose voice is utterly lost. "[A]bortion" suggests simultaneously political language that eludes the reach of this housebound woman, or the termination of a pregnancy, or, instead, the termination of a self through the loss of voice and aspirations. This woman is not the femme artiste manquée; she is an aborted woman whose lost potential—beyond "children in a house"—is a site of inspiration for the speaker, who is moved to write about the challenges of motherhood and to encourage another maternal writer. Contrary to Johnson's assertion that the poem casts children and art as a "rivalry," I see this poem (re)claiming motherhood as poetic material—even when the subject is the taboo topic of abortion or maternal regret. The spectral unknowability of the third woman's fate is reflected in the gaps and spacing of the poem's structure, which strands individual words and images in suspended isolation. Rich's poem is haunted by this figure of the aborted woman, whose ghost can only point mutely to the oppressive costs of heteronormative motherhood.

A ghost, Avery Gordon suggests, is not "simply a dead or missing person, but a social figure, and investigating it can lead to that dense site where history and subjectivity make social life" (8). In attending to figures that are "lost, barely visible, or simply not there to our supposedly well-trained eyes" (8), Gordon's sociological approach draws on ghosts to understand history, power, and subjectivity. She writes, "Haunting is one way in which abusive systems of power make themselves known and their impacts felt in everyday life, especially when they are supposedly over and done with . . . or when their oppressive nature is denied" (xvi). Gordon's fruitful use of ghostly figures in literature for understanding history and power provides insight into the violent omissions and repressions in the historical record that literature might fill. Rich's poem reminds us to see mothers as women in their reproductive historical context. In her imaginings, she conjures the aborted woman but also refuses to diminish the agency of the woman as a mother. Spectral studies[10] offers a new way to think about Rich's poem in which the third woman, whom Johnson referred to as a "nonperson" (196) is a kind of ghost—an absent presence—that reminds the addressee and reader that pronatalism and normative motherhood do violence to women.

The rhetorical figure of the aborted woman is also a means for thinking through maternal regret, which is a highly taboo subject. The essays in Andrea O'Reilly's *Maternal Regret: Resistances, Renunciations, and Reflections* (2022), for example, trace a renewed interest in expressions of maternal regret, women who wish that they had not had children. In her essay in this volume, O'Reilly observes, "Regretful mothers are the quintessential mother outlaws; in their acknowledgement and articulation of maternal regret, they flip the patriarchal script of normative motherhood to expose that maternal desire, ability, and fulfilment are not innate to women; rather, they are constructed to

10. I do not mean to invoke the ideas of the uncanny or fetish that are part of Derrida's hauntology. Nor am I directly engaging the figure of the ghost that appears in trauma studies or the ghostly figures that haunt postcolonial, magical realist texts as forms of alternative knowledge. Instead, I am interested in the idea of "ghosts" in the sense created by Terry Castle and Avery Gordon. Castle's work of identifying lesbian figures in nineteenth-century texts requires a certain queer perspective to "see" such ghosts and their erasure. I am drawing on a similar feminist and queer perspective when I say that Rich allows readers to "see" ghosts of aborted women. Avery Gordon reminds us of the importance of social context for understanding the presence and role of ghosts. Seeing the aborted women requires knowledge of social context. Together, Castle and Gordon explain how certain women writers use a feminist and/or queer perspective to see the aborted woman.

regulate women's and mothers' lives" ("'Out of Bounds'" 31). This regret is rhetorically important to defend abortion. For example, in an essay in O'Reilly's volume, Alesha Doan and Shoshana Ehrlich compare antiabortion websites that feature postabortion testimonials to testimony on the Facebook group "I Regret Having Children" and find similarities: "Across both sets of narratives, women express a longing for a reimagined life, unburdened by their reproductive decision" (58). The authors contend that feeling "diminished well-being" and "loss" (58) as a result of having children needs to be acknowledged for its own sake as well as for defending abortion. They write, "Although the antiabortion movement has weaponized abortion regret narratives for political gains, we contend that the reproductive rights movement has been missing an opportunity to use maternal regret narratives to combat hegemonic ideals of motherhood and challenge the essentialized construction of patriarchal motherhood" (58). Although speaking of maternal regret breaks a deep-seated taboo, rhetorically it is a potential means for defending abortion.

The aborted woman is also a rhetorically queer disruption of heteronormative temporality. Weighing, valuing, and mourning the loss of women's potential to childbearing and conjuring ghostly alternative, counterfactual pasts and futures destabilizes the hegemony of reproductive futurity. Uchronia, the use of counterfactual thought in literature, is typically used by writers for social commentary. Although uchronia is not always rhetorically queer, its use to decentralize the role of Edelman's Child in our collective imaginations and the role of motherhood in women's lives challenges heteronormative roles and timekeeping. Beginning with the premise *What if—?*, uchronia takes a historical fact but veers into experimental thought. Texts may be set entirely in an alternate history, like Philip Roth's novel *The Plot Against America*, or they may include moments or spaces of uchronia where the narration speculates about an alternative outcome to something that happened in the past. The most recognizable use of this device from a feminist perspective is Virginia Woolf's *A Room of One's Own* (1928), in which she observes that "we think back through our mothers if we are women" (79) and proceeds to imagine what might have been the life of Shakespeare's equally talented sister.[11]

11. Saloman argues that *A Room of One's Own* relies on "counterfactual thinking" to make Woolf's point that women's exclusion from the literary canon resulted from material conditions and not a lack of talent. Following Woolf's example, counterfactual thinking about the reproductive and literary lives of foremothers abounds in twentieth-century feminist writings. Alice Walker, in her celebrated volume *In Search of Our Mothers' Gardens* (1983), for example, asks why there are not more signs of African American women's artistic talent. The answer, she famously observes, is "cruel enough to stop the blood" (233). She goes on to explore how the creative potential of Black women was lost to enslavement and forced childbearing. Another feminist classic, Maxine Hong Kingston's *The Woman Warrior: Memoirs of a Girlhood Among Ghosts* (1976), makes extensive use of counterfactual thinking to

Following the models of Woolf and Rich, twenty-first-century women writers see the ghostly figure of the aborted woman haunting counterfactual futures. Ghosts, Jeffrey Weinstock observes, disrupt the "linearity of historical chronology" and remind us that "beneath the surface of received history, there lurks another narrative, an untold story that calls into question the veracity of the authorized version of events" (63). According to Weinstock, ghosts "violate conceptual thinking based on dichotomous oppositions" (64) by being here / not here. The aborted woman challenges the dichotomies of aborted child / aborted mother as well as fulfilled mother / dissatisfied childless woman. Merritt Tierce's essay for *The New York Times*, "The Abortion I Didn't Have," for example, invokes the trope of the aborted woman when she recounts her own failure to have an abortion as a nineteen-year-old. Tierce discovered she was pregnant just as she was finishing her undergraduate degree (which she started at the age of sixteen) and had been accepted to Yale Divinity School. The daughter of fundamentalist Christian parents, she recalls how using birth control, practicing abstinence, having an abortion, and putting a child up for adoption were all equally impossible for her immature imagination, but so was having a baby, although that is ultimately what she did, at her family's urging. Her essay is a reflection on her experience as a young, unprepared mother whose budding intellectual and creative life was interrupted by unplanned pregnancy.

Now a successful writer, Tierce notes, "It took 15 years to dig myself out, after having children so young." Since attending the Iowa Writers' Workshop and receiving her MFA in 2011, she has published short stories, essays, and a novel; taught at the University of Iowa; and was a writer for two seasons on the HBO series *Orange Is the New Black*. Reflecting her lifelong love of reading and writing, her article is rife with references to women's poetry (including Brooks's "The Mother"). Tierce rejects the comment she often hears that her life and her children's lives turned out fine. As the phrase "dig myself out" implies, Tierce sees her life of creative, meaningful work and parenting

---

connect with her Chinese foremothers. The counterfactual figure of "No Name Aunt"—like Judith Shakespeare—relies on the trope of the aborted woman to show how the absence of reproductive control results in tragedy for women. Similarly, Bone Boatwright in Dorothy Allison's *Bastard out of Carolina* (1992) uses the healing power of storytelling to imagine the counterfactual life of her mother, Anney, and her own illegitimate birth:

> Who had Mama been, what had she wanted to be or do before I was born? Once I was born, her hopes had turned, and I had climbed up her life like a flower reaching for the sun. Fourteen and terrified, fifteen and a mother, just past twenty-one when she married Glen. Her life had folded into mine. (309)

Bone's epiphany that her mother was once a girl like her sparks compassion for Anney (despite her failings) as an aborted woman.

happening despite, not because, she had children when she did. Tierce's essay challenges many taboos against speaking about abortion and motherhood by discussing how her unplanned pregnancy derailed her education, career plans, family planning, and subsequently her identity. The essay enumerates her losses: She did not go to Yale; the compelled marriage to her son's father failed; he took the first job available to him, not the job he dreamed of; she lost her religious faith; she lost her sense of personhood as it was subsumed under the social label of "mother"; she lost her mental health and dealt with depression for the first ten years of her son's life because not going to graduate school meant losing her feelings of "accomplishment, contribution, confidence, and curiosity"; and, equally costly in her estimation, she lost the opportunity to be the kind of parent she wanted to be on her own time and terms, acknowledging that she has done her best parenting now that her children are teenagers. Tierce sums up her experience saying, "I did have to abort the life I imagined for myself."

Tierce's essay flips the antiabortion script that tells women they will regret having abortions. Tierce challenges the truism that the act of having a child is beyond reproach, and although she wrestles with the knowledge that her children may read her article and be disturbed by her argument, she notes that children are not responsible for a woman's maternal experience:

> But it's not poetic to say that dealing with the consequences of an unplanned pregnancy gave me some perspective. Or at least it's not nearly as poetic as it is to say to your children, You gave me my life, or to say about them, They made me who I am. It's a mistake to hang this on the children, even to feel gratitude toward them. They have no agency, no design in mind; they aren't responsible for our experience of them. They have nothing to do with it.

In her essay, Tierce directly muses on the counterfactual. At first she notes, "I can't imagine life without [her son] because the counterfactual does not exist," but then she goes on to say, "Forget the counterfactual, because it actually does exist, at least as a concept: In that other life, I would have accepted the loss of control and turned myself fully toward my children. In real life, I turned toward them only halfway, so I could keep watch on what I'd lost, and what I still wanted. But that meant my children lost, too." She admits that she was consumed with damaging doubts and regret for what she lost. Later in the essay she claims that when her friends—now in their forties—ask her advice about whether or not to have children, she knows what she is supposed to say: "I can't imagine life without my kids." But, she clarifies,

> I feel something like an obligation to hedge—even if I can't imagine life without my kids, even if they have made me who I am, the narrative is so overpromoted, especially to women, that I feel a duty to throw a pebble on the other side of the scale. Maybe that instinct is perverse, but I think of it as asking for a world in which a woman who doesn't have children is worth as much as a woman who does.

As a rhetorical strategy, Tierce's construction is full of tensions and broken taboos: Although she can't admit imagining her life without her children (who will be her readers), she does wish for a world in which she could imagine this counterfactual self.

Tierce's essay is haunted by the counterfactual and the aborted woman. Challenging the myth that mothers don't have abortions, she notes that she had two terminations after having her son and daughter. Like the speaker in Olds's poem who honors the "boon of absence," Tierce is grateful to those not-children: "If I imagine the counterfactual, I can say I have strong and loving relationships with both of my children now in large part because I didn't have those other children." And in concluding, Tierce wishes she had chosen adoption for her first child and imagines "alternate futures" for her younger self. In defense of her son, she cannot claim the abortion she didn't have, but she can claim it on behalf of other women: "When I help someone get an abortion, or even help someone think about abortion in a new way, I'm going back, choosing an alternate future and affirming the worth of that concept itself." Both Tierce and the speaker in Rich's poem challenge hegemonic notions of reproductive lives not by questioning the value of the fetus but by reminding readers of the value of women. By flipping the script on the antiabortion dualism of aborted child / aborted mother, their work draws on the epistemology of abortion and the knowledge of the ways that unplanned pregnancy and coerced childbearing can damage the lives of women and men.

## Conclusion

It's worth noting that several of the twenty-first-century writings discussed in this chapter were published in the years around the passage of the Partial-Birth Abortion Ban Act (2003). This ban on late–second trimester procedures succeeded in part because of campaigns of misinformation and stigma that promoted fetal primacy over women's lives. After years of witnessing the erosion of abortion rights, proabortion groups (such as the Abortion Conversation

Projects) understood that this proposed ban and subsequent law demanded a change in rhetorical strategies for defending abortion rights (Ludlow, "Love"). These changes have included discursive wanderings into territory formerly conceded to antiabortion rhetoric: the nature of the fetus, the maternal, spirituality, men's involvement, and a panoply of emotions ranging from regret to relief. This chapter has considered how the change in strategy is reflected in the literature of the twenty-first century that is deeply informed by an epistemology of abortion derived from the experience of patients, providers, and defenders. In the hands of contemporary writers, abortion is defended through the strategies of flipping the scripts on antiabortion rhetoric and conjuring the counterfactual aborted woman.

In the next chapter, I consider how bio-autographies by feminist writers see motherhood and heteronormative reproductive time as posing challenges to women's selves and art. More than the fear of "not being," the authors considered in chapter 2 fear becoming the artiste manquée who fails to live up to her artistic potential. This threat is felt through the haunting figure of the aborted woman—a counterfactual fantasy of the author's mother, who might have had children at a different time, in a smaller number, or who might never have had children. She might not have become an artist, but she would have had a different life, her daughter imagines. The question of abortion is structurally central to these memoirs and their temporal awareness of their mothers' reproductive lives.

CHAPTER 2

# Women's Time in Feminist Bio-Autography

## The Abortions Their Mothers Did Not Have

In a 2013 NPR interview following the publication of her novel *The Woman Upstairs,* Clare Messud described her mother as having missed the women's movement, noting that by the time Germaine Greer's book *The Female Eunuch* and *Ms.* magazine were both published, in 1970, her mother already had three children, and by 1973, when *Roe v. Wade* was decided, her life was dominated by the demands of her family. Messud explained, "I think she always felt a sort of wistful longing, as if she had been left on the shore watching the boat go." It's significant that Messud locates her mother temporally in relation to the legalization of abortion and two feminist publications, as these are iconic and related achievements of the mid-twentieth-century women's movement that signal—to white, middle-class feminists in particular—both reproductive control and the struggle to voice muted experiences. Messud's account of her mid-twentieth-century mother implies an imagined counterfactual: What might her mother's life have been with alternatives to the gendered expectations of heteronormativity and patriarchal motherhood? In telling her mother's story, Messud implicitly conjures the ghost of her mother's alternative life.

The legalization of abortion in 1973 has served as a significant temporal marker in white, middle-class US feminism, and it is probably safe to say that its importance cannot be overstated. US feminist consciousness is built around an awareness that pre-1973, women's lives were determined by what Adrienne Rich, in *On Lies, Secrets, and Silence* (1979), called "compulsory heterosexuality," the belief that normative sex is heterosexual and procreative, and childbearing and motherhood are women's destiny. In the foreword, Rich asserts the feminist challenge to this view of women: "The question finally . . . is whether women's bodies are to be viewed as essentially at the service of men; and to what extent the institution of heterosexuality promotes and fosters the belief that they are. Both abortion and lesbianism have been and still are defined as perverse and criminal behavior" (17). *Roe* signaled the denaturalization of motherhood and sexuality and presented resistance to compelled motherhood and steps toward sexual liberation and comprehensive women's healthcare. After *Roe,* more women had greater reproductive control, bodily sovereignty, and sexual freedom, not to mention a confidence in the feminist movement's ability to act—even if the benefits of those actions were unevenly experienced (Solinger, *Pregnancy*). Significantly, the post-*Roe* era meant that many women could determine the course of their own lives to a degree not enjoyed previously. In the eyes of many, the ability to exercise sexual and reproductive freedom signifies citizenship. Anything less is a denial of women's humanity and full participation in society.

This chapter considers the dominant role that 1973 specifically, and legalized abortion generally, plays in US feminist periodization. It considers this role by examining what Janet Beizer terms *bio-autography,* a genre of life-writing combining the author's and subject's voices. The bio-autographies in this study disrupt traditional ideas of authority and timekeeping through interweaving the reproductive histories of a feminist daughter and her mother: Cheryl Strayed's *Wild: From Lost to Found on the Pacific Crest Trail*; Terry Tempest Williams's *When Women Were Birds: Fifty-Four Meditations on Voice*; and Alison Bechdel's *Are You My Mother? A Comic Drama.* Like Messud, these authors reflect on the pre-*Roe* lives of their mothers to consider how they might have been different to understand their own artists' journeys to finding their voices. These mothers are not necessarily regretful, but their daughters apply an awareness of the reproductive choices that were not available to them to distinguish their lives. Rather than serving as a plot device in their texts, the legalization of abortion access is a temporal marker for a feminist daughter's comparison to and recognition of her mother as a woman. In this chapter, I will use the term *pre-Roe* to indicate coming of age and family-making stories that largely took place before 1973 and *post-Roe* to indicate stories about coming of age after 1973.

The two gestures of recuperating a mother's life in relation to 1973 and wondering about her counterfactual life—the hypothetical abortion she didn't have—reflect another version of the rhetorical trope, introduced in chapter 1, of the aborted woman, the imagined, uchronic figure of the woman who might have been. This figure is rhetorical, not literal—it is not an identity—and is born of collective knowledge that not having reproductive control may lead to families that are sometimes formed too quickly, that have more children than intended or wanted, or that are characterized by violence or abuse.

The figure may also simply point to a path not taken because it wasn't even visible. The mothers in these texts are not depicted as having unhappy lives (nor do the authors wish they had *not* been born or their mothers *had* had abortions). Rhetorically these authors compare their mothers' pre-*Roe* coming of age and family-making stories to their own post-*Roe* coming of age stories as artists. In making this comparison, they expand on Katie Watson's idea of "abortion beneficiaries" (26). Watson describes beneficiaries as people who have not had abortions themselves but have benefitted from other people's abortions or from the certainty of access. This includes partners and siblings, as well as heterosexual couples who enjoy their sex lives without fear of contraceptive failure. They are "stakeholders in the abortion debate" (29) who have been largely silenced by stigma. The post-*Roe* authors in this chapter readily identify as such stakeholders and acknowledge that they became writers because they had control over their bodies, sexuality, and reproduction.

My argument in this work is that twenty-first-century literature by women depicts abortion as ordinary. By *ordinary* I mean that literature captures the everydayness of abortion in US women's experience and imaginary. This everydayness is in contrast to the extraordinary abortion stories that populate public policy debates. The epistemology of abortion—the knowledge gleaned from fifty years of legalized access that supports continued access—has altered literary expression not just thematically but also formally. The texts examined in this chapter reveal that the use of feminist pre-/post-1973 periodization to imagine literal and figurative foremothers has become ordinary. These texts do not formally dramatize access: With the exception of Strayed, no one has an abortion, and even *Wild* downplays the importance of her decision to have one. Instead, these authors depict the abortions that women did *not* have pre-1973 as normal points of interest in a mother's biography.

## 1973 as a Feminist Inflection Point

Critical time studies calls attention to how chronotopic organization is related to power. The dominant temporal regime of nation-time frames the subjective experience of time. The texts by Strayed, Williams, and Bechdel subvert normative temporalities and instead reflect alternative structures, such as those explored by Julia Kristeva. In "Women's Time" (1979), Kristeva identifies female subjectivity as characterized by both natural cycles (somatic, repetitive, related to reproduction) and what she calls monumental time (eternity, resurrection myths, cult of maternity). She contrasts women's time to the linear history of progress and teleology of nation-time. To this consideration she adds a discussion of feminist movement in the twentieth century, including one branch that sought to include women in linear time accounts of progress and another branch that sought to disruptively recuperate the muted feminine Other. Kristeva anticipated the legacy of the two branches being a form of feminism that could accomplish two goals. First it would reclaim motherhood—rather than rejecting it. Important to Kristeva's formulation is the critique of traditional, selfless maternity and the exploration of "guiltless" motherhood—a type of motherhood that allows women to retain a sense of self rather than being subsumed by a maternal selflessness (30). Second, this new form of feminism could devise aesthetic practices to reveal the repressed and unsaid with patriarchal cultural symbolism (30) that would "break the code, to shatter language, to find a specific discourse closer to the body and emotions, to the unnamable repressed by the social contract" (25). This form of feminism, according to Kristeva, would privilege creative time (cyclic, aesthetic, generative) over the epic time of patriarchal periodization and literature. The "un-timing" of "historical periodizing frames" that Kristeva sought can be seen in women's art that privileges temporal fluidity and synchronicity, as well as "evanescence and contingency" (Apter 4) rather than fixity and certainty. Time, motherhood, and art are central concerns in the three works considered in this chapter.

Power shapes individual histories in addition to national histories, as recent queer theories of temporality demonstrate through interrogations of heteronormative timekeeping—the normative march of compulsory heterosexuality from courtship through marriage and childbearing. Sara Ahmed, for example, describes the (almost) irresistible process of being shaped by heteronormative time as "the path of happiness," the way that subjects are directed to pursue norms: "Somethings are assumed to lead to happiness" (48). This path is a normative temporal track that simultaneously guides and speeds subjects along unthinkingly. Ahmed observes that "we are directed by what is in front of us; and what is in front of us depends on how we are directed" (48). Raising consciousness to heteronormativity entails recognition that "happiness can thus also be a form of pressure," an awareness that can come as a (belated) shock, as in the case of Woolf's Mrs. Dalloway, who, Ahmed notes, "becomes alienated from her own life, conscious of possibilities only after they have been given up, possibilities that shimmer like the old friends she remembers in the passage of her day" (57). Similar to Ahmed's interpretation of Mrs. Dalloway, Strayed, Williams, and Bechdel wonder if their mothers had feelings of alienation or, like Messud's mother, the experience of standing on the shore "watching the boat go." The legalization of abortion in 1973 disrupts heteronormative timekeeping by providing a way of stepping off that path.

The conjured rhetorical figure of the uchronic aborted woman throws the hegemony of heteronormative timekeeping into question by revealing a queer trace or question of what might have been.

In her best-selling 2012 memoir *Wild,* Cheryl Strayed, who was born in 1968, recounts a period of despair in her mid-twenties following her mother's death from lung cancer. During this time, Strayed begins a dangerous spiral that threatens to end her writing career before it even starts. Shortly after her mother, Bobbi Lambrecht, is diagnosed, Strayed is unable to complete her final college term paper, which prevents her from graduating. After her mother's death, she ends her youthful marriage, moves to Oregon from her home in Minnesota, distracts herself with sexual affairs, and flirts with a heroin addiction. During a brief return to Minnesota, she discovers she is pregnant on the same day she impulsively purchases a book about the Pacific Crest Trail (PCT). She decides to abort the pregnancy and to hike the trail, thus beginning a grueling summerlong journey through California and Oregon, during which she confronts her mother's death and the direction her own life has taken. Concluding her adventure in the week that would have been her mother's fiftieth birthday and the due date of her terminated pregnancy, Strayed arrives at the Bridge of the Gods in Oregon rebalanced and free from her emotional baggage.

The narrative relies on both cyclical and monumental time for its structure. The extradiegetic narrator of *Wild* struggles to identify the beginning of the story of her hike, ultimately selecting the day Strayed learns her mother's cancer is terminal (although she does not start walking until two years later), noting that she was twenty-two years old, the same age as Bobbi when Strayed was born. By noting the nine months of her preparation and hiking, as well as the coincidence of her mother's birthday in the week she completed the hike and would have given birth, the narrative structure of *Wild* creates an overlap of beginnings and endings, and connections between birth, death, and rebirth:

> As I walked, I thought that if I'd continued with the pregnancy I'd learned about in that motel room in Sioux Falls the night before I decided to hike the PCT, I'd be giving birth to a baby right about now. The week of my mother's birthday would've been my due date. The rushing coalescence of those dates felt like a punch in the gut at the time, but it didn't compel me to waver in my decision to end my pregnancy. It only made me beg the universe to give me another chance. To let me become who I needed to before I became a mother: a woman whose life was profoundly different than my mother's had been. (272)

*Wild* is also structured around a healing period—not so much from her abortion as from the loss of her mother—and a period for her own rebirth as a mother and a writer. In this manner, *Wild* privileges the timekeeping of grief as well as rebirth and aesthetic creation.

Underpinning the narrative of her hike is the entwined story of two women, Bobbi and Strayed, one who came of age before *Roe v. Wade* and one after. Bobbi, who had gotten pregnant with Cheryl's sister when she was only nineteen, married their father and endured several years of abuse. After leaving the relationship in her late twenties, Bobbi struggled to support her children: "She worked and worked and worked and still we were poor" (14). When she met Eddie, Strayed's stepfather, they moved to the northern Minnesota woods, where Bobbi raised her children back-to-the-earth and later enrolled in college at the same time as Strayed. Strayed writes, "We were her kids, her comrades, the end of her and the beginning" (13), suggesting that having children so young was in some way "the end" of Bobbi. Strayed, like Messud, recounts the life of a mother who came of age before the mid-twentieth-century women's movement and legalized abortion:

> "I never got to be in the driver's seat of my own life," she'd wept to me once, in the days after she learned she was going to die. "I always did what someone else wanted me to do. I've always been someone's daughter or mother or wife. I've never just been me."
>
> "Oh, Mom," was all I could say as I stroked her hand.
>
> I was too young to say anything else. (272–73)

Unconventional and tough, Strayed's mother models one woman's ability to remake herself—repeatedly. Her story of escaping from abuse, surviving single motherhood, and pursuing a midlife return to education, is a model of strength, a strength that was gained from surviving the failed promise of compulsory heterosexuality. Nevertheless, Bobbi's lament motivates her daughter:

> Much as I loved and admired my mother, I'd spent my childhood planning not to become her. I knew why she'd married my father at nineteen, pregnant and only a tiny bit in love. . . . When she'd learned she was pregnant, she'd pondered two options: an illegal abortion in Denver or hiding out in a distant city during her pregnancy, then handing over my sister to her mother. . . . But my mother hadn't done either of those things. She decided to have her baby, so she'd married my dad instead. (272)

The illegal abortion that Strayed's mother did not have becomes important to how Strayed thinks about her mother and herself.

Terry Tempest Williams similarly uses a pre-/post-*Roe* periodization for reflecting on the life of her mother. A prolific nature writer and environmentalist, Williams, who was born in 1955, is known for exploring the similarities between the social position of women and the natural environment. The author and editor of numerous books and articles, Williams, who was born in 1955, is perhaps best known for her 1991 memoir *Refuge: An Unnatural History of Family and Place,* which connects nuclear weapons testing in Nevada to the cancers killing the women in her family in Utah. *When Women Were Birds* (2012) recounts how her mother, Diane Dixon Tempest, who was dying of ovarian cancer, bequeathed her journals (occupying three library shelves) to Williams. The matriarch of her Mormon family, Diane had five children before 1973, and she died when Williams was thirty-two years old, leaving her to make the heartbreaking discovery that the journals were all blank. The "Fifty-Four" of the subtitle refers to Diane's age when she died and the age when Williams begins writing the text, a textual echo reflecting a repetitive women's timekeeping. *When Women Were Birds* explores the politics of voice, motherhood, and reproduction. Two features of the text, in particular, develop these themes: the use of blank space and a discussion of the legalization of abortion in the central, twenty-seventh chapter.

Indebted to the theories of Tillie Olsen, Muriel Rukeyser, Claudine Herrman, and Helene Cixous, *When Women Were Birds* employs nonlinearity, gaps, and spaces that evoke the silences and secrets characteristic of the patriarchal suppression of women's voices. The first chapter narrates Williams's discovery that her mother's journals were empty, which is then shockingly followed by twelve blank pages. Readers enter Williams's surprise, loss, and bemusement when they turn page after blank page, wondering over their own disappointed expectations and frustrated pleasures ("Did I buy a book that's entirely blank?" "Is that it?" "What was unwritten?"). Readers are also invited to consider what they would do with these blank pages—Fill them? With what? The book's form thus considers the questions Williams explores: Why did her mother leave her journals empty, and what is the significance of that silence—is it hostile or inviting? Did her mother intend Williams to fill them? Or did her busy mother simply not have time to write? Did she seek to protect her family from her struggle with cancer? What other secrets did her mother keep? Diane's motivations are made more mysterious when Williams observes that "in Mormon culture, women are expected to do two things: keep a journal and bear children. Both gestures are a participatory bow to the past and the future" (18). The expectation was that Diane's journal-keeping would be in service to patriarchal families and normative timekeeping—minus personal reflection and voice. Were the empty journals a silent rebellion against this cultural expectation? The blank pages of *When Women*

*Were Birds* and the invitation to imagine what Diane might have said point to the figure of the aborted woman. Williams observes, "What my mother wanted to do and what she was able to do remains her secret" (16).

Chapter 27 is an impassioned defense of abortion and reproductive freedom that identifies 1973 as the point of departure for Williams's life from her mother's life. In this chapter Williams defends abortion as "our spiritual and legal right in the United States of America" (102). The structural and temporal midpoint of the fifty-four chapters, which would have been the midpoint of Diane's life, recounts her decision to have a tubal ligation procedure (birth control), something uncharacteristic of her peers. Williams contrasts this act in the same chapter with her memory of when abortion was legalized: "Birth control gave me my voice. . . . I have never had an abortion, but I was grateful to have that choice before me. I was a senior at Highland High School in 1973, when the landmark case *Roe v. Wade* was decided in the Supreme Court. It was a decision that gave us confidence as young women entering sexual maturity that we did have control over our own bodies" (101). She recalls thinking to herself as a young woman, "I am my mother, but I'm not," prompting the recognition that "my path would be my own" (57). This statement leads her to a momentous decision: "Having children could wait. Finding my voice could not" (91). Like Strayed, Williams compares her mother's pre-*Roe* life to her own post-*Roe* choices. Abortion is shown to be ordinary in this text not because Williams had one but because 1973 structures the temporal consciousness of the text.

The use of blank space and the defense of abortion prompts consideration of women's reproductive freedom through awareness of women's silences—imposed or chosen—and the ghosts that haunt these spaces. Asked to contemplate the twelve blank pages provided by Williams, the reader is positioned to contemplate maternal lives and reproductive histories—including their own. This invitation is powerfully disruptive. Williams quotes Muriel Rukeyser's famous line, "What would happen if one woman told the truth about / her life? / The world would split open," as a comment on the power in women's stories to disturb larger familial and cultural narratives. At the same time as Williams's text acknowledges the threatening power of women's truth, it also validates the maternal choice to remain silent. The chapter suggests that mothers protect their families by withholding certain truths and thereby shield individuals from threatening details. Knowledge of one's mother's reproductive history—including abortion—could indeed "split open" an individual's or family's world and thus is guarded with care. The temporal structure of the text reveals that 1973 marks a shift away from the silencing of women's voices through compelled childbearing to a new era of balancing the individual's need for privacy with the collective need to hear stigma-busting stories that help to defend reproductive rights.

Similarly, in *Are You My Mother?* legal access to birth control and abortion provide a temporal marker for Bechdel's reflection on her mother's life. Bechdel's graphic memoirs about growing up in a family headed by her closeted gay father expose the traditional family and its secrets as breeding grounds for toxic shame and abuse (a different response to familial secrecy than Williams had). Following her best-selling *Fun Home: A Family Tragicomic* (2006), in which she reveals not only her father's sexuality but also his suicide, Bechdel, who was born in 1960, published *Are You My Mother? A Comic Drama* (2012) about her relationship with her mother, Helen Bechdel. *Are You My Mother?* reveals that Bechdel's first memoir almost wasn't completed due to her paralyzing writer's block, which she gradually recognizes as arising from anger at her mother. The nature of this anger and how she overcomes it to publish *Fun Home* builds the narrative tension in *Are You My Mother?*

Repetition and reproductive cycles shape Bechdel's account of her relationship with her mother, as in the bio-autographies Strayed and Williams. The extradiegetic narrator of *Are You My Mother?* self-reflexively debates whether her first menstrual period or her coming out as a lesbian should serve as the beginning of the diegesis of their relationship: "I see that perhaps the real problem with this memoir about my mother is that it has no beginning. Sort of like how I'd understood human reproduction as a child. I was an egg inside my mother when she was still an egg inside her mother, and so forth and so on" (6–7). Bechdel interrupts this image with the announcement of her menopause: "There's a certain relief in knowing I'm a terminus" (7). She goes on to explain, "Even if I'd ever had the slightest urge to reproduce, it's too late now. I'm running out of eggs. My clockworklike menstrual cycle skipped its first beat the very week, in my forty-fifth year, that I sat down to begin writing about my mother" (7). The coincidence of her reproductive years ending at the same time as she produces this text about Helen privileges both cyclic and creative time. She also notes, "It had been five months since this book was due, and six since my last period. Like my mother, I keep a log of the events of daily external life. But unlike her, I also record a great deal of information about my internal life. Although I'm often confused about precisely where the demarcation lies" (17). Two differences between them, however, are made clear by the text: sexuality and reproductive political views.

In the text's central chapter, "Mind," Bechdel contemplates an abortion her mother didn't have pre-*Roe*. "Mind" begins with Bechdel's memory of sorting through a box of her father's letters that also contains a few of Helen's poems. These documents provide Bechdel with insight into her parents' life in the 1960s as a young, child-free couple in Germany, where her father was stationed. Bechdel reflects on the cool, detached tone of her mother's poems, but the letters reveal that, at the time her mother wrote these poems, she was unhappily pregnant with Alison. Her unhappiness is due to something vaguely referred to as her father's hostility and "crassness" (128). When asked, Helen evasively acknowledges that Bechdel's father, Bruce, laughed "inappropriately" when she announced her pregnancy and then punished her with the silent treatment (139). Surmising that her own conception was six months earlier than the FDA's approval of the birth control pill, Alison muses that her father may have proposed an abortion: "My mother did not tell me, did not suggest in any way, that my father had proposed an abortion. But I can't help suspecting this was the 'crassness' he stooped to. Apparently, he took the news of mom's pregnancies with my brothers just as badly" (140). In the same panel, Helen is depicted walking through German streets alone, with a forlorn expression, but the narrative does not speculate on why she did not have an abortion and neither lauds her as heroic nor condemns her as shortsighted. The possibility that an abortion would have prevented the subsequent suffering endured by Bechdel and her parents is invoked by Bechdel's "relief of being a terminus" and prompts speculation about the woman and artist Helen might have become under different circumstances. Neither Bechdel nor her mother had an abortion, but "Mind" puts the issue centrally in the text of *Are You My Mother?* and in so doing highlights how reproductive and sexual freedom are vital for women's art. Bechdel can be seen as an abortion beneficiary in how she uses the trope of the aborted woman to contrast her post-*Roe* life of greater freedom from compulsory heterosexuality to her mother's muted life.

Bechdel's contemplation of her mother's poetry in "Mind" shows that Helen's pre-1973 impersonal style was a reflection of her lifestyle. She suggests Helen was a frustrated artist—she returns to poetry writing late in life but refuses to identify as a poet (30)—whose Catholic upbringing and obeisance to mid-twentieth-century compulsory heterosexuality cost her dearly. While Bruce attended graduate school and pursued his career and sexual affairs with young men, Helen supported him and cared for their children (174), and while she was well-intentioned, dutiful, and "good enough" as a mother, the troubled dynamic of her marriage prevented her from being "enough" for her daughter. Bechdel compares her mother's pre-*Roe* life to her own post-*Roe* choices. The abortion that Helen Bechdel did not have looms large in "Mind," as one of several discrete decisions that she made as part of the heteronormative path of happiness even as that path demanded more secrets and silences from her.

## A Post-1973 Claiming of Voice Through Embodiment

In addition to telling the pre-*Roe* stories of their mothers, these writers tell their own post-*Roe* stories—specifically how they became writers. Feminist periodization is important to this theme, as the ordinary feminist periodization of abortion access and women's control over their bodies is invoked to mark the point of inflection from their mothers' (silenced) lives. Strayed, Williams, and Bechdel use the marker of legalized abortion and women's gaining control over their bodies as a means for understanding how they became artists.

For Strayed, legal abortion access is key to her transformation. Although the path through her loss and back to herself is not clear, her abortion decision is straightforward and unequivocal: "That I would get an abortion was a fact so apparent it seemed silly to discuss anything else" (56). Through the haze of unprocessed grief and drug use, the unplanned pregnancy is a recognizable danger: "I was crying over all of it, over the sick mire I'd made of my life since my mother died; over the stupid existence that had become my own. I was not meant to be this way, to live this way, to fail so darkly" (56). The unplanned pregnancy is a wake-up call, but the abortion Strayed procures barely merits mention in the text:

> I got an abortion and learned how to make dehydrated tuna flakes and turkey jerky and took a refresher course on basic first aid and practiced using my water purifier in my kitchen sink. I had to change. I had to change was the thought that drove me in those months of planning. Not into a different person, but back to the person I used to be—strong and responsible, clear-eyed and driven, ethical and good. And the PCT would make me that way. There, I'd walk and think about my entire life. I'd find my strength again, far from everything that had made my life ridiculous. (57)

In the first sentence of this passage, the text buries the lede, downplaying the abortion and equating it to other pre-trip activities. *Wild* illustrates how abortion is ordinary or undramatic in the sense that the decision to have one does not dominate the narrative's plot; instead, the action is driven by Strayed's journey, how she will be transformed by it, and how much of her symbolically overburdened pack (named "monster") she will shed.

The abortion initiates Strayed's recovery and reclaimed vocation as a writer. She recalls how she began her first novel during the hike, reminding herself, "Of all the versions of myself I'd lived out, there was one that had never changed: I was a writer" (189). After her hike, she subsequently graduated magna cum laude with a double major in English and women's studies from the University of Minnesota and went on to complete an MFA from Syracuse University. She has written fiction and essays, publishing in *The New York Times* and elsewhere. In 2010, she started the popular advice column "Dear Sugar" for *The Rumpus,* which has since become a podcast that she hosts. She has published two advice books, one of which, *Tiny Beautiful Things,* has been adapted to stage, while *Wild* became an international bestseller, won accolades for her writing, and was adapted in 2014 into an Oscar-nominated movie starring Reese Witherspoon as Strayed and Laura Dern as Bobbi, her mother. Although Stayed does not make much of her identity as a writer in *Wild,* the existence of the text attests to the primacy of writing in her life.

In *When Women Were Birds,* Williams describes her own silence and her fight to find her voice. As a child, she overcame a stutter that still threatens to return as an adult during public speaking (33). When as a young bird-watcher, she reported an unusual sighting to her local Audubon society, she was told her sighting was not "credible" (43) due to her young age. Additionally, she shares the memory of showing her poetry to her formidable father, whose crushing assessment—"a bit flowery" (33)—hushed her, and in later writing she practices self-censorship: "I didn't want to criticize my father" (45). She describes her childhood fondness for writing with "invisible ink" (lemon juice on parchment) (39), and, as an adult, her self-named practice of "repetations": "When I want to see the furthest into my soul, I will write a sentence by hand and then write another sentence over it, followed by another. An entire paragraph will live in one line, and no one else can read it. That is the point. . . . A friend of mine calls it my disease. I call it my confessional" (178–80). Finally, Williams writes of occasions when her political voice has been silenced, such as when she quit the governing council of the Wilderness Society after learning that her voice was being discounted as "extreme" (147).

In chapter 27, however, Williams shares that although she never had an abortion, the certainty of access gave her confidence in herself: "Birth control gave me my voice" (101). The confidence that abortion access gives to Williams combines with the mystery of her mother's silence to lead her to express her grief through Diane's blank journals: "When I opened my mother's journals and read emptiness, it translated to longing, that same hunger and thirst Mother translated to me. I will rewrite this story, create my own story on the pages of my mother's journals" (20). She suggests that, if there is a subversive motivation behind her mother's silence in response to the Mormon cultural expectation that she keep a journal about her family, it is this impulse that motivates her to write: "I am writing the creation story of my own voice through the blank pages my mother has bequeathed to me. Transgression is transmission" (97). Williams declares: "Mother gave me my voice by withholding hers, both in life and in death" (163). Williams identifies with elements of her mother's life and character, but access to birth control and abortion distinguishes her ability to find and use her voice from her mother's muted one.

*When Women Were Birds* uses the feminist periodization of pre– and post–*Roe v. Wade* as a point of inflection between Diane and Williams, who remains child-free and who chooses language over silence: "To withhold words is power. But to share our words with others openly and honestly, is also power" (16). In chapter 27, she uses her voice to defend abortion access by reflecting on the belated knowledge of the abortions that her friends have had:

> No, I have never had an abortion, but I know the tenderness of many women who have. It is much more common than we choose to admit. We have gone underground. This is the conversation we are not having. The abortions we have are an intrinsic part of who we are and what we have become. And it is deeply private. Just recently I learned that three of my closest friends have had abortions. It is not something we ever discussed. (102)

These friends had abortions to finish educations, for health reasons, and to care for their families. This passage reveals the power in hearing previously untold stories from the women close to Williams, and it provides readers with an allegory of listening for the muted abortion stories of mothers, friends, sisters, and partners. By listening, as Williams does, for the silenced stories of the women in our lives, she learns and shares facts that counter the popular myths about abortions: Abortion is not rare, there is no one type of woman who has an abortion, mothers have abortions, spiritual and religious women have abortions, conservative women have abortions, and so on. These truths do indeed have the power to "split open" the world. Recent research suggests that hearing someone's abortion story produces a positive change in one's abortion politics (Cockrill et al.). Other research finds that Americans who hold antiabortion views are 21 percent less likely to have heard someone's abortion story (Cowan). Taken together, these studies suggest that those who oppose abortion rights are less likely to hear the stories—from the women closest to them—that would challenge the misperceptions and abortion myths invoked in social policies designed to curtail reproductive freedom.

Like Williams, Bechdel claims her voice by claiming her body. This means rejecting her mother's overvaluation of the mind. Bechdel fears being silenced, but unlike Williams, she fears she will be silenced by her mother's compliance with heteronormativity. "Mind" begins in 2002 with Bechdel's recollection of a dream in which she impotently seeks to make an emergency phone call. The emergency dream is painfully close to her reality at that time: She is in dire financial shape prior to the publication of *Fun Home* but equally distraught by the knowledge that the book's publication (and subsequent outing of her father's queer secrets) will upset her mother, as happened years prior when she announced her sexuality and her decision to publish a lesbian comic series (229). "Mind" becomes an exploration of what seems like a life-threatening dilemma: Will she publish the book (telling her father's queer secrets) and save herself financially but risk her mother's disapproval? Or will she delay publication and face financial ruin to retain her mother's approval?

Resolving this emergency requires claiming her anger at Helen for Helen's betrayal of women and their bodies. In "Mind" Bechdel considers how Helen's detached poetic tone reminds Bechdel of how her mother encouraged her to develop an unhealthy overreliance on her own mind—to the neglect of her body and its demands. She recalls her mother's twentieth-century disregard for the body generally and the female body specifically when she asks Helen for the name for female genitalia. Helen uses the dictionary to look up the term *vagina,* which she delivers with distaste (169). Similarly, Helen's letter responding to Bechdel's coming out as a lesbian in college exudes a repressive shaming of the body and its disruptive desires: "Couldn't you just get on with your work? You are young, you have talent, you have a mind. The rest, whatever it is, can wait" (156). "The rest" in this sentence includes Bechdel's sexuality, against which Helen applies the kind of pressure Ahmed describes as characterizing compulsory heterosexuality. Helen similarly discourages Bechdel from making art that reflects her identity as a lesbian, saying that by doing so, Bechdel was "limiting" herself. Bechdel takes a developmental turn when she recognizes that, as a child, winning her mother's love meant participating in her heteronormative front, suppressing any inconvenient desires (those arising in the body, in particular), and overinvesting in her mind as an instrument of her false self (156). "Mind," like the other chapters in Bechdel's memoir, is named for a psychoanalytic concept explored by D. W. Winnicott, whose theories of object relations lead Bechdel to see that the unhealthy overreliance on her intellectual abilities encouraged by her mother's heteronormative expectations required a silencing of her body in life and art. In her pre-1973 life, Helen privileges the mind as something she can control, whereas the body—and specifically the female body subjugated by patriarchy—was out of her control. Bechdel credits her post-1973 lesbian identity—the disruptive desires of her body—with breaking the hold of her internalized mother-editor: "If it weren't for the unconventionality of my desires, my mind might never have been forced to reckon with my body" (156). By claiming her anger at her mother's demand for a false self, Bechdel overcomes the writer's block that was preventing her from finishing *Fun Home.*

Strayed's, Williams's, and Bechdel's memoirs draw on a white, middle-class, feminist periodization to explain their journeys to becoming writers. The Supreme Court decision in 1973 that legalized abortion signals a defiance of compulsory heterosexuality, the subversion of normative procreative sex, and a challenge to women's predetermined roles as wives and mothers. In this sense, legalized abortion is an index of sexual and reproductive freedom and bodily sovereignty, the prerequisites for women's expression. These writers can think about claiming their voices through the trope of reclaiming women's bodies from compulsory heterosexuality.

Despite contrasting post-1973 daughterly voices with pre-1973 maternal silences, these texts subvert notions of progressive linearity. The decision in *Roe v. Wade* in 1973 may have presented these daughters with different options than what their mothers had, but their texts are not willing to depict their entwined stories as a teleology or to reduce their mothers' lives to oversimplified foils for their own feminist identities and desires. In what follows, I want to discuss how feminist biography seeks to destabilize the relationships of power between authors and subjects as a way of understanding how Strayed, Williams, and Bechdel resist an oversimplified comparison of pre-/post-1973 women's lives.

## The Politics of Recovery and Bio-Autography

The life-writing by Strayed, Williams, and Bechdel seek to recuperate their mother's pre-1973 biographies, an act that aligns with the feminist critical practice of recovering the historically and canonically lost, suppressed, and muted voices of women. While Strayed, Williams, and Bechdel do not identify as scholars in this tradition—they identify as writers—their stories about how they became writers are intertwined with the biographies of their literal and figurative mothers, and they cast the recovery of their mothers' lives and voices as an expression of their own post-1973 empowerment and voices.

In an essay on recuperative readings, Carla Kaplan describes recovery as the "archeological imperative" of feminist literary criticism. Feminist writers and critics sought to identify a women's literary tradition, and in its absence, they imagined their foremothers' talents were thwarted by having limited or no access to education, opportunity, or role models and by being wives and mothers, leading them to produce "aborted work, deferred, denied" (Olsen).

Early feminist critics such as Virginia Woolf, Tillie Olsen, Adrienne Rich, and Alice Walker and those who followed sought to "rescue . . . silenced, marginalized women, from history or from critical traditions" (Kaplan 169). Susan Gubar describes the practice as a "fantastic collaboration" between critic and subject (qtd. in Kaplan 172). Nancy Miller describes the feminist critic's role as developing "a strategy for reading between the lines (of texts and lives), deciphering silence, decoding double-talk and filling in gaps to correct and compensate for the double silence of repressed expression and critical misunderstanding that we might identify with all revisionary, recuperative work" (qtd. in Kaplan 177). She calls this strategy "overreading."

Subsequent critics, however, have identified unexamined premises in recuperative biographical works by feminists. Kaplan contends that the rescue of women who were omitted from historical texts and canons by feminist scholars "often imparted much of the sense of the heroic, the image of misunderstood, abandoned, neglected women finally rescued and released by their stronger, bolder daughters" (169). Some critics note the outsized role the feminist critic assigned herself in saving other women. Teleological bias—here, the belief in feminist progress—enables the assumption that the feminist daughter is stronger than her mother. By assuming the role of hero, the feminist critic may un/intentionally reduce their subject to the role of a victim who lacks agency. As Mariane Hirsch cautions, "To speak for the mother . . . is at once to give voice to her discourse and to silence and marginalize her" (16).

Furthermore, in *The Mother/Daughter Plot: Narrative, Psychoanalysis, Feminism,* Hirsch explains that the literal mother's voice is difficult to hear in Western culture. Hirsch's work on mother–daughter plots in nineteenth- and twentieth-century novels by women traces the unspeakable quality of maternal lives even as women gain greater agency. She posits that the maternal perspective is muted in these texts due to an androcentric identification with the subject position of the (male) child: "While psychoanalytic feminism can add the female child to the male, allowing women to speak as daughters, it has difficulty accounting for the experience and the voice of the adult woman who is a mother" (12). Due to the dominance of psychoanalytic models for understanding selfhood, Western narrative is dominated by the voice and perspective of the child. Hirsch's work points to the difficulty in thinking and writing about the lives of women without letting the maternal role silence other aspects of their lives.

Janet Beizer echoes this concern in *Thinking Through the Mothers: Reimagining Women's Biographies,* which examines feminist biography and the rhetoric used to express the desire for a feminine literary lineage. Beizer observes that feminist writers and critics are always thinking about their literal mothers, even as they search for figurative, literary ones, and that "listening for the mother's voice" may be compromised by daughterly projections of disappointments and unmet needs. She refers to this as "biography as tale of desire" (16), which produces mixed results: "Efforts to revive the buried lives of women in the hope of finding spiritual foremothers tend to wake maternal phantoms who are alternately wrestled to the ground and embraced" (3). She concludes that the projection of these desires interferes with any pure understanding of lost literal or figurative mothers: "As I unpacked the maternal metaphor, I was led to wonder if, as women, we have any greater access to our mothers' lives than to the lives of other women whose stories have been swept away like dust in the debris of the past" (4).

Beizer and other subsequent critics point to new strategies to recover literal and figurative maternal voices in twenty-first-century feminist biographies. Beizer, for example, observes a self-conscious merger of searches for literal and figurative mothers that foregrounds and explores the author's desires rather than sublimating them: "Quests for the lives of metaphorical mothers and hunts for the lives of real-life mothers are often not only congruent but also significantly intertwined" (3). By merging their mothers' lives with their own experience and the voices of feminist othermothers across generations, these authors tell a complex story of feminist movement and periodization. Additionally, Kaye Mitchell, in "This Is Not a Memoir: Feminist Writings from Life" in *The New Feminist Literary Studies*, observes a shift in feminist life-writing conventions that deemphasize the heroic individualism of the author. She identifies "more experimental forms of life writing which juxtapose stories of self with stories of others, and which presume neither the existence of a knowable self nor the necessary desirability of self-knowledge as the outcome of the act of autobiographical writing" (208). This type of feminist life-writing resists the individualism of neoliberalism and instead emphasizes collective politics. Beizer similarly identifies a desire for interconnection (rather than individualism) that leads to new forms of writing:

> The ways in which the quest for foremothers, for many feminist biographers, New Historians, and literary critics, is personally motivated, becomes a search for the self and its biological maternal origins, and itself becomes part of the story. Biography and autobiography then fuse, often flirting with the fictional, blurring generic boundaries, and creating an intergenre I named "bio-autography": the writing of the self through the representation of another's life. (2–3)

Women writers have increasingly found ways to foreground maternal voices in their texts and call attention to the limitations and ethical problems of representing another's voice. In addition to Beizer's concept of bio-autography, Jo Malin's *The Voice of the Mother: Embedded Maternal Narratives in Twentieth-Century Women's Autobiographies* examines contemporary women's autobiographies for how daughters inseparably weave their mothers' stories into their own. Mothers become what she calls "intersubjects." Rather than daughters assuming authority over their mother's stories, a dialogic relationship emerges through these embedded maternal biographies. This narrative strategy subverts the monologic "word of the father" of male autobiography and its characteristic tale of great deeds and accomplishments (10). Finally, in *Contemporary Feminist Life-Writing: The New Audacity* (2020), Jennifer Cooke explores stylistic and formal elements that call attention to a text's craft and structure, thereby disrupting assumptions that women's life-writing is always unmediated, confessional writing. Mitchell, Beizer, Malin, and Cooke all point to ways that twenty-first-century feminist writers of biography and autobiography are resisting patriarchal forms and regimes to recover maternal voices.

Strayed's, Williams's, and Bechdel's bio-autographies demonstrate a similar concern for not resilencing the voices of the pre-*Roe* women they seek to recover. The assumption might be that because abortion access empowered the daughters of Bobbi, Diane, and Helen to become writers, they experience greater agency and ability to speak truth to power. Their texts, however, resist an oversimplified linear account of women's empowerment. These texts reveal the ongoing silencing of women's voices, thereby resisting the neat binary of silenced mother and empowered daughter. This resistance to progressive linearity reflects Kristeva's argument against thinking about generations of feminists as discrete or advancing: "My usage of the word 'generation' implies less a chronology than a signifying space, a corporeal and desiring mental space. So it can be argued that as of now a third attitude is possible, thus a third generation, which does not exclude—quite to the contrary—the *parallel* existence of all three in the same historical tie, or even that they be interwoven with the other" (33). The relationships between generations of women that are represented in the works by Strayed, Williams, and Bechdel attest to the coexistence of generations of women who are fighting multiple battles on multiple fronts for themselves and for other women.

These texts also downplay the authors' individualism and authorial heroism by elevating the voices and perspectives of their biographical intersubjects and feminist othermothers. The textual mapping of their mothers' ages onto their own lives, the confusion over the beginnings of mother–daughter relationships, and the rejection of their ending (even after death) are all details that reinforce how their stories cannot be separated from their mothers' biographies. The introduction of feminist othermothers into their accounts further downplays the individualism of these authors and builds a sense of feminist narrative collaboration. In particular, the figure of Adrienne Rich serves as a feminist othermother to Strayed, Williams, and Bechdel, on whom they draw to tell their multi-/anti-generational feminist stories. Each text in this study was published in 2012, the year that Rich died, and each alludes directly to her oeuvre and specifically to *The Dream of a Common Language,* the first book of poetry Rich published after she came out as a lesbian in 1976. Rich came of age in the 1940s—a decade before their own mothers—and unquestioningly started down the path of a heteronormative life. After receiving her education and accolades for her poetry, she was married and had three sons by the late 1950s. Her involvement in the feminist movement of the 1960s, however, led her to revise her life and art radically. Rich divorced her husband and came out as a lesbian, and as she embraced the theory that the personal is political, her poetry became increasingly subjective—disappointing some critics (as described in "When We Dead Awaken"). Rich's raised consciousness and alienation from her earlier life resulted in her writing essays that probed silences and that recuperated women's voices and experiences. For Rich, sexual freedom and abortion are the foundation of women's liberation in part because she appreciated how patriarchal motherhood could bury a woman and her voice. Like Kristeva, she perceived the need to revise—not reject—motherhood. Her subsequent work, *Of Woman Born* (1976), critiques the patriarchal institution of motherhood and praises the radical potential of mothering, which she denaturalizes by arguing, "The 'childless woman' and the 'mother' are a false polarity, which has served the institutions both of motherhood and heterosexuality. There are no such simple categories" (250). She goes on to observe, "Many of the great mothers have not been biological" (252). Rich's life spanned more than one generation of feminists, and her work offers a way for feminists across generations to recognize shared struggle. Her work presents to Strayed, Williams, and Bechdel the consolation that while they may not identify with their pre-1973 mothers and their limitations, they can appreciate their strength.

For Strayed, recovering her mother's voice means celebrating her mother's strength as a mother, which she herself lacks until her hike. Although her goal is to "not be her," Strayed clearly craves her mother's strength to remake herself. Some might argue that the lesson Strayed takes away from reflecting on her mother's life is the hegemonic directive to be what feminist historian Rickie Solinger has called "a good-choice-maker" (*Beggars*) one whose reproductive decisions are informed by neoliberal norms. Kaye Mitchell considers how the neoliberal overprivileging of autonomy, self-reliance, and individualism has played a role in shaping contemporary feminism and recent feminist life-writing. By misreading "the personal is political" as an invitation to overemphasize their individual battles to overcome oppressive structures, some authors, Mitchell notes, celebrate their micro-triumphs over sexism at the cost of appreciation for how collective struggle benefits all women. Feminist life-writing, she notes, runs the risk of only telling stories about winning and overcoming adversity. The challenge, she speculates, is in recounting personal stories that connect empathetically to others (including maternal subjects) rather than serving the ego of the writer. Strayed, however, demonstrates her reliance on foremothers. Autonomy and self-reliance—while necessary for attempting a solo hike—are not privileged over the traits that her mother possessed, including the strength it took to leave an abuser, to transform her life, and to be a single mother. The text affirms that Strayed is "a good choice-maker," but it simultaneously refuses to ignore her mother's agency or reduce Bobbi to her regrets. Strayed's embrace of her mother can be seen in her embrace of her own desire to become a mother. Her desire to "not be her" is not a rejection of motherhood. Her narrative concludes with her seated on the bridge in Oregon and with a moment of prolepsis: "In four years I'd cross the Bridge of the Gods with another man and marry him in a spot almost visible from where I now sat. . . . In nine years that man and I would have a son named Carver, and a year and a half after that, a daughter named Bobbi" (310). Significantly, her goal in hiking the PCT, which she first articulated simply as "I had to change. I had to change," becomes more clearly focused on claiming her desire to become a mother, like Bobbi, who conveyed her love fiercely. But unlike Bobbi, Strayed (re)claims her sense of self first.

The importance of Adrienne Rich's work can be seen in Strayed's stashing a copy of *The Dream of a Common Language* in her already symbolically overburdened pack. As she hikes, Strayed sheds much of her symbolic and literal baggage but retains her copy of Rich's work, affirming, "The PCT book was my bible; *Dream* was my religion" (60). Strayed describes Rich's work as "the mix-tape running through my head," and says that as she "chanted the lines" (304), it compelled the realization that "fear is a story women tell themselves" (51) and that by rewriting it, "power begets power" (51). These lines allow Strayed to reflect on her own fears (losing her mother, losing her way) as well as the fears that her mother confronted (losing herself and then losing her marriage). In addition to borrowing two poem titles for her chapter titles ("Power" and "The Dream"), Strayed appears to have found inspiration for her own name (which she assumes after her divorce) in the poem "The Lioness," in which a speaker reflects on the dangers of uncharted territory: "[T]he problem is always / one of straying too far, not of staying / within bounds." She claims the identity of a motherless stray but also the strength to stray outside social norms—even outside one's current identity—with the help of other women in search of transformation. In Strayed's case, these women are Rich and her mother.

In *When Women Were Birds* Williams also alludes to Rich's *The Dream of a Common Language* (168), drawing on "Cartographies of Silence" to understand her mother's blank journals. In this poem, the speaker identifies how a silence can be strategic, "a plan / rigorously executed," and cautions against confusing these silences "with any kind of absence," suggesting a presence that can only be surmised (16). Williams recognizes her mother's silence as deliberate, tactical: "I will never know what she was trying to tell me by telling me nothing" (168). Additionally, by starting with the twelve blank pages in the first chapter, Williams introduces Diane's strategy into the text: "Her absence became her presence" (1). Similarly, her respect for Diane's privacy seems borrowed from a different poem by Rich, "A Woman Dead in Her Forties," in which the speaker, who is dying of cancer, observes, "There are things I will not share / with everyone." Like Strayed's bio-autography of her mother, *When Women Were Birds* recovers and elevates the story of an ordinary woman—Williams's mother—without muting her voice or lending undue authority to Williams. Williams accomplishes this through balancing what her mother does say with the knowledge that her mother's silences may be chosen.

*When Women Were Birds* disrupts Williams's authority not only by giving space to her mother's silence but also by throwing her ownership of the text into question. The 2012 Picador edition of *When Women Were Birds*, which uses rough-cut paper edges to create the impression of its being a primitive book, begins with the facsimile of a bookplate, "This Journal Belongs To ______." As Cooke notes about other strategies for challenging the assumption that women's life-writing reflects unmediated confessions, this blank space provokes questions about the ownership of the text to destabilize Williams's claim on it: Who owns this book? Williams? Her mother? The reader? Diane's presence is also given power by the instances when readers hear her voice. In chapter 27, Williams describes her mother's unorthodox decision to control her fertility, recalling, "When we were children, we visited Mother in the hospital. We were told she was having 'corrective surgery.' Later I learned she had made the decision to have her tubes tied, not a common practice among her peers. 'Freedom,' she said" (180). The contrast between the sexist euphemism "correcting" and her mother's own term, "freedom" (provided in direct dialogue), is noteworthy. Diane's term bespeaks an insubordinate consciousness of the constraints posed by compulsory heterosexuality and patriarchal motherhood. Additionally, it reminds readers of the pre-1973 context in which Diane made her reproductive decisions, contributing to an understanding of Diane's silence as a form of agency. In *Of Woman Born,* Rich describes mid-twentieth-century childbirth as a form of alienated labor, and disempowerment of women by the medical establishment. In an article examining the silences of women who were traumatized by their mid-twentieth-century childbirth experiences, D'Arcy Randall considers how such patients made bids for self-empowerment through the use of their silence, as well as why it was important for writers like Rich to speak out:

> Few would argue that these unfortunate mothers' tactics [of silence] are, in the long run, helpful or useful. Speaking out is surely a more effective strategy to secure authority. But one also needs to be heard, and for the profoundly disempowered at a time of crisis, silence may appear the only dignified option. Note that [these] mothers cling to precious "knowledge" withheld from the doctors. Rich does not deny the limited options faced by most real mothers, but *Of Woman Born* gives women space to imagine themselves reclaiming the institutional frameworks in which we give birth. (200)

Rich's assertion that women's silence can be a form of resistance to mid-twentieth-century patriarchy and misogyny reveals their agency, even as Rich emphasized the importance for women—particularly women artists—in finding their voices. In this way, *When Women Were Birds* discourages overreading and filling the gaps of Diane's silences.

*Are You My Mother?* has numerous direct allusions to Rich's work, establishing her as Bechdel's feminist and queer othermother. In the chapter titled "Hate," Bechdel depicts a scene from college showing her girlfriend reading *The Dream of a Common Language* and *On Lies, Secrets, and Silence.* The narrator recalls: "Adrienne Rich was not assigned reading for any of my classes. My new lesbian friends had turned me on to her. She was apparently a respected poet of my mother's generation, but she'd recently come out as a lesbian. A radical one. And a really smart one" (170). While her mother, a product of her mid-twentieth-century education, admired the impersonal style of new critics and poets who sought to avoid the political and personal, Bechdel recalls thrilling to not only Rich's reputation as an intellectual but also her pivot away from stylistic detachment and its hidden politics and unexamined privilege (186–87). In so doing, she recognizes her mother's ignorance about and distaste for women and their bodies as internationalized sexism. Bechdel relates her indirect literary relationship with Rich—attending her lectures

(185) and submitting poetry to her publications (180)—but her indebtedness to Rich for her ideas about language, women's bodies, and feminism was clearly lifelong and life-changing. Indeed, Bechdel's assertion that her body and its desires saved her from her unhealthy overinvestment in her mind (156) echoes Rich's biographical note in *Of Woman Born*: "I knew I was not an incorporeal intellect. My mind and body might be divided, as if between father and mother; but I had both" (220).

Rich also serves as an intergenerational mediator who supplies Bechdel with a way of thinking about anger at and hate for her mother. Early in the text, Helen unnerves Bechdel by criticizing Sylvia Plath for "hating" her mother (34), which only intensifies Bechdel's internal conflict. Winnicott's theory of hate provides the title for a chapter in *Are You My Mother?*, but Adrienne Rich's discussion of matrophobia could be applicable as well to Bechdel's situation. According to Rich, feminist daughters often experience matrophobia, which she defines as fear of becoming their mother, and insists should not be confused with hating their mother:

> Thousands of daughters see their mothers as having taught a compromise and self-hatred they are struggling to win free of, the one through whom the restrictions and degradations of a female existence were perforce transmitted. Easier by far to hate and reject a mother outright than to see beyond her to the forces acting upon her. (*Of Woman Born* 235)

Rich goes on to explain that feminist daughters may have a sense that their mothers betrayed them by selling out to heteronormative patriarchy. In "Mothers and Daughters," she argues that in order to build a strong women's movement, women need to do more than analyze and reject their mothers' participation in patriarchy. She writes,

> It was too simple, early in the twentieth-century wave of feminism, for us to analyze our mothers' oppression, to understand "rationally"—and correctly—why our mothers did not teach us to be Amazons, why they bound our feet or simply left us. It was accurate and even radical, that analysis; and yet, like all politics narrowly interpreted, it assumed that consciousness knows everything. . . . It was not enough to understand our mothers; more than ever, in the effort to touch our own strength as women, we needed them. (*Of Woman Born* 224–25)

Rich laments that while seeking the strength necessary to revise gender roles, her generation lacked models, but it also lacked a connection to their mothers: "easier by far to hate and reject a mother outright than to see beyond her to the forces acting upon her." She asserts that while this new generation of women forges the models they need, they also need to recognize that, while they don't need to identify with or become their mothers, their mothers *were* a source of strength—"Our mothers were in some incalculable way on our side" (225)—and women need strength to resist heteronormativity, to remake themselves midlife if necessary, and to imagine a world free of gender-based oppressions.

*Are You My Mother?* shows that Bechdel does not hate Helen, and it honors Helen's strength by representing her agency and voice. In another strategy that Cooke would appreciate for its self-reflexivity, Bechdel includes her mother's voice in the narrative through transcribed phone calls: "I must confess that I have taken to transcribing what she says. I don't think she knows I'm doing it, which makes it a bit unethical. But I want to capture her voice, her precise wording, her deadpan humor. I don't think I could possibly re-create it on my own" (11–12). She recalls how as a child when her obsessive-compulsive disorder kicked in and prevented her from writing in her diary, her mother took dictation, anticipating their flipped roles: "My mother composed me as I now compose her" (14). In addition to hearing Helen's voice, readers are also made aware that Bechdel invited her mother's editorial suggestions on early drafts of *Are You My Mother?* (164, 284), thereby disrupting her authority, exposing her writerly desires, and foregrounding the process of crafting the text. Like Strayed's and Williams's memoirs, *Are You My Mother?* reflects a merging of memoir and maternal biography that destabilizes the daughter-biographer's authority. The narrative offers numerous scenes where Helen contributes to Bechdel's work on *Fun Home* and *Are You My Mother?* (126) and includes depictions of them discussing the texts over phone calls (250). Readers are left with an equally strong sense of both mother's and daughter's agency.

Bechdel also represents her mother's agency by showing their divergent political perspectives, including Helen's antiabortion views. In "Mind," Bechdel depicts her mother's appreciation for an article by Norah Vincent, the libertarian, lesbian writer and alleged gay rights movement sellout. Her mother approvingly observes, "[Norah Vincent] was talking about abortion, and she said fetuses are more endangered than gays right now" (124). The narration conveys both Bechdel's pain at this remark and her pride for her mother's integrity:

> I had long since given up trying to debate abortion with mom. None of my feminist arguments could sway her. My childhood, despite the [Vietnam] war and social chaos unfolding on the nightly news, had been serenely

> apolitical. My family didn't discuss current events. There was something embarrassing, it seemed, about the outside world. I'd never known anyone to take a stand about anything. So it was highly unusual when mom took a bus to Washington to protest the fourth anniversary of *Roe v. Wade.* I was sixteen. She didn't say much when she got home late that night. But I was deeply impressed by her quiet, principled act. (124–25)

This passage further emphasizes the difference in their political views, but it also suggests Bechdel's appreciation for what she may not know about the experiences informing her mother's reproductive politics and that she recognizes they both are activists in their own way.

The life writing of all three authors employs the feminist practice of recovering women's voices to seek out the strength of literal and figurative foremothers. These texts invoke the trope of the aborted women to think about their mothers without reducing them to being victims. Their texts revise recovery for the twenty-first century and throw into question their writerly authority and their ability to know their mothers. Rather than engaging in a heroic act of overreading, Strayed, Williams, and Bechdel are at pains to show how much they don't know about their mother's lives. Instead, the texts celebrate their mothers and acknowledge their agency through their secrets, their disapprovals, their differences, and—most importantly—the contexts and the "forces acting upon her" that make collaboration with a daughter-biographer imperfect and powerful. In these texts, Adrienne Rich's words provide for mediation and reparative readings of their mothers. By engaging with Rich's work, these writers navigate matrophobia—the fear of becoming their pre-1973 mothers—and disidentify with them while simultaneously recognizing their agency and strength. Compulsory heterosexuality reduces women to the role of mothers, but these texts, I suggest, depict and celebrate mothers as women without reducing them to their maternal role. These gestures serve to destabilize the pre-/post-1973 temporality that underlies their stories about their mothers and to disrupt the idea that their post-1973 lives are somehow more empowered.

## Conclusion

In "Telling Time in Feminist Theory" (2002), Rita Felski claims that feminists tell "many different stories about women and time," observing that while some feminists may think of themselves as "allies of the new, fervent proponents of radical change," others are skeptical of the "fetish of the new" and its basis in a vision of the past that sees "an enemy to be vanquished" (21). Surveying feminist scholarship, Felski offers a taxonomy of four theoretical frameworks for thinking about feminism, women, and time—redemption, regression, repetition, and rupture—which she links to affect (hope, sadness, boredom, and surprise). Each framework for telling time has uses and limitations, leading her to conclude that "there can be no single time for women. We need a pragmatics, not a metaphysics of time. The many times of feminism make it clear that no one time can do justice to the complexities of feminism or the world" (27). Felski's account of how feminists tell time is useful to thinking about the current moment in legalized abortion access in the US, and a reminder that the pre-/post-1973 periodization relied upon by Strayed, Williams, and Bechdel in their stories about their mothers and their lives as writers is only one way of telling feminist time.

The Supreme Court decision in *Dobbs v. Jackson Women's Health Organization,* which overruled the decision in *Roe* and the constitutional right to abortion, presents a demarcation of what could now be called the *Roe* era: 1973 to 2022. It remains to be seen to what use feminists will put this periodization. Felski's regression framework could apply to early scholarly reactions to the end of almost five decades of legalized abortion access, which reflects a sense of fear, sadness, and anger. Krystale Littlejohn and Rickie Solinger's edited volume, *Fighting Mad,* offers those feelings, as does Jessica Valenti's *Abortion,* which begins with her desperate concern for the future of her teenage daughter's reproductive freedom. The *Roe* era represented decades of safe, accessible reproductive healthcare for many women. However, there are other ways that this periodization may be put to use in the wake of the *Dobbs* decision. The subtitle of Valenti's work, *Our Bodies, Their Lies, and the Truths We Use to Win,* for example, is also a call to action, as is *Fighting Mad,* suggesting that *Dobbs* may provide a galvanizing moment in feminist activism and the hope of a new wave. Additionally, as the next chapter in this work will show, the *Roe* era was characterized by dynamic and relentless antiabortion activism.

Perhaps future feminists will discuss the *Roe* era in terms of the failure of privacy, long believed by many feminists to be an inadequate defense of the right to abortion (Latimer 19–20), and its welcome demise as the beginning of a more robust defense of women's humanity. Yet again, the *Roe* era may be seen as a failure of intersectional feminist praxis for how the desires of white, middle-class women excluded the voices, experiences, and needs of BIPOC women, thereby preventing a diverse coalition of feminists from coming together to fight for reproductive justice.

Indeed, the pre-/post-1973 periodization discussed in this chapter reflects the interests of middle-class, white feminists, whose enjoyment of legalized abortion access was never fully shared by all women. While women of color and poor women access abortion and therefore share the sense that 1973 was an important year, the *Roe* era did not necessarily reflect a period of reproductive freedom for these communities. As numerous reproductive justice advocates have observed, the Hyde Amendment (enacted shortly after 1973) blocked and continues to obstruct meaningful access to abortion for poor women, while BIPOC communities, facing legacies of racialized biopolitics, continue to seek freedom from coerced sterilization as well as protections for the right to parent. From this perspective, the significance of the pre-/post-1973 chronotope reflects a form of what Tanya Ann Kennedy calls "white time" (5), which is "implicitly based on the dominance of race . . . and the reproduction of social domination" and is made up of "chrononormative regimes that regulate the social collective and thus the social imaginary" (5).

Nevertheless, the *Roe* era meant something to many women, as the texts discussed in this chapter reveal. Strayed, Williams, and Bechel identify as beneficiaries of *Roe*'s feminist challenge to compulsory heterosexuality because it granted them the ability to claim a writer's voice and vocation. This freedom of expression contrasts with the lives of their mothers, who, while not unhappy, married too soon, married difficult partners, and leapt at birth control when it was made available. These texts, which recover maternal stories and illustrate the numerous ways the authors benefitted from abortion (even without having one), attest to the importance of women's writing, which now may be imperiled by the decision in *Dobbs*. It is therefore perhaps encouraging that Strayed, Williams, and Bechdel refuse the idea of feminism as progressive and themselves as somehow freer or stronger than their mothers. Women's strength defies periodization.

CHAPTER 3

# "How Can You Work There?"

## Violence and Care Work in Twenty-First-Century Abortion Clinic Thrillers

In *Scarlet A*, Katie Watson argues that the American public needs to hear more stories about ordinary abortion to counter the extraordinary stories that circulate in political and policy debates. Ordinary abortion stories reflect the mundane and varied reasons that lead women to end pregnancies, as well as the overwhelming safety of the procedure and caring work of the providers. She speculates that abortion providers would be the perfect source for these narratives were it not for the silencing effect of antiabortion stigma:

> The simple fact that abortion providers spend a significant amount of their time doing this work might also create more natural opportunities for storytelling. Yet providers don't discuss it much either. . . . Public discourse stigmatizes abortion providers as dangerous, deviant, or illegitimate. Abortion stigma and the constant threat of violence and personal harassment lead providers to discuss their work only within small circles. Their silence means abortion work is not seen as the type of work a neighbor, soccer club acquaintance, or colleague would do. (74)

This chapter considers how antiabortion violence has shaped twenty-first-century thrillers by US women writers by providing both settings and characters. While the thriller, conventionally characterized by criminality, suspenseful atmospheres, sinister environments, and dramatic moral dilemmas may not appear to be a vehicle for telling "ordinary" stories, it does offer a platform for exploring widespread misogyny and antiabortion violence. Rather than making abortion into the narrative moral dilemma, these texts instead turn a critical gaze on white male anger while relating stories about ordinary abortion in contexts of antiabortion violence. The texts that I examine—Elisabeth Hyde's *The Abortionist's Daughter,* Jodi Picoult's *A Spark of Light,* Joyce Carol Oates's *A Book of American Martyrs,* and Jennifer Haigh's *Mercy Street*—depict clinics as imperiled shelters for women and providers as professional and caring. In this chapter I will first discuss antiabortion violence directed at clinics, as well as the stigma that prevents the appreciation of abortion care work as work, before analyzing these novels for depictions of teenage-girl sexuality, toxic masculinity, denaturalized motherhood, religious hypocrisy, toxic masculinity, and the use of literary realism to depict ordinary abortions.

## History of Antiabortion Violence

In *Bearing Right: How Conservatives Won the Abortion War,* William Saletan argues that the Supreme Court decision in *Roe v. Wade,* which decriminalized abortion in 1973, galvanized the New (religious) Right and refueled antiabortion activism. These activists adopted direct-action strategies to disrupt abortion services and to garner maximum media attention (Ginsburg 51). A blueprint for their approach is found in *Closed: 99 Ways to Stop Abortion,* in which Joseph Scheidler gathered and systemized direct-action strategies to target patients and physical clinics. Scheidler, the founder of the Pro-Life Action League, promoted a "doctrine of necessity" that argued "violence is permissible as a last resort when it must be used to stop or prevent greater violence (i.e., abortion)" (Ginsburg). Scheidler was a mentor to Randall Terry, the founder of Operation Rescue, which made a national name for itself in the 1990s by blockading and invading clinics in Atlanta and Wichita. Operation Rescue, whose slogan was, "If you believe abortion is murder, act like it's murder," coached its members in direct-action techniques that included physically blocking clinic entrances and so-called sidewalk counseling, including haranguing, shaming, following, misinforming, admonishing, browbeating, waving signs, and shouting at patients. These tactics continue today as routine forms of antiabortion violence.

In 1994 the Freedom of Access to Clinic Entrances (FACE) Act levied fines on protesters who use violence, obstruct entrances, or damage clinics. The FACE Act awakened hope in abortion defenders, but as Lauren Rankin has documented in her history of clinic escorts—volunteers who walk with patients from the parking lot into the clinic to shield them from protesters—the hope of relief from Operation Rescue's tactics quickly faded (Rankin; Pridemore and Freilich). According to Rankin, the law—and subsequent policies like it—is unevenly enforced and does little to quell the harassment perpetrated by groups such as 40 Days for Life, Love Life, and Operation Save America. Antiabortion harassment of patients entering clinics has prompted a patchwork of state "buffer zone" laws that create fixed areas around clinics or floating areas around patients and staff. These laws continue to be challenged in the courts ("Protecting"; see also Wirken et al.; Doan). Additionally, in *The Turnaway Study,* Foster notes that sidewalk activism may have an alternative purpose: "Even if protesters are not effective in stopping a significant number of people from getting abortions," they give supporters a way to be involved (79).

As Foster's observation suggests, direct-action strategies have not proven successful in deterring patients seeking abortions.[1] Mireille Jacobson and Heather Royer conclude that patients who are deterred by direct-action techniques in one area will travel to another: "Our findings imply that anti-abortion terrorists are ultimately unsuccessful in obstructing the market for abortion services. But the terrorism does impose a cost. Where terrorists have effectively reduced abortion services or instilled significant fear, and where alternative abortion facilities exist, many women respond by traveling elsewhere to terminate their pregnancies" (Jacobson and Royer 193). The gap between those who have the means to travel elsewhere and those who don't is widening, however (Lindo et al.; Gerdts et al.; McGowan et al.; Wirken et al.). Additionally, McGowan et al. find that the uncertainty produced by the changing laws causes clinics to yo-yo between being open and closed and creates a disruptive "abortion churn" that discourages patients.

In response to the persistent demand for abortions, the antiabortion movement developed additional direct-action strategies that focused on providers. If women can't be dissuaded from having abortions, their logic seems to be, then providers must be prevented from performing them. Neal Horsely's Nuremberg Files website, for example, which he launched in 1997, posted a "wanted" list of more than two hundred providers, including their photos and addresses: "This website was finally removed from the internet in 2002 as a result of lawsuits from Planned Parenthood and targeted doctors" (Jacobson and Royer 195). As the name of the site implies, providers were cast as genocidal murderers, and visitors to the site were incited to hunt them. Operation Rescue still regularly targets abortion providers by distributing identifying flyers in their neighborhoods (Watson 75), creating a climate that

1. As scholars point out, "Demand for abortions is quite inelastic" (Jacobson and Royer 192), and as Watson reports, "Americans have voted with their feet" (21) in support of abortion access: One in five American pregnancies are terminated, thirty million abortions have happened since *Roe*, and one million abortions happen annually in the US.

encourages violence against clinic structures, doctors, and staff. According to the National Abortion Federation (NAF), the largest organization of abortion providers, "since 1977, there have been 11 murders, 42 bombings, 200 arsons, 531 assaults, 492 clinic invasions, 375 burglaries, and thousands of other incidents of criminal activities directed at patients, providers, and volunteers" ("Violence"). Such activities include butyric acid attacks on clinics as well as anthrax threats, attempted murders, woundings, and kidnappings. To date, four abortion-providing doctors have been murdered in the US: in 1993 David Gunn, in Florida; in 1994 John Britton, in Florida; in 1998 Barnett Slepian, in New York; and in 2009 George Tiller, in Kansas.

The sociologist Carol Joffe, who has studied abortion provision for decades, observes that "virtually every clinic that provides abortions today is preoccupied with issues of security" (*Dispatches* 51), and she argues that if freestanding clinics are to survive, "you need a community with you" (21). How, in a climate rife with antiabortion stigma, is such a community built? Alessandro Piazza and Grace Augustine analyzed the conditions that enable abortion clinics to remain open despite policy attacks and threats of violence. In their article in *The Journal of Management Studies,* they examine data reported by NARAL (now named Reproductive Freedom for All), NAF, and Planned Parenthood as well as reporting retrieved from *Bloomberg News.* They find that there is no one "combination of conditions necessary for the survival of clinics," but "the lack of public opposition alone appears to be sufficient for survival in most cases," and "that clinics tend to thrive in the absence of staunch opposition to abortion rights either from the general public or from elected officials . . . while active support does not play a role one way or the other" (2141). Even clinics in low-demand areas "can still survive provided that anti-abortion legislation and anti-abortion activism are absent"; "in some areas where there is potentially not enough demand to sustain a clinic, by virtue of public support for abortion clinics, they are nonetheless able to survive (by means of fundraising, volunteering, and donations, for example)" (2143).

Nevertheless, there is a sense that a post-*Dobbs* world holds increasing threats of violence to abortion providers, clinics, and patients. In *Man Up: The New Misogyny & the Rise of Violent Extremism,* Cynthia Miller-Idriss argues that public discussions of violent extremism consistently understate or ignore the role of misogyny in supremacist extremists' rhetoric and actions, in which antiabortion ideology is a key trait. Furthermore, as Arielle Schechtman notes in *The Georgetown Journal of Gender and the Law,* "in the wake of *Dobbs* . . . analysts warn of a rising threat of violence in the realm of abortion protesting, with the Department of Homeland Security highlighting the potential for violence by domestic extremists" (255). The unfairness of expecting abortion providers to supply patient care *and* respond to these threats of violence simultaneously has become an untenable expectation, according to Katie Watson:

> One result of our public and private silence about the experience of abortion is that doctors and clinic managers have become the public face of abortion. Unlike other health issues, in which patients and families advocate for future patients and doctors and institutions that helped them, in abortion we ask those who provide something millions of women and families want and need to also shoulder most of the burden of its defense. That doesn't seem fair, and I don't think it's sustainable. (6)

The novels discussed in this chapter draw on this history and context of violence to provide the setting for their narratives. This depiction exposes the violent misogyny behind antiabortion ideology, and by focusing critically on the violence perpetrated by men, these portrayals normalize and dedramatize abortion decision-making.

## Stigma and Clinic Workers

This chapter's title is taken from Jennifer Haigh's *Mercy Street,* in which the protagonist, an abortion clinic employee, is repeatedly asked, "How can you work there?" by people who oppose abortion but also by family and friends who know how taxing and dangerous her work is. Both groups (enemies and allies) are responding to the way stigma and violence are interwoven into abortion-providing.

The *there* is somewhat unique in terms of women's healthcare, and so some information about freestanding clinics is necessary. Independent abortion clinics have a unique history in the US. In most of the developed world, abortions are provided in hospitals, but after *Roe,* US hospitals (many of which are Catholic-affiliated) avoided doing procedures to appease their funders, their communities, or their local government authorities (Ginsburg 55). Additionally, many pro-choice activists, informed by the women's health movement, sought to move abortion away from the male-dominated medical establishment, which had, in the nineteenth century, usurped the power of abortion-providing midwives to assert its own authority. This gave rise to women-owned clinics in the 1970s (Ginsburg 55; Solinger, *Pregnancy*). Piazza and Augustine note that "by the late 1980s, more than 90 per cent of abortions in the US were performed in standalone clinics, and this figure eventually rose to 95 per cent by 2000 and held almost steady until 2011." According to 2024 findings from the Guttmacher Institute, 63 percent of abortions are medical ("Medication Abortions"), but of the clinician-provided abortions, 80 percent are still performed in brick-and-mortar clinics (Jones et al.). In a recent study drawing on semistructured interviews, Weitz and Cockrill report that "women's preferences for abortion care centered on privacy, cost, empathy, ability to control their image, and desire for safe quality care" (413). The interview subjects "assumed their general provider did not 'do abortion' and many believed those providers were opposed to abortion." Additionally, they describe how "women who had delivered a baby were concerned with their image in their general provider's eyes. Two women were denied care by their general providers" (413). These findings lead Weitz and Cockrill to recommend that "general providers should proactively make patients aware of their positions on abortion and if supportive indicate that they can provide that care and/or a referral" (412), and they also explain the enduring popularity of freestanding clinics for women who do not wish to rely on their primary care providers for care. In the absence of abortion care offered by general providers, women turn to clinics.

In their study, Piazza and Augustine note that although patients prefer standalone clinics, an unintended consequence is that clinics "created visible organizational targets for disapproval that were isolated from the mainstream medical establishment" (2128). Because of stereotypes and myths, abortion-providing is considered what sociologists term "dirty work," a type of organizational stigma "'that evokes a collective perception that the organization is deeply flawed or discredited' . . . as a result of their engagement in practices that society devalues or views with distaste" (2126). Illegal abortions before *Roe* were dangerous, and the term *back-alley abortion* invoked this illegality and historical association with criminal organizations like the mob. Since legalization, however, this association remains fixed in antiabortion rhetoric, casting providers as immoral, greedy, and duplicitous monsters who prey on vulnerable women. They are assumed to be not only depraved but also incompetent, operating without training or oversight, indifferent to the women they treat, and motivated solely by profiteering (Ginsburg; Solinger, *Beggars*). This myth is disproven by the vast majority of providers (doctors, nurses, advocates, and escorts) who are trained professionals and who care deeply about patients. Katie Watson laments that "despite the fact a highly trained, compassionate cadre of health care professionals have for forty-five years provided safe abortion care that many millions of American women desperately wanted, providers continue to be stereotyped as rogue doctors who the state is justified in regulating out of existence" (74–75).

This stigma has implications not only for patients but also for the workers—doctors, nurses, advocates, escorts, and others—in abortion clinics. Stigma and mythologies prevent the broader population from sometimes appreciating the work performed in these spaces. Beyond abortion care, staff may engage in outreach, pregnancy tests, sexually transmitted infection scans, birth control provision, and adoption counseling, as well as the work of connecting abortion patients with funding sources, obtaining judicial bypasses, pre- and post-abortion counseling, monitoring and security, escorting, connecting patients with survivor resources, and more. Clinic workers perform this physical and emotional labor in a context of regular threats of violence. In "Secrecy and Safety: Healthcare Workers in Abortion Clinics," Sarah Todd, Andrew Parnaby, and Todd MacCullum expose the lack of research into workplace safety in clinics, observing that cultural ambivalence, silence, and stigma "make it difficult to position issues facing abortion workers in relation to more general workplace safety concerns" (401). Although "abortion workers' daily tasks . . . differ little from the employment experiences of any health care provider," they explain, "the daily practices of abortion workers take place within a hostile, often dangerous environment," which results in "the fear and actual experience of physical harm and a pervading social stigmatization" (403). The association with "dirty work" contributes to an isolation experienced by workers who find it "difficult, if not impossible, to tell friends, neighbours, and often even family members about our jobs" (Todd et al. 403) and to an internalization and normalization of this violence as "just part of the job" (405). Todd and her colleagues conclude that the cultural ambivalence and stigma of dirty work "is to the detriment of all workers, but particularly the nurses, social workers, ultrasound technicians, receptionists, security staff, housekeeping staff, and physicians who are struggling through the day-to-day safety issues involved in abortion work" (406).

Todd, Joffe, and other scholars celebrate the care work of abortion providers and how they prioritize their patients' well-being outside and inside the clinic. In recounting the successful passage of the FACE Act, Rankin, for example, cites her interview with Jeanne Clark, a veteran clinic escort, who framed the victory in terms of patient experience: "We made the woman visible in the issue" (Rankin 49). Clark's comment reflects the provider focus on praxis. Inside clinics, providers have adapted their methods to meet patients where they are. Joffe describes clinic workers' beliefs that "every woman is different" and that "good abortion care" is a combination of calibrating language, showing regard for the fetus, respecting decision-making, and welcoming spirituality into the process (*Dispatches*). Similar research by Katie Gallagher, Davina Porock, and Alison Edgley and the scholarship in Krista Jacob's *Our*

*Choices, Our Lives: Unapologetic Writings on Abortion* (2004), in addition to Jeannie Ludlow's scholarship ("Sometimes"), provide accounts of abortion care work that is nuanced and that seeks to empower patients by openly discussing feelings, including those about the fetus, motherhood, guilt, and grief.

The praxis of abortion care work inside and outside of clinics is a type of emotional labor that, in the context of antiabortion stigma, can be draining for providers. For example, hostile patients—those who seek abortion but who also express antiabortion views—are particularly challenging and not uncommon. Joffe shares the observation made by providers that "many women who are showing up for abortions these days are not immune to the gross misinformation and stigma that now surround the procedure" (*Dispatches* 113). Antiabortion attitudes show up in clinics in the form of what Watson calls "fundamental attribution error," or a situation where individuals attribute their own behavior to circumstances ("I'm having an abortion because this is the wrong time for me to have a baby") but they attribute someone else's similar behavior to bad values ("She's using abortion as birth control"). Encountering the seeming hypocrisy of patients who oppose abortion access for others but access it for themselves can be exhausting for providers. In "Helping Women and Protecting the Self: The Challenge of Emotional Labor in an Abortion Clinic," Michelle Wolkomir and Jennifer Powers write about their interviews with abortion clinic employees that revealed "interactive processes by which workers . . . developed specific strategies, along a continuum from investment to detachment, that enabled them to cope effectively with each type of patient" (153). Detachment in this case does not mean providing inferior care but rather performing to professional requirements while fulfilling important commitments to self (167–68).

Providers also do the work of combatting "the palpable sense of isolation and corresponding lack of solidarity with other abortion patients" (*Dispatches* 116). Misinformation and stigma have not only divided abortion patients, they also serve to divide those who can access reproductive services and those who cannot. Indeed, the Guttmacher Institute coined the term "the two Americas" to describe its own research that shows the overrepresentation of poor women and women of color in abortion statistics due to economic and racial inequality ("Tale"). A woman living in poverty is four times as likely to have an unplanned pregnancy, which points to gaps in education and access to birth control (Joffe, *Dispatches* 108). Abortion advocacy is not failing, Joffe states, but "there is a clear gap—of class and of education—between those who work in this increasingly professionalized movement and the majority of women now getting abortions" (118); she concludes that the challenge "is to make the isolated women in the heartland waiting rooms feel that they are part of the struggle" (118). These are enormous problems, and the literary thrillers discussed in this chapter alone cannot solve them. They may, however, help to lessen stigma and misinformation, while building support through an empathetic community of educated readers.

In what follows I examine how psychological thrillers set in clinics use the conventional focus on criminal mindsets to expose the pervasive misogyny that informs antiabortion ideology. This misogyny, as Miller-Idriss argues, is underresearched and underrecognized for its role in all forms of contemporary extremist violence. Its integration of other supremacist belief systems such as white supremacy, she notes, is also underexamined. While many antiabortion activists may disavow racist groups, "it's not a stretch to see how mainstream arguments about the need for more babies to counter 'replacement' or produce a sufficient 'supply of infants' benefit white supremacist extremists, their obsession with demographic change, and their desire to increase white birth rates" (118). The abortion clinic thrillers in this study help to connect these dots for readers and educate a community about the violence directed at patients and providers.

Literature set in and about abortion clinics is also a particularly apt mechanism for representing nuance, transporting readers to unfamiliar situations, and building empathy. Public conversations around abortion have been dominated by a framework of two sides: pro or anti. Joffe, for one, laments this framework and the current state of the national discussion: "The most fanatical elements of the antiabortion movement have established the contours of the abortion wars. These true believers have sought to eliminate from public conversation about abortion what I believe the issue most cries out for: a recognition of nuance" (*Dispatches* xiv). In addition to Joffe's call for more nuance in discussions of abortion, Katie Watson calls for stories that explore the complexity of the private decision to have an abortion without challenging the right to privacy to make that decision (4). Arguably, clinic literature supplies an excellent way into conversations about abortion that allow insight into private decision-making and the nuances of those decisions.

Additionally, literature set in clinics allows for a depiction of the scope of ordinary abortions—those safe, legal, straightforward terminations sought by one million women each year in the US, which contrast with the extraordinary stories that are used to fuel public policy debates. As noted above, Watson argues that providers could tell stories about ordinary abortion, but they have been careful with whom they share them. She asks,

> Is there a *Will & Grace* of abortion? It would have to be a show about abortion providers. . . . Given all providers already do, it's too much to ask

> for them to also "come out" if they would prefer not to. But humanizing them and their patients through fictional characters with recognizable lives would accomplish similar goals. (76)

In this reference to the popular television series that normalized queer-identifying characters to a mainstream American audience, Watson is calling for narrative that can overcome stigma. The novels discussed in this chapter fulfill Watson's call by drawing on abortion providers and clinics as their characters and settings. In this chapter I examine *The Abortionist's Daughter, The Book of American Martyrs, A Spark of Light,* and *Mercy Street.* The provider characters in these novels are granted humanity—meaning they possess heroic traits and flaws in equal measure. In addition to their humanity, these novels expose the threat to patriarchal authority posed by teenage-girl sexuality and denaturalized motherhood, and the problems of toxic masculinity and patriarchal religious hypocrisy. Finally, these texts use the conventions of literary realism to depict the inside of clinics and the scope and complexity of abortion decision-making.

## Teenage-Girl Sexuality and the Threat to Patriarchal Authority

In *Dubious Conceptions,* Kristin Luker reported that late twentieth-century teens were having more sex compared to earlier decades; they were using birth control and using it more effectively; and as a result of this use, they were getting pregnant less often, but when they did, they were less likely to put the baby up for adoption or to get married (10). This shift in the rate of unwed teen motherhood continues into the twenty-first century (Office of Justice Programs) and has caused an uproar among conservatives, who see it as a failure of morals and a contributing factor to "insufficient supply" of infants to meet the adoption demand (Miller-Idriss 117). Liberals and conservatives share concern over negative outcomes for teen mothers, which leads liberals to support access to abortion, something conservatives have opposed through the promotion in various states of parental notification laws for minors and abstinence-only sex education. These measures are promoted through the negative rhetorical figure of the promiscuous teenager seeking an abortion of convenience (Watson 42–43; Dreweke). Underlying this conservative opposition is the religious ideology that sex should take place within marriage and should be for procreation (Solinger, *Pregnancy;* Valenti). The association of abortion with youthful sexuality in the cultural imaginary, however, is not factually accurate. The majority of women seeking abortions *are* young, but two-thirds are in their twenties and not their teenage years. The Guttmacher Institute reports: "Adolescents made up 10% of people obtaining an abortion; 2% of people obtaining an abortion were 17 or younger" ("Abortion in the United States"). Moreover, most abortion patients are mothers who already have children, which is not to say they can't be teenagers, but it reveals their decisions to be something other than a matter of convenience.

The thrillers by Hyde and Picoult do not fully counter this stereotype. Instead, they depict characters who are teenage girls thinking about and having sex; however, they defuse the stereotype by condemning men as sources of violence and criminality and as more dangerous than "bad" teenage morals. In these two novels, fathers, husbands, and boyfriends respond violently to female sexuality that they cannot control. Hyde's *The Abortionist's Daughter* is an uneven novel (with a 3.2-star rating on *Goodreads* and decidedly mixed reviews) that offers a stronger denunciation of male violence than satisfying defense of female sexuality or abortion, but its focus on the actions of men—and the harm they perpetrate—is significant. Set in wintery Boulder, Colorado, it begins with the murder of an abortion provider, Dr. Diana Duprey, in her own home. Initially it is suspected that she was killed in a domestic fight with her husband, Frank Thompson, a local prosecutor, who resents Diana's lax restrictions on their nineteen-year-old daughter, Megan. Diana has fostered Megan's intelligence and independence—including her sexuality—which doesn't prevent Megan's youthful misjudgments. Prior to the novel's action, Megan had her first sexual relationship while still in high school with Bill, her pro-choice, "ideal" high school boyfriend, and she experienced a newfound sense of her autonomy: "She was no longer a virgin, and that, under her logic, meant she was no longer her parents' child. It was the coolest thing that had ever happened to her" (42). At one point, Megan and Bill take ecstasy, and Bill photographs Megan in the nude, but she is convinced he erases the images. When Megan grows tired of Bill's possessive behavior—"He had a jealous streak that both irritated and flattered her" (49)—she dumps him and heads off to college, relieved to put some distance between herself and his controlling attitude, which includes stalking. In revenge, however, Bill sells the nude photos online (52).

The backstory of Megan's relationship with Bill is interwoven with the present moment and the search for Diana's killer. A conventional thriller, *The Abortionist's Daughter* supplies several red herrings, and initially readers are led to suspect Diana was murdered by her husband or by someone reacting to her work as an abortion provider. Frank's anger at Diana's parenting extends beyond her permissiveness toward Megan. Years before, contrary to Frank's wishes, Diana decided to continue a pregnancy with a trisomy, knowing that the child would be born with severe disability. Frank believes Diana made this choice to disprove antiabortion critics (267). Their son, Ben, was born with Down syndrome and died before the action in the novel. Frank does not forgive Diana for this (in his mind) unnecessary loss. There is another possible suspect, however: the antiabortion activist Reverend Steven O'Connell. O'Connell, Diana's longtime adversary, had recently and unsuccessfully pressured her to intervene between his teenage son's pregnant girlfriend, Rose, and her parents, who wanted her to abort the pregnancy. O'Connell is enraged by Diana's refusal to share information about Rose and by her insistence that the girl should be allowed to make her own decision (267).

Despite the seemingly stereotypical stories of teenage girls having promiscuous sex (Megan has a sexual relationship with a teacher and later the detective investigating her mother's murder), the narrative challenges the stereotype by asserting that youthful female sexuality is not the narrative crime; instead, it is the response of men to the seeming threat of this sexuality that causes Diana's death. The penultimate chapter, belatedly focalized through Diana's perspective, provides the final narrative plot twist: three men are linked in her death. Rose's father, Jack, blames Diana for refusing to counsel her to have an abortion, and on the day of her death he attacked Diana in her office, violently shaking her and snapping her neck (259). Later that same day, Frank confronts Diana with the nude images of Megan, accusing her, "You were never willing to impose any limits" and shaking Diana violently, causing her neck to snap again (264). Finally, that same day, Diana is attacked in her home by Bill, who wants her to intervene on his behalf with Megan. When Diana refuses, he grabs her by the hair, snaps her neck yet again—this time paralyzing her—and leaves her to drown in her indoor pool (265). While youthful female sexuality is a theme in the novel, it is the men's responses to that sexuality that are foregrounded. The narrative does not condemn Rose's and Megan's sexual behaviors and is sympathetic to Diana's efforts to be a good mother, wife, and abortion provider (253). The men, however, are all implicated through the repeated image of snapping Diana's neck in a murderous response to female sexual agency.

Picoult's *A Spark of Light* similarly examines patriarchal entitlement through the characters of Hugh McElroy and George Goddard, two white men who are confronted with their daughters' sexuality and whose responses drive the plot. *A Spark of Light* is set at The Center, the last remaining abortion clinic in contemporary Jackson, Mississippi. In addition to abortions, the clinic staff provide women's general and reproductive healthcare, including birth control. For this reason, when the novel begins, fifteen-year-old Wren McElroy is at the clinic with her aunt Bex after telling her she is considering having sex. Shortly following their arrival, the clinic is attacked by Goddard, who is bent on revenge after learning that his teenage daughter has had an abortion. Goddard kills two people (the clinic owner and a social worker) and gravely injures two others, including the doctor. Goddard then barricades himself with a group of hostages—including Wren—inside the clinic, which is then surrounded by local law enforcement. Wren's father, Detective McElroy, an experienced hostage negotiator, is called to the scene before anyone knows that his daughter is inside.

Goddard's and McElroy's characters are foils. Goddard has been raising Beth as a single parent with the help of his religious fundamentalist community since his wife left him (8). Beth, who is intimidated by her father, a veteran with PTSD who served in Bosnia, became pregnant after a consensual but brief encounter with a boy she never sees again. After failing to obtain the judicial bypass that would allow her to have an abortion without telling her hair-trigger father, she self-manages her abortion: "She had bought misoprostol and mifepristone, the pills used in medication abortion, off the Internet. That was illegal in the United States, which Beth hadn't known at the time" (99). When Beth hemorrhages, her unsuspecting father takes her to the hospital, where she confesses her abortion to a nurse, who subsequently reports her. Goddard overhears this confession and rushes off righteously but mistakenly to The Center to avenge his daughter: "She had never seen him as anything but a hero" (159). Deluded by this self-perception, Goddard lashes out and commits murder, but he has misread Beth's vulnerability and has, in fact, left her defenseless at the hospital, where, under a new fetal rights policy, she is being charged with murder: "The only love [she] had ever known was conditional. . . . Even if her father came back, it wouldn't be to apologize. It would be to tell Beth how disappointed he was in her" (40). In the final scene, Goddard is shot and killed by McElroy, leaving Beth orphaned as she faces criminal charges.

McElroy is also a single parent, after the failure of his disastrous youthful marriage (Hugh "got a girl pregnant" [5]), and he raises Wren with the help of her aunt Bex. McElroy is similarly confounded by the news of his daughter's sexuality. Upon learning that Wren is inside the clinic, he ponders, "Why was Wren in there? Why was Bex in there?" (213). Wren has struggled to voice her needs to her father: "How could she ask a man who couldn't even say the word cramps to bring her somewhere to get birth control?" (88). Although Wren's quest for birth control is preemptive (she and her boyfriend are only discussing having sex), her father's initial response is regret at his loss of control:

"She should have stayed a little girl" (88). In the final scene, McElroy is made sympathetic through the revelation of the circumstances of his birth: Bex, whom he believed was his sister, is in fact his biological mother. She too had a teen pregnancy and was forced by her Catholic mother to carry it: "Bex, who had *not* terminated her pregnancy, had still lost a potential life that day—her own" (349). Through learning about and reflecting on these events, McElroy accepts Wren's maturity and bodily autonomy, and the novel concludes with an image of their new relationship: "As she left with her father, it was the first time she held his hand, instead of the other way around" (356). By focusing on the stories of teenage sexuality, the novels by Hyde and Picoult could be said to reinforce the stereotype that abortions encourage teenage promiscuity; however, these novels instead condemn controlling patriarchal overreactions to that sexuality.

Jennifer Haigh's naturalist thriller *Mercy Street* depicts the politics of reproduction under the slow violence of antiabortion misogyny and represents teenage-girl sexuality through secondary characters, who, along with other women, are threatened by the disastrous consequences of falling pregnant. The novel is named for a fictional street in Boston, in the former sex work district, where an abortion clinic, Women's Options, is besieged daily by protesters. A series of crushing nor'easter snowstorms paralyze the city and highlight Haigh's characters' struggle to survive against the force of an indifferent fate and their desires for love and security. *Mercy Street* criticizes how neoliberal ideology keeps characters—especially women—locked into false promises of happiness and security and arrives to girls and young women through magazines, television shows, social media, and children's games promising romantic salvation as balm and reward. Agency and free will are reflected in moments of fleeting control and choice, but characters are more likely to find themselves spinning the wheel of fortune: Girls and women "fall" pregnant—a term mulled over by the protagonist, Claudia Birch, that is reminiscent of other literary fallen women, like Stephen Crane's Maggie. Sexuality is depicted as one of many instinctual needs these characters—young and old—struggle to satisfy.

Teenage girls are depicted as among the most vulnerable characters in the novel. Claudia, a forty-three-year-old social worker, is employed at Women's Options, and at one point in the narrative she recalls a media story involving Baby Doe, an infant murdered by her teen mother's boyfriend. She struggles to remember if the girl was turned away by Women's Options for being too far along in her pregnancy to receive a legal abortion (129). Claudia is attuned to the challenges facing teenage girls because her own mother was a teen and she grew up helping her raise foster children for income. The novel abounds with secondary stories of children born to parents—young and old—who are ill-suited to their care, highlighting repeatedly how the lack of reproductive control facilitates different forms of abandonment, neglect, and violence against women, teens, and children. Like the mother of Baby Doe, the women who come to the clinic are "fallen"; however, incredibly, Women's Options and Claudia help some of them get back up again. While the novels by Hyde and Picoult explore retaliation against threats to patriarchal control posed by teenage-girl sexuality, Haigh's novel explores how girls' sexuality is exploited and not protected under patriarchal, capitalist slow violence.

It could be said that these novels fail to capture ordinary abortion by choosing to depict teenage girls as patients at abortion clinics. As noted, a teenage girl is not the average patient at US abortion clinics. However, there is increasingly the sense that teen girls are, as Jessica Valenti notes, "the canaries in the coal mine" of antiabortion legislation. Proposed laws would protect teens from so-called trafficking, an inflammatory term that is being applied to anyone aiding a minor in obtaining an abortion—including through supplying information, medication, or transportation. Valenti elaborates her point that "antichoice groups and politicians know their bans are incredibly unpopular. . . . To counter that opposition, legislators hope that feigning concern over children will distract Americans from the terror their laws are causing" (106). These laws are a stealthy step in a broader and wildly unpopular attempt to limit all women's access. So while teenagers accessing abortion are not ordinary, they occupy a disproportionately important role in the cultural imaginary for legislating abortion access. For this reason, they appear in these texts.

## Toxic Masculinity and Clinic Violence

Contemporary cultural rhetoric and narrative often depict a post-9/11 crisis in masculinity (Kennedy; Donnar). The abortion clinic thrillers discussed in this chapter explore this crisis through a feminist perspective that is critical of hegemonic masculinity. As the previous section suggests, if masculinity is in trouble, it is a crisis of patriarchy's own making. In particular, these novels explore and critique a kind of white masculinity that is entitled, aggrieved, individualistic, and misogynist—a noxious brew popularly referred to as *toxic masculinity.* Masculinity studies provides this now-popularized term to capture the gender ideology of male superiority and entitlement, which not only harms women but also interlocks with racism, cisgenderism, and heterosexism and which is ultimately poisonous to men themselves (Kimmel et al.; Miller-Idriss). Toxic masculinity aims to control the sexuality and reproductive lives of white women specifically and all women generally (Kimmel; Miller-Idriss).

Within the scholarship of abortion-providing, critical analysis of masculinity is beginning to make an overdue appearance. Whitney Arey's analysis of gender, rhetoric, and antiabortion direct-action strategies, for example, provides one approach to thinking about masculinity outside and inside clinics. Arey notes, "The abortion clinic itself is a place where social meanings of masculinity and fatherhood are enacted, challenged and socially reproduced both through language and social interactions between protesters and male companions" (3). Examining the rhetoric addressed to men accompanying women into clinics, Arey concludes there is no one definition of masculinity being invoked: "By mixing various constructions of masculinity, anti-abortion protesters attempt to create affective responses in male companions by drawing on cultural discourses on masculinity, fatherhood, and strength" (13). This rhetoric draws on a patchwork of messages about men and masculinity, as Arey describes:

> The examples I use from anti-abortion speech present men's participation in abortion as emasculating, shameful, weak and irresponsible, while simultaneously emphasizing male patriarchy, toxic masculinity, responsible fatherhood, and strength as characteristics that men inherently possess. To illustrate the ways that anti-abortion speech at clinics reproduces and mixes gender stereotypes about masculinity and reproduction, I analyze how protest speech deals with themes such as choice, responsible fatherhood, strength, and violence, in order to convince men to prevent the abortion of the woman they accompanied. (208)

In addition to studying the antiabortion rhetoric, Arey also observed the reactions of the targeted men that were often aggressive or violent and that simultaneously "reify conceptions of toxic or patriarchal masculinity as well as perform supportive reproductive partnership" (4). This leads Avey to conclude that toxic masculinity sometimes begets toxic masculinity: "Men's attempts to reject constructions of masculinity articulated by protesters may be performed through the same patriarchal gender ideologies they purport to contradict" (4).

The novels by Hyde, Picoult, Oates, and Haigh not only explore masculinity, they critique it. That the abortion clinic serves as a literary site of contested gender roles and identities is not surprising, but the focus on and critique of masculinity in these novels feels new and pointed. The male antagonists in the thrillers discussed in this chapter are burdened by their rage, an anger that

Michael Kimmel has described in *Angry White Men: American Masculinity at the End of an Era* as "real but not true" (9). They feel entitled and ripped off—victimized—but rather than directing these feelings self-destructively toward an indifferent neoliberal state, they focus their anger on women and the abortion clinics that help them.

As discussed above, Picoult's two father figures, Goddard and McElroy, illustrate the point that men could be heroes to women if they didn't allow toxic masculinity to cloud their appreciation of women's humanity, and three male characters in Hyde's novel are implicated in the murder of Diana Duprey. Joyce Carol Oates's *A Book of American Martyrs* satirizes martyrs—both men and women—using the US abortion debate as a backdrop, but it gives particular attention to the impact of patriarchal egos on families and women. In this novel, the premature deaths of two fathers who are consumed with their pursuits—an abortion provider and his murderer—leave their daughters to make sense of their loss. The narrative begins with the murder of Augustus "Gus" Voorhees in front of his Broome County abortion clinic in Ohio in 1999 and shifts between the perspectives of Luther Dunphy, the failed evangelical lay minister who kills him, and acquaintances and members of the families of the two men. Despite being a novel that is sympathetic to abortion access, *American Martyrs* casts pro-choice Voorhees and antiabortion Dunphy as more alike than their different political stances would suggest. While women martyrs are satirized too, the foiling of these two male characters results in a dark portrait of the lasting damage to women (wives and daughters) that normative masculinity inflicts.

Prior to the novel's action, young Dunphy rebelled against his father's authority, spending his twenties fighting, drinking, and abusing women. While he perceives his marriage to Edna Mae and introduction to her evangelical faith as a transformational moment, religion provides a thin veil of respectable discourse for his misogyny and sanctimoniousness. Luther settles down with Edna, her faith, his work as a carpenter, and their children, who arrive with alarming rapidity—including an infant daughter with Down syndrome—but after a less-than-successful enrollment at ministry school, during which Luther has several sexual affairs, the facade of his stable life unravels. His road rage causes a terrible car accident, in which his disabled daughter is killed, traumatizing the entire family. Edna Mae, in her grief, becomes addicted to opiates, which are prescribed to help her sleep, and as her addiction grows, she loses touch with her roles as wife and mother. Dunphy, who suffered a head trauma in the accident, believes that he cares solicitously for his wife, even as he contemplates killing her.

The narration reveals that Luther is a cagey narrator, possessed of a damaged memory that enables and reflects his toxic masculinity: It does not allow him to remember barroom fights that he lost during his wild youth (instead he recalls winning them); he does not remember his infant daughter being in the car accident that he caused; nor does he recall killing Timothy Barron, Voorhees's innocent bodyguard (268). Each of these memories is shameful to his sense of self and manhood. His ability to recall his shameful treatment of women, however, is not impaired, because he blames them for his abuse—including the girl in high school whom he repeatedly assaults, the women with whom he has affairs, and drug-addled Edna Mae, whom he eventually attempts to smother in her sleep.

As Dunphy's delayed execution draws near, a chapter focalized through Edna Mae's perspective, "Unclean," reveals her anger at her husband, whose criminal actions—which previously she had only permitted herself to praise as sanctified—have left the family broken. This revelation is followed by the recognition of her anger at Luther for the death of their disabled daughter:

> There was no one she dared tell: her knowledge that Luther had not protected their little girl as she'd needed to be protected. For Luther had not loved Daphne, really. He'd been embarrassed and ashamed of their youngest child because she was not "right"—as other children her age were "right"—she had seen it in his face. A man cannot disguise his emotions looking upon his own child. . . . Sometimes it seemed to her—(though she told no one this, not even Reverend Dennis)—that Luther had killed two men in cold blood as a way of ending his marriage and changing his life utterly. (413)

Edna too is guilty of a selfish, feminine martyrdom and of abandoning her family through her grief, addiction, and subsequent embrace of the antiabortion movement. Dunphy's martyrdom is specific to his gender as well, and reflects the greater damage that is inflicted by toxic masculinity through its access to power.

The Voorheeses are similarly a family of martyrs who suffer from their patriarch's narcissism. Because Voorhees dies at the beginning of the narrative, the narration does not focalize through him, making it more difficult to assess his character compared to Dunphy's. Nevertheless, it becomes apparent that he is a martyr to the same toxic masculinity as Dunphy, only with a veneer of class privilege. At first his actions and intentions appear selfless and philanthropic, but as the narrative progresses, readers see a masculine ego that demands his family's entire support. Voorhees descended from a wealthy, educated family. His father was a doctor and his mother is a professor, who left him with his father to pursue her own career in another state. Radicalized by protests against the Vietnam War, Voorhees elects to use his obstetric and gynecological training to perform abortions, although his parents lament that this "sacrifice" is not only less lucrative but also significantly more dangerous (193, 304). His surviving family and friends speculate that his sense of occupying the moral high ground often blinded him to the risks he was taking, believing that he could persuade his enemies to his side or provoke them to assassinate him, thus making him a martyr to the abortion cause (194–95, 542).

Just as Luther's wife, Edna Mae, once out of her husband's shadow, retrospectively finds her sense of self, so does Gus's wife. Jenna Matheson met Voorhees in her final year of law school when he was a second-year resident (203–4). Despite her own promising career, Jenna subsumed her work and identity to his to the extent that, as her children recall, she valorizes his absence from their family as a noble, mutual sacrifice: "By the age of forty he'd virtually surrendered a private life. So our mother would say wistfully yet with an air (we thought) of pride" (165). In another parallel to the Dunphy family, the Voorheeses also have a youngest child who embodies a conflict between the parents. After having two biological children, the Voorheeses decide at Gus's urging to adopt. It's not revealed until later in the narrative that Jenna had any doubts about this action. But after her husband's death, readers learn her most private thoughts:

> She did not want to think that Gus's wish for another child, an adopted child, preferably Chinese, had something in it deeply irrational, unexamined. She did not want to think that her acquiescence to her husband's wish had something in it deeply craven, insecure. Or that her fear of displeasing Gus Voorhees in virtually any way, small, large, petty, profound was a fear that was justified. (201)

Here Jenna admits to herself that adopting Melissa was ignoble virtue-signaling. Voorhees's specific desire to adopt a Chinese girl arose from witnessing sex-selective abortions in China and performed to his enemies his ability to discern unjust abortion practices and his valuing of human life. To Jenna this gesture seems calculated, ideological, and selfish rather than loving. Additionally, Jenna recognizes how Voorhees prevailed in this family decision as in others, and she recognizes that despite being married to a progressive man who espoused feminist ideas, she had no power in the relationship. This fact is reflected when she learns of her husband's murder, and her emotional response is one of relief. Both male characters in *American Martyrs* are satirized for having selfish, masculine egos. Their views on abortion are less important to the novel than its critique of toxic masculinity and the damage it inflicts.

Violence against women is enacted by men indirectly and directly in *Mercy Street*. Unlike the women characters, who fall and sometimes rise with resilience, the men in *Mercy Street* stay fallen. The first of the three main male characters is Timmy, Claudia's weed dealer. An ex-Marine, Timmy is divorced from his son's mother and has made a career for himself as a dealer after returning to Boston and failing to join the stagehands union. He has fantasies that his remote parenting rivals his ex-wife's and longs to raise his estranged son in Boston (67). Timmy also supplies weed to Winky/Anthony, a part-time protester outside Woman's Options. Winky's participation in the antiabortion fray is motivated by nostalgia for a potent Catholic church: "The thing with the priests was bad, very bad. Innocent children had been approached sexually. Anthony didn't doubt this, and yet he couldn't help feeling that the average person was better off not knowing" (105). An incel, he is also motivated by a pitiful need for belonging and connection. Incapacitated by a head injury sustained while working construction, Winky "got paid just for staying alive" (114), and lives in his mother's basement imagining his online life and connections are real. Although he fantasizes about having a family, the narrator wryly notes, "To Anthony, who had never impregnated anyone and had little hope of doing so, abortion was a distant, abstract problem—a thing you were supposed to care about, like the national debt" (119). To fill his days, Winky passes along photos and video of Women's Options and Claudia to the web designer of the Hall of Shame, a website of images of women entering abortion clinics. Both Timmy and Winky are depicted as deluded by fantasies of their own importance and nostalgia for patriarchal authority.

The Hall of Shame was created by the more deeply misogynist character of Victor. Older and more bitter than Timmy and Winky, Victor went to prison for burning down his girlfriend's house after learning she had an abortion (196). Victor idolizes Timothy McVeigh after becoming radicalized online: "With his dial-up modem he'd ventured onto the information superhighway, not understanding that his life was about to change. In the Usenet groups he was no longer Victor Prine, a backwoods trucker hauling loads across the continent. He became Excelsior11, a renegade soldier for good" (146). In addition to his ex-girlfriend, Victor is angry at his mother, Audrey, who left his father: "His mother was a whore because what other kind of woman would leave her child?" (181). His hatred of women is informed by this early loss—"They killed their babies so they could go on fucking" (184)—as well as his identification with the unborn. At one point, his internal thoughts about his mother are narrated: "If Audrey went inside the clinic, he himself would be aborted. He was running for his life" (184). Victor sees women as the enemy of men's identities and egos. Unlike Timmy and Winky, Victor's misogyny is explicitly entangled with racism and his worries about population:

> If you looked at historical birth rates, as Victor had done, the roots of the problem were clear. A Black female born in 1950 . . . produced, on average, four viable offspring. A White female born that year produced only two. Since then, the situation had only worsened. Today's underachieving White female produced only one precious Caucasian child. The numbers were abysmal. (149)

In a symbolic scene, Victor attempts to shore up his threatened masculine vitality by going hunting, despite the fact that, as a convicted felon, he is banned from owning firearms. He bungles his shot, however, and wounds an out-of-season doe, redoubling his shame. He abandons his pursuit of the young animal, leaving her to die of her wounds (237–39). Finally, Victor's violence culminates in his plan to harm Claudia after obsessing for weeks over the images of her sent to him by Winky.

The link between the out-of-season deer, Baby Doe, and the women who appear on Victor's Hall of Shame (including Claudia) reinforces the image of imperiled women and violent, misguided men in the novel. Broken in body or mind, the men are incels, criminals, deadbeats, addicts, and victimizers. They drift through the novel's environment equally buffeted by fate as the female characters, but they are unburdened by responsibilities and care for others. Instead, they are encumbered by their rage and what Kimmel calls "ressentiment," a term he borrows from George Sorrel to describe a potent mixture of hatred, envy, and the sense of being a victim (38). Women become an easy target for displacing this rage. Life in *Mercy Street* is short and brutish for some, like Baby Doe. Violence is dealt out by the state equally to all but is suffered disproportionately by women who must also contend with the men in their lives, who burn down houses; stalk, abandon, and abuse partners and children; and threaten safe spaces for women like Women's Options.

## Denaturalized Motherhood

In *Man Up*, Miller-Idriss observes that the new misogyny that fuels violent extremism is characterized by the belief that men are biologically and genetically superior to women, which legitimizes their domination by men. The violence directed against women is intended not to eliminate them but rather to punish them for rejecting their "rightful roles" (104) as men's inferiors and whose reproductive capacity is not theirs to control (116). This gender essentialist belief system simultaneously devalues and reduces women to their "natural" roles as mothers.

The novels by Picoult, Hyde, Oates, and Haigh abound with examples of mothers who reject motherhood or revise its "natural" meaning. These maternal characters abandon families outright or at least distance themselves to pursue careers. This behavior denaturalizes motherhood and the idea of maternal instincts and thereby lends support to legalized abortion access. By depicting women who reject motherhood, who deprioritize it, or who value it equally with other aspects of their lives, these novels assert the right of women to live outside the normalizing ideas of how women *should* behave sexually and maternally. In *Abortion and the Politics of Motherhood,* Kristin Luker points out, "This round of the abortion debate is so passionate and hard-fought because it is a referendum on the place and meaning of motherhood" (193). She goes on to put a finer point on this claim: "While on the surface it is the embryo's fate that seems to be at stake, the abortion debate is actually about the meanings of women's lives" (194).

Feminists critics and scholars reiterate that motherhood—not just gender—is a social construction that was rewritten by *Roe,* a revision that abortion literature both reflects and performs. The subtitle of Judith Wilt's monograph about abortion literature in the late twentieth century, *The Armageddon of the Maternal Instinct,* is evidence of this trend. In her introduction, Wilt argues that "the makeshift seals of culture over maternity have now been split wide for a generation over the issue called abortion in the political and medical arena. The issue is in fact maternal choice. Though some element of maternal choice has been part of the lore of women back to its traceable dawn, in this generation, 'the maternal' exists no longer repressed in the unconscious, or as 'the natural,' operating as biological or psychological 'instinct'" (2). The novels considered in this chapter depict abortion's role in exposing motherhood as a social construction.

In *The Abortionist's Daughter,* Diana Duprey's husband, Frank, criticizes her mothering for having Ben, their son with Down syndrome, and for allowing their daughter, Megan, more freedom than he thought appropriate. The narrative structure of the novel, which begins after Diana's death, privileges his perspective until her perspective is heard in one of the concluding chapters. In this chapter Diana's love for Ben (267) and hope for Megan (264) is depicted, in addition to her dedication to providing sound healthcare to her patients (250). She is a woman with a career, who fights back when her mothering is critiqued, but she is killed by men who oppose her.

*A Spark of Light* presents several women who abandon motherhood for a variety of reasons. Wren's mother, Annabelle McElroy, leaves Hugh and Wren to be in a new relationship. This shocking decision is tempered by the revelation that the marriage was never compatible. Hugh "got a girl pregnant" (5) and they felt obligated to marry despite their differences. Instead of being a critique of Annabelle, her departure is attributed to unplanned pregnancy and coerced marriage. Goddard, McElroy's foil, is left by his wife when his PTSD threatens her life (116). The mothers of both characters also denaturalize ideas of maternal devotion. Goddard's mother attempts to murder his father in retaliation for his implied abuse (7), and Bex, who was a teen when she became pregnant with Hugh, elects not to raise her child but rather to pose as his sister in order to pursue her education and career as an artist (348–49).

*A Book of American Martyrs* exemplifies the denaturalization of motherhood through its study of the ways that men and women are blinded by their own obsessions to the exclusion of other priorities, including motherhood. After the fatal encounter between Gus Voorhees and Luther Dunphy, their widows become martyrs to their own causes, leaving their fatherless daughters to fend for themselves. Edna Mae Dunphy regularly travels with antiabortion church members to protest at abortion clinics, where in one instance, she roots through medical waste in an alley in the middle of the night to retrieve products of conception to bury properly. To the horror of her eldest daughter, Dawn, she encourages her children to help her and ignores their entreaties to go home. As a result, Dawn begins to drift from her mother's unfocused care. Jenna Voorhees becomes detached from parenting following the loss of her husband. Consumed with her new work as a much-in-demand speaker spreading Gus's story, she tells her daughter, "I can't be 'there' for you any longer, Naomi. You and the others. All of the others—Gus's others. I am just too tired. You will have to make your own way" (329). Even Gus's mother, Madelena, is depicted as uninterested in motherhood. She left Gus and his father when he was eight years old and left a second son with a different man years later. When she married Gus's father, she tried to settle into being the wife of a doctor and a mother, but she confesses to her granddaughter, Naomi, "I loved Gus, that he was the person he was. I just did not want to be 'his' mother and I did not think that it was necessary for his development and his happiness, that I pretend to be this person" (549). She even tells Gus that if she could have, she would have aborted him. About these revelations, Naomi marvels, "Abandoning her son and his father, leaving to establish a 'career' for herself—she is not apologetic, she feels no guilt. But is this so?—Madelena Klein feels no guilt? I adore her. I want to be her. I hate her. She is a monster!" (526). Naomi's thoughts reflect the disruption that revisions of normative motherhood can cause.

*Mercy Street* represents the impact of oppressive conditions on the bodily well-being of its characters, but especially women characters who, like men, are struggling to survive unemployment, low-wage work, and a floundering healthcare system, but who, unlike men, face gender-based violence and are responsible for the well-being of children. Motherhood is represented as imperiling and imperiled by a social environment that privileges men and undervalues the care work of women. While care work and caring have been naturalized as something women and especially mothers instinctually do, *Mercy Street* reveals and elevates caring as work and in so doing contributes to a demythologizing and denaturalizing of motherhood. It exposes how devaluing care work is a type of patriarchal state violence. When the novel begins, Claudia, a social worker, has been working at the Mercy Street clinic for nine years as an options counselor (26, 29). She cares for women by shepherding them through first- and second-trimester terminations, providing referrals, and acquiring bypasses of the Massachusetts parental consent requirement. In doing so, she provides patients with the opportunity to control their reproduction—something not available to her mother. Her labor as a social worker is better compensated than Deb's work in a nursing home and as a foster parent, but Claudia recognizes the devalued status of all care work: "Deb raised other people's kids because it was one of only a few things she could earn money doing. The world was full of discarded people, sickly old ones and damaged young ones, and she was a paid caretaker. It said something about the world that this was the worst paying job around" (17–18). The novel calls attention to care work as a form of labor and its devaluation as another form of violence against women. As this passage illustrates, motherhood is denaturalized not only through the abundance of "discarded" children but also through the mothering provided by nonbiological mothers.

Additionally, motherhood and mothering are not depicted as conditions that naturally fulfill women. Claudia's mother (as well as Bex in *Spark* and Madelena in *American Martyrs*), for example, exemplifies the violence of the aborted woman discussed in chapter 1. Pregnant with Claudia while still a teenager in rural Maine in the 1970s, Deb dropped out of high school and survived (barely) on subsistence employment at a nursing home (17–18, 50, 61). The narration shares Claudia's musings about Deb's nonchoices: "In the spring of 1971, abortion was still illegal in Maine. If Claudia had been conceived a year later, would she even be here? She had never asked her mother that question. The answer was none of her business, and anyway, she didn't want to know" (47). The desire not to know, while ambiguous, suggests that Claudia finds the idea painful because her mother's counterfactual life would have been happier. Claudia suspects that her "out of wedlock" (24, 45) birth sealed her mother's fate and her own. Deb took in foster children to supplement her food stamps and depended on Claudia—still a child herself—to care for the children while she worked outside the home (16, 58–59). Claudia grew up feeling the early loss of her distracted and absent mother as well as her childhood: "Deb said, often, that she treated them [the fosters] like her own children, and Claudia can attest that this was true" (18). She recalls Deb's exhaustion and need for the distraction of television (87, 183) and her own fight to break free of Deb's life and attend college on a scholarship.

*Mercy Street* further demythologizes motherhood by having Claudia revise normative, patriarchal ideas of how and when to mother. As spring approaches and the nor'easter storms dwindle, she discovers that she too has fallen pregnant after a one-night affair with Timmy. Surprised by pregnancy and perimenopausal at forty-three, Claudia chooses to keep her pregnancy and embraces her single-mother status—an identity that brings her closer to Deb, who has died from breast cancer just prior to the novel's action. In the concluding chapters, Claudia has a series of pregnancy dreams about her mother:

> The first time it happened, Claudia woke up laughing. In the dream she caried her mother inside her, the baby version of Deb, mother and daughter nested inside each other like a set of Russian dolls. Soon, soon, she would give birth to her mother. In the dream she found this ridiculous, but also correct and delightful. (338)

Claudia recognizes that Deb did not share her daughter's sense that her life was a tragedy. She realizes that her mother, who fell pregnant pre-*Roe* at seventeen, enjoyed motherhood—even if she was compelled into it—and that she loved Claudia. Claudia's recognition of her own stability, satisfaction at being single (Timmy is arrested on drug charges and disappears from the narrative), and her free choice to be a mother allow her to embrace motherhood as the clinic encircles her with its care and protection. In this novel, women's sexuality and motherhood can avoid punishment, and while masculinity is large, dangerous, and unpredictable, it is, like the weather, navigated and outlasted.

A final important way in which essentialized ideas about motherhood are challenged is found in the statistical fact of adult mothers who comprise the six out of ten women seeking abortions. Picoult's *A Spark of Light* offers one such story in the character of Dr. Louie Ward, an African American man.

In one scene, Ward is moved by hearing the homily of the Good Samaritan, which prompts him to remember his mother, who died after having an abortion, and to reflect on her motives. As a young man, he suspected his mother had an abortion because she was having an affair with a white man. After hearing the homily, he revises this belief:

> At that moment Louie realized why his mama had gone to see Sebby Cherise. It wasn't because she was having the child of a prominent white man. It was because she had been protecting the child she already had, at the expense of the one she hadn't wanted to conceive. This was a variation on a theme he had heard from patients: I have a child with a disability; I don't have the time to parent another one. I can barely feed my son; what will I do with a second baby? I already work three jobs and take care of my family—there isn't any more of me to go around. (56)

This story of a mother having an abortion to better support the child she already has is assigned to a figure who never appears as a character in the novel, but its presence—along with its amplification through Ward's observations of similar stories—is another powerful depiction of ordinary abortion that affirms that such stories can be told.

The novels by Hyde, Picoult, Oates, and Haigh expose "natural" motherhood as a social construction. They depict women abandoning children cruelly, unintentionally, and sometimes lovingly. Sometimes they depict motherhood as an empowering choice. These depictions work to defend abortion against the violence of essentialized motherhood.

## Satire of Religious Hypocrisy

Much feminist scholarship has traced the rise of the religious right in the years following *Roe v. Wade* (Ginsburg; Luker, *Abortion*; Saletan; Fried; Petchesky; Solinger, *Abortion Wars*). Religious fundamentalism dominates the antiabortion movement, taking the closure of clinics as its cause and the fetus as its focus. The rhetoric of this movement espouses concern for women, but its actions reflect an unrelenting agenda of controlling women's identities, bodies, and roles. In her chapter in *Fundamentalism and Gender*, "Fundamentalism and the Control of Women," Karen McCarthy Brown makes the point that misogyny is not inherent to fundamentalism but that current fundamentalist thought is informed primarily by the sense of "a world out of order" caused by the failed promise of Enlightenment rationalism, and that the control of women is important to regaining a sense of order. The growing ideology of Christian nationalism, however, according to Miller-Idriss, is deeply patriarchal and misogynistic. She notes, "Christian nationalists espouse a militant defense of biblical, patriarchal authority, situating husbands as the breadwinning head of the household and wives as submissive, supportive homemakers and mothers who will raise children in an environment promoting chastity, purity, heritage, tradition, and family values" (46). This worldview, which at its core is threatened by perceived "unfair" advances in women's and LGBTQ rights, is informing a mainstreaming of antifeminist thought, and "when that backlash to gendered social change evolves toward violence—including support for violent extremism—it can expand into a full-blown embrace of the use of sexual and gender-based violence as a strategic and ideological aim" (50).

The novels by Hyde, Picoult, and Oates depict fundamentalist attempts at reordering a disordered world through controlling women while exposing how these efforts are motivated by fear, compromised integrity, and self-serving, patriarchal righteousness. A recurring theme in these twenty-first-century thrillers is religious hypocrisy. In the novels considered in this chapter, stridently antiabortion religious figures are depicted as motivated less by spiritual values and more by messy human desires and misogyny. At the same time, an insurgent spirituality is (re)appropriated in service to abortion patients.

In *The Abortionist's Daughter,* Reverend O'Connell sought out Diana to learn if his high school–aged son, Scott, and his pregnant teenage girlfriend, Rose, were her patients. Rose's parents want her to have an abortion, but O'Connell tries to coerce her into keeping the baby and tries to pressure Diana into intervening between Rose and her parents. When Rose changes her mind and tries to abort the pregnancy herself, O'Connell is exposed as callously blind to her well-being. Upon hearing Rose described as the kind of person who could not give up a baby for adoption, he responds, "I consider that a character flaw" (254). Due to his machinations, Rose self-induces an abortion, which results in her near-death and a hysterectomy. O'Connell's character is satirized in the novel for valuing fetal life over the well-being of a young woman.

In *A Spark of Light,* Goddard's attempt to raise his daughter correctly following her mother's departure is warped by a focus on her purity informed by his fundamentalist religious beliefs (316). This focus blinds him to her emotional and physical well-being as well as to the consequences of his arrest—namely, leaving her fatherless as well as motherless while facing murder charges. After seeing her in the hospital and learning that she was pregnant, the last words Goddard says to his daughter are "I don't even know who you are" (316). Similar to O'Connell's character, Goddard's character fails to recognize the humanity of his young daughter.

By contrast, the character of Louie Ward, a fifty-four-year-old African American abortion provider in *A Spark of Light,* is informed by a deep spiritual conviction in his work that allows him to connect with his patients and with others (324–25). He converses amiably with Allen, his harasser and the antiabortion leader of the local religious Right to Life group, who is depicted as incapable of the give-and-take that characterizes true dialogue and who seeks only to antagonize and assert his opinions (343). Allen is depicted as unsavory due to his insensitivity and blind devotion to faith and cause. He likes to joke that because he's fat, "he kn[ows] what it's like to be pregnant" (17); when asked about the need for abortion in cases of rape, he dismisses the question with a shrug, "Really, how big a percentage is that?" (343) Ironically, the woman he sends undercover into the clinic on the day it is taken hostage by Goddard (Janine) is a rape survivor and former abortion patient, although she can barely admit it to herself. Not only has Janine repressed the memory of her assault, she has hidden the memory of the abortion she had afterward and embraces her fundamentalist faith and antiabortion politics: "She knew that there were plenty of people who wouldn't understand, who would call her a hypocrite. Maybe she was. But to her, that just meant she had something to make up for, and this was how she was going to do it" (336). These characters represent organized religion as flawed by hypocrisy, blindness, and sanctimony, while Louie's spirituality is the lifeblood of his compassionate care for his patients.

In *A Book of American Martyrs,* religious hypocrisy in abortion activism is illustrated through the character of Dunphy as well as the antiabortion movement that eggs him to be a martyr only to abandon him when his story becomes media-unfriendly. Dunphy himself is rife with hypocritical views. He identifies himself as "a loving Christian husband and father" (6), but he has had affairs, his actions have led to the death of his daughter, and he has murdered not just Voorhees, but also Voorhees's bodyguard, Tim Barrons, an honorable Vietnam veteran (330). Furthermore, the novel exposes the supporters who encourage Dunphy as less devout than they are political. They are part of "the Coalition" (25), a partnership of political activists whose common goal is antiabortion and not spiritual. One member, sensing Dunphy's naivete, sets him up to murder Voorhees by "confiding" to him the time of the doctor's arrival at his clinic (9, 99). While Dunphy is in prison, his brother laments that Operation Rescue may be "using my brother to make money" (367) by promoting his image as a martyr. At the request of the prison chaplain, Dunphy signs copies of the Bible believing profits from their sale will benefit the

Christian Youth League; however, the chaplain and warden work a deal to sell the books "on eBay after his death," noting that Dunphy was "worth more to the cause dead than alive" (449, 451). In *American Martyrs* the religious right cares more about winning the abortion war than it cares about a man like Dunphy. Rather than being guided by a sense of religious integrity, the characters in the novels by Hyde, Picoult, and Oates, who represent fundamentalist religious authority and, by extension, the antiabortion movement's professed belief that all life is sacred, are revealed to be motivated by other factors, including the need to control women.

## Thriller, Realism, Naturalism: Depicting Antiabortion Slow Violence

Rob Nixon coined the term *slow violence* as part of a call for new ways of thinking about and depicting the violence of environmental destruction and its impact on people who have been socially marginalized. For Nixon, traditional narration of violence is too "immediate in time; explosive and spectacular in space" and immediately visible; he calls instead for representations that capture violence as "incremental and accretive" to expose invisible legacies of damage caused by violence and the complicity of the privileged that facilitates it (2). Nixon's call for action is a question: "How can we convert into image and narrative the disasters that are slow moving?" (16). His aim is for depictions that humanize and make suffering visible rather than rendering it into entertaining spectacles that leave audiences unmoved and the status quo undisturbed (3). Although Nixon's work focuses on environmental crisis, the concept of slow violence captures the enduring and multifaceted problem of antiabortion violence against girls, women, and providers. Nixon's call to action aligns with Watson's call for a *Will & Grace* of abortion narratives that could humanize and demythologize.

The novels by Hyde, Picoult, Oates, and Haigh use elements of literary realism to depict the day-to-day workings of abortion clinics and the conventions of literary naturalism to reveal an environment of misogyny. The thrillers considered in this chapter counter antiabortion stereotypes and misinformation by realistically depicting patients, staff, and procedures inside clinics. In doing so, they expose how antiabortion stereotypes, stigma, and misinformation are another form of violence—like physical attacks on clinics and restrictive policies—enacted by the antiabortion movement against girls and women.

Using elements of literary naturalism (impersonal forces, oppressive natural and social environments, human behavior), *Mercy Street* depicts a social environment that is unrelentingly hostile to girls, women, and mothers. At turns filled with all-too-human characters who struggle against fate, and a feminist survival narrative in which women outwit their hapless male antagonists, *Mercy Street* depicts abortion as integral to women's day-to-day survival. It also depicts the daily heroism of freestanding abortion clinics and their resourcefulness in supporting these women. The unrelentingly grim New England weather, storm after winter storm, reinforces the idea that a woman's life—Deb's, Claudia's, her patients'—is a series of more or less devastating events that make action and forward movement almost impossible. A single misstep can prove fatal.

*Mercy Street* brings readers into the clinic setting in realistic detail. Claudia's daily work as an abortion counselor is detailed: She educates patients about the morning-after treatment and IUD insertions as methods of pregnancy prevention after unprotected sex (83), counsels a minor on the judicial bypass process (21), counsels an addict who has repeated abortions (28), counsels a mother who accompanies her daughter to the clinic but who hasn't revealed that she herself had an abortion (176), reports domestic and sexual assault, counsels trans men about abortion, and finds funding for Landon, a woman with a late second-trimester pregnancy who will need a procedure in a different state (201). Her character not only educates readers about the types of work abortion providers perform, but she also educates readers about patients. As the following narration reveals, Claudia has heard countless patients explain their decisions, making her character a repository for the epistemology of abortion:

> My son is autistic and day care won't take him. I can't handle another kid.
> I got fired. Evicted. I got into law school.
> I just need to finish (high school, chemo, probation. My PhD. My tour of duty).
> My mother would never forgive me.
> I want a different kind of life. (92)

Through Claudia's perspective, readers also witness the realities of how clinics confront antiabortion actions. Claudia and her colleagues discuss the return of a Crisis Pregnancy Center nearby, which provided Landon with misleading information that led to her needing a second-trimester procedure (207). In addition to a full-time security guard named Luis, the clinic has codified procedures for handling threatening messages and figures (86) and meets to discuss security updates and new threats (275). Despite the lack of gratitude and outright hostility from patients that she and her colleagues often face, Claudia and the workers at Woman's Options support patients and their choices. Claudia describes overhearing her colleague Naomi on the phone with someone asking about emergency contraception: "'These girls,' Naomi said, shaking her head. She spoke of the callers as if they were her own daughters: What are these girls thinking? Exasperation in her voice; affection, amusement, a grudging admiration. She seemed to be rooting for them" (84). Above all, *Mercy Street* depicts abortion care work as work and abortion clinics as workplaces. Significantly, Claudia notes in passing that even though her position "was stressful," she had "a retirement plan and health benefits and what passed for a full-time salary in the nonprofit world" (26–27). In other words, Claudia's work is a job like any other job. It is exceptional only for the way it is stigmatized.

In addition to Claudia's counseling work inside the clinic, her character's backstory educates readers by countering antiabortion mythology. In one scene, a protester outside the clinic waves a sign that (falsely) claims abortion causes breast cancer, and Claudia uncharacteristically snaps, confronting the man. The scene is fueled by the knowledge that Claudia has been grieving the loss of her mother, Deb, who died of breast cancer in her early fifties (98, 242, 252). Her anger is as much a response to the sign's falsehood as it is to the tragedy of her mother's death: Deb, who disastrously did not have access to abortion in 1971, nevertheless died of breast cancer. Contrary to the protester's message, childbirth, not abortion, robbed her mother of a fulfilling life and instead doomed her to impoverished, stigmatized, single motherhood and care work—an early death of sorts.

Oates's *A Book of American Martyrs* does not dwell on the ethics of the abortion debate (it is, instead, focused on the personalities attracted to the debate), but the novel does provide realistic details about clinics, patients, and providers, including about the ordinary encounters and dangers of abortion-providing. One scene of rare narrative focalization through Voorhees's perspective lists the reasons he heard from patients for having abortions:

> Because the father is gone. Because he is not coming back.
> Because the father would kill me, if he knew.
> Because the father is married.
> Because the father has too many children already.
> Because the father would deny it, he would say that I am lying . . .
> Because I don't know how this happened. I did not want it to happen.

> Because it is the same man as with my sister. Because he is engaged to my sister. Because my sister cannot know! . . .
> Because he is so old.
> Because he is too young. (189)

The epic catalogs of reasons for having an abortion in thrillers by Oates and Haigh provide an important trope in the depiction of ordinary abortion. Rather than narrating one patient's experience seeking abortion, thrillers that are set in clinics do the work of representing a variety of reasons for seeking terminations. The ensemble cast of characters who arrive at the clinic in *A Spark of Light* provide a similar assortment of reasons for seeking abortion. These accounts do the work of countering antiabortion stigma and demystifying abortion. They reveal the ordinariness of abortion as well as the silencing power of stigma.

In addition to offering the myriad reasons for why women terminate pregnancies, these thrillers also demythologize and destigmatize abortion and providers by taking readers into procedure rooms. In *A Spark of Light,* Dr. Louie Ward travels to clinics in different states—including The Center—to perform procedures when he is not busy teaching young medical students how to perform abortions. In one crucial scene, the narrative lingers on an abortion procedure that he performs on a woman who is fourteen weeks pregnant, going into specific detail about each step of the procedure as he performs it and as he counsels her (295–300). A similar moment in *The Abortionist's Daughter* describes abortion procedures in a neutral, nonsensationalized manner (250). The stereotype of the back-alley abortionist is also debunked in *A Spark of Light.* Dr. Ward's character is shot in the initial moments of Goddard's assault on the clinic, and although he survives his wounds, his narrative moments are filled with retrospective memories of his time as a provider. Through his perspective, the novel builds a sympathetic viewpoint on providers as it records the numerous obstacles, wrongs, and threats that they endure. Ward is portrayed as kind and respectful, willing to talk with antiabortion activists, but frequently met with hostility and hypocrisy (272, 341, 190). His character exposes and debunks myths about abortion providers as greedy and transactional by describing the reality of how procedures are funded and reflecting on the damage that efforts to defund Planned Parenthood would produce: "It wouldn't stop abortions. Abortions would literally be the only things they could afford to do" (312). His character withstands racist attacks by antiabortion activists, witnesses everyday heroism from pro-choice nonactivists (57–58), provides care for rape victims, and educates patients about the facts of abortion (324).

These thrillers portray providers and clinics in ways that counter stigma. The realism of these novels portrays abortion-providing as ordinary healthcare and medical office work—not the stigmatized, secretive doings of shady characters. They seek to depict the psychological and physical tolls on abortion workers and patients that come with continuing attacks on clinics and abortion access. Finally, they perform the heavy lifting of countering the slow violence of antiabortion myths, misinformation, and stereotypes.

## Conclusion

The genre of the psychological thriller may not initially appear to be a likely choice for grounding an argument that abortion is ordinary. The thriller conventionally depicts extraordinary crimes and criminal mentalities. To this objection, I argue that these novels do the work of dedramatizing and destigmatizing the decision to have an abortion by making the psychology of the men who enact violence against patients, clinics, and providers the source of narrative drama and pathology. It is significant that the decision to have an abortion is not the driving plot element in these texts, nor does having an abortion reflect a deviant mind or morality. By depicting the psychology of misogyny, these novels, whose publication dates span the first three decades of the twenty-first century, reveal instead the gradual evolution and intensification of misogyny's role in violent extremism. From Hyde's depiction of resentful husbands, fathers, and boyfriends, to Oates's depiction of warring male egos, to Picoult's and Haigh's explicit defense of clinics as safe spaces for women until they become targets of patriarchal and Christian nationalist hate, these novels represent and condemn how "control of women's bodies—and entitlement to them" (Miller-Idriss 117) has emerged as an integral belief in violent extremism.

Additionally, some readers have objected that these novels are not sufficiently proabortion or feminist, presumably because they lack a sympathetic figure who represents the experience of having an abortion or they represent teenage girls who appear to be punished for their sexual activity. As I've acknowledged, the use of teenage-girl sexuality and abortion access in these novels does not represent the statistical reality of ordinary abortion; however, they exist to critique the paranoid misogyny that is provoked by the idea of "uncontrolled" teenage sexuality and pregnancy and how that paranoia is connected to other fears over threats to normative gender roles, normative motherhood, and patriarchal authority to which violent extremism purports to respond. Plots and dramatization in the texts are driven by male responses to teenage-girl behaviors that the texts frame as ordinary.

By exposing toxic masculinity and violent extremism to censure, in addition to depicting and elevating the day-to-day reality of abortion clinics and the mundane reasons that motivate women to have abortions, these novels capture elements of ordinary abortion in ways that support abortion and reproductive freedom.

CHAPTER 4

# Resisting Responsibilization

## Abortion and Disability in Twenty-First-Century Mommy Memoirs and Fiction

The exploration of twenty-first-century thrillers in chapter 3 examined Elisabeth Hyde's *The Abortionist's Daughter*, a novel about the murder of an abortion doctor, Diana Duprey, whose husband resented her decision to give birth to a baby they knew would have disabilities. The husband, Frank, misreads his wife's motives for having this child, and in one scene he makes the following accusation: "You had to go and prove you weren't just a heartless baby killer. Oh no, you were the great Dr. Duprey, the abortion doctor who decided not to abort her retarded child. Great way to refute the pro-lifers. Hey, it's a matter of choice, see? What a photo op" (267). Frank is mistaken about his wife's reasons for having their son, but his accusation reflects the intersection of abortion and disability politics. Diana was determined to keep her pregnancy because she wanted it, but Frank believed that a termination would avoid unnecessary suffering and that Diana had the baby only to make an ideological statement: "Great way to refute the pro-lifers." Hyde's novel exposes the complicated politics of abortion and disability through the characters' conflicted reproductive decision-making.

In fact, three of the thrillers discussed in chapter 3—*The Abortionist's Daughter, A Spark of Light,* and *The Book of American Martyrs*—represent the entwined politics of abortion and disability in the twenty-first century. The presence of disability in each of these novels serves to highlight this entwinement and to depict the moral complexity of decisions and outcomes. In Jodi Picoult's *A Spark of Light*, for example, the antiabortion views of one character, Janine, are informed by her childhood memories of a brother with Down syndrome. Although the family cherished this brother, Janine's childhood was spent subordinating her needs to his. When she is sexually assaulted at a party, she tells no one about the assault or the subsequent pregnancy, which she terminates at a local clinic. Janine is traumatized, blaming herself for the rape, which she suppresses the memory of, along with that of the abortion, by undertaking a personal crusade to "whitewash the stain with years of pro-life activism" (235). *A Spark of Light* is complexly proabortion and pro-disability. Rather than being easily dismissed for her hypocrisy, Janine's character is tragic due to the polarization of both the abortion and the disability debates, which prevents her from admitting the abortion to her family or herself. Another novel, Joyce Carol Oates's *A Book of American Martyrs*, explores the stigmatization of both abortion and disability. The character of Luther Dunphy, a failed lay evangelical minister, murders an abortion provider in the belief that he is "defending the defenseless," but ironically, he fails to protect his disabled daughter. In Dunphy's religion, ability and disability are signs of God's (dis)favor. When his wife's pregnancy is diagnosed with a fetal anomaly, they pray for a nondisabled child: "Jesus would take care of her and her baby, she had had only healthy babies in the past and Jesus would look after her now" (62). After their daughter is born with Down syndrome, Dunphy forgoes her corrective heart surgery, which must be funded through aid, something that mortifies his sense of self-reliance. He "worried this was some kind of welfare or federal government program he did not believe in" (60). Luther's ability to "defend" his daughter ultimately fails when he causes the car accident in which she dies. He suppresses the memory of his role in her death, but his wife believes "he had not loved Daphne, really. He'd been embarrassed and ashamed of their youngest child because she was not 'right'" (413). While Janine's loyalty to her disabled brother makes her ashamed of her abortion, Dunphy is ashamed of his daughter's disability, which his antiabortion views prevent him from exploring. The intersection of abortion and disability politics has produced an ongoing debate in this century, explored in the three thrillers by Hyde, Picoult, and Oates. These novels depict how (in the case of Dunphy) holding extreme antiabortion views does not lead to greater respect for disability, and how (in the case of Janine), holding rigid pro-disability views can lead to denying abortion access.

More recently, those who defend abortion in cases of fetal anomaly have debated those who argue that such cases are discriminatorily based in ableist worldviews. In the public imaginary, this debate sometimes collapses into an oversimplified question: Does abortion in cases of fetal anomaly constitute a kind of neo-eugenics? The biopolitics of this question concern this chapter's analysis of recent mommy memoirs and fiction. By *biopolitics* I am referring to the neoliberal responsibilization of mothers and the influence of social stigma and public policy on family-making decisions. I use biopolitics to counter the popular assumption that family-making is natural and private. Increasingly, families and women, in particular, are presented with expanded and normalized fetal testing, in addition to the social expectation that they make responsible choices based on the results. Their decisions are shaping and are shaped by how inclusive of disability society is, and they are inherently political and not private.

This chapter examines two mommy memoirs and a novel that center and deconstruct those tensions. In what follows, this chapter turns to an examination of mommy memoirs to consider responsibilized decision-making after a diagnosis of fetal anomaly. Martha Beck's *Expecting Adam: A True Story of Birth, Rebirth, and Everyday Magic* and Ayelet Waldman's *Bad Mother: A Chronicle of Maternal Crimes, Minor Calamities, and Occasional Moments of Grace* rely on the warm, pronatalist approbation for this genre to authorize disruptive discussions of disability and abortion and to depict mothers who arrive at different decisions: Waldman has an abortion after an amniocentesis reveals her fetus has a trisomy disorder, while Beck, after a similar discovery, decides to continue her pregnancy. In Lois-Anne Yamanaka's novel, *Father of the Four Passages,* the actions of grieving and accepting previous abortions becomes the catalyst for a mother's feminist acceptance of her son's disability and her resistance to being responsibilized. Before exploring these three texts, this chapter first considers the biopolitics of disability and abortion in the twenty-first century, as well as the mommy memoir genre.

## Disability Is a Biopolitical Issue

The twentieth-century normalization of prenatal testing and selective abortion was informed by ideas—long in circulation—about disability and motherhood. These ideas are explored by Claire McKinney in her essay in *Hypatia* about the story of Sherri Finkbine, the TV host of the children's series *Romper Room* in the early 1960s. In 1962, Finkbine was "a married, white, middle-class mother of four who was two months pregnant when she heard of the possibility of birth defects associated with thalidomide, an ingredient in sleeping pills her husband had brought back from England and that she had ingested" (273). The ensuing media representations depicting her situation as a "tragic narrative" contributed to the political context that "made abortion-law liberalization a priority across the US" (273). Because abortion was illegal at the time, Finkbine had to obtain permission for a therapeutic termination from her local hospital's board. In the process, she also tried to alert local news media anonymously about the dangers of thalidomide. When her name was leaked, sparking a national debate over the morality of abortions in cases of fetal anomaly, the hospital reversed its decision, and Finkbine had to leave the US to terminate her pregnancy in Sweden. Her experience was later recounted as a *Life Magazine* cover story and a speech to the Society for Humane Abortion, which was reprinted in *Time Magazine* and in Alan Guttmacher's *The Case for Legalized Abortion Now* (McKinney 273). McKinney argues that Finkbine's story garnered popular support for abortion, which was illegal except in rare cases and still highly stigmatized, through the rhetorical trope of fit motherhood, a construct that relies on its opposite for its significance: the trope of unfit motherhood (comprising teen mothers, single mothers, and mothers on welfare). Finkbine's status as a white, middle-class, married mother and the circumstances of her wanted pregnancy were used to frame her abortion as tragic, a moral choice, and a reflection of fit motherhood: "Finkbine's narrative displaced abortion stigma onto disability stigma, working to normalize therapeutic abortion while leaving intact the more generalized stigma of both nontherapeutic abortion and the supposed tragedy of disability" (273). McKinney's account illuminates how Finkbine's story garnered support for abortion access by creating distinct categories of legitimacy and illegitimacy, while uncritically drawing on disability stigma to do so.

In the decades immediately after Finkbine's case, prenatal testing was recommended only for high-risk pregnancies, but as the safety and accuracy of tests increased, as well as the range of tests for genetic anomalies, so did the normalization of testing. Doctors now routinely screen pregnant people for chromosomal alterations, duplications, and deletions that are associated with disabilities such as Down syndrome, muscular dystrophy, Tay-Sachs disease, spina bifida, sickle cell anemia, and many others. Stefanija Giric in her article in the *Journal of Law and the Biosciences* reports that by the early 2000s, "the American College of Obstetricians and Gynecologists (ACOG) amended its guidelines on chromosomal abnormalities to recommend that all pregnant women in the first trimester of pregnancy be screened for certain biochemical markers associated with risk of their fetus having Down syndrome as well as other chromosomal abnormalities and defects" (736). She notes that in 2016, "it is possible to both screen for and diagnose many heterogeneous conditions via different techniques, one of which (cell-free fetal DNA testing) can yield results even as early as after 9 weeks of gestation" (737).

Alongside developments in prenatal testing, the disability rights movement has progressively evolved. In 1990, disability advocates celebrated the passage of the Americans with Disabilities Act, which protects members of the disabled community from discrimination in housing, employment, communications, and transportation. Social justice advocates argue that disability is a socially constructed form of Otherness, which requires exposing and rethinking ableist norms and privileges to achieve full social access by members of the disabled community. Part of this rethinking involves deconstructing and destigmatizing notions of dependence. Over the course of a human lifespan, these advocates point out, everyone experiences periods of dependence and disability; recognizing our mutual dependence deconstructs the two poles of dis/ability to encourage new and more just ways of organizing our social world and physical environment. Giric describes this perspective as follows:

> Disability rights advocates argue that it is not the limitations caused by disability itself but societal discrimination against individuals with disabilities that constitutes the major problem; therefore, it is imperative that individuals with disabilities and their caregivers have access to the support necessary to overcome the challenges of a living in a society that may not meet their needs. (741)

Destigmatization exposes the idea of self-reliance as a myth and counters its overprivileging as a neoliberal value. Social justice advocacy challenges the idea of disability as a social burden and instead promotes diversity and new modes for sociability.

Some disability rights activists have argued that prenatal testing only intensifies antidisability stigma and reflects a kind of neo-eugenic thinking. Rosemarie Garland Thomson, for example, argues that therapeutic abortion is a mechanism for erasing the social diversity represented by people with disabilities as well as the experiences of those who care for them. Other critics point to the long US history of "racial hygiene" that was intended "to stem the perpetuation of 'defects'" (Hubbard 93) by preventing people with disabilities from engaging in sex or having children. Ruth Hubbard links contemporary genetic testing directly to the history of the racial hygiene policies of Hitler's Nazi Germany and similar early twentieth-century practices in Britain and the US. In her analysis of Finkbine's story, McKinney does not go as far as Hubbard in making a straight throughline from early twentieth-century eugenics to mid-twentieth-century ideas of fit motherhood, but, she notes, they "share some conceptual affinities" (270).

The concerns voiced by Thomson and Hubbard are poignantly exemplified in Sarah Zhang's 2020 essay for *The Atlantic*, "The Last Children of Down Syndrome." Zhang writes about the startlingly low birth numbers of children with Down syndrome in Denmark, where prenatal testing for the condition has been available to all since 2004 and where 95 percent of diagnoses lead to abortion. In 2019, only eighteen people with Down syndrome were born in Denmark (44), even though, Zhang claims, the culture can be broadly described as accepting of disability and there are no state policies compelling parents to terminate:

> In wealthy countries, it seems to be at once the best and the worst time for Down syndrome. Better health care has more than doubled life expectancy. Better access to education means most children with Down syndrome will learn to read and write. Few people speak publicly about wanting to "eliminate" Down syndrome. Yet individual choices are adding up to something very close to that. (46)

Zhang cites Thomson's term for this phenomenon: *velvet eugenics.* She quotes the genetic counselor, Laura Hercher, who asks, "If our world didn't have people with special needs and these vulnerabilities, . . . would we be missing a part of our humanity?" (46). Also disturbing is the possibility that, as prenatal testing expands, so too will the deselection process. Zhang points out that "Down syndrome is frequently called the 'canary in the coal mine' for selective reproduction. It was one of the first genetic conditions to be routinely screened for in utero, and it remains the most morally troubling because it is among the least severe. It is very much compatible with life—even a long, happy life" (44). The possibility in the near future of deselecting children with autism, for example, should be alarming. Additionally, Zhang observes that in the US, where there is no national healthcare system, testing and genetic counseling are uneven across regions, a situation that may lead to an "empathy gap": "If only the wealthy can afford to routinely screen out certain genetic conditions, then those conditions can become proxies of class. They can become, in other words, other people's problems" (51).

The difference between the explicit state policies of the twentieth century and the twenty-first-century private decisions to have therapeutic abortions reflects responsibilization, Wendy Brown's term for describing neoliberal governmentality under which individuals are expected to take responsibility for their own well-being (*Undoing*). Responsibilization, according to Brown, reflects a social process of shifting responsibilities from the state to individuals and communities. Fetal testing has become part of the responsibilization of women/mothers. In her groundbreaking anthropological study of fetal testing and decision-making, *Testing Women, Testing the Fetus: The Social Impact of Amniocentesis in America,* Rayna Rapp argues that advancements in fetal testing and the social expectation that families act on their results has made women into "moral pioneers," her term for the seemingly sudden way "a new power was thrust into the hands of ordinary people—the power to decide what kind of life is worth bringing into the world" (46). The task falls to women, according to Rapp, because their bodily sovereignty entitles them to have a choice and their social roles as caregivers require them to make it. Individual women now bear the weight of making decisions about how inclusive our society will be.

Framed in the liberating rhetoric of "offering women a choice" (Zhang 46), these decisions are heavy. In a pair of posts on *The New York Times* blog *Motherlode,* Alison Piepmeier describes learning with her husband that their wanted pregnancy had a higher-than-average chance of resulting in a child with Down syndrome, compelling them to make a decision based on their desire for a child and their comfort with disability. Her experience with making the uncommon decision to continue her pregnancy—she notes that nationally "up to 92 percent of [these pregnancies] are terminated"—led her to interview other parents making the same choice ("Choosing"). Piepmeier names herself and her subjects "the 8%-ers." Media coverage that lauds new screening as "the holy grail of prenatal testing" and "a game changer" represents the decision-making following testing and diagnosis as a clear choice, but Piepmeier argues that the ethics are more nuanced ("Choosing"). Although antiabortion groups have ethical objections to the normalization of selective abortion, her argument calls for an ethical rethinking of the social stigmatization of disability. Piepmeier, who is adamantly proabortion (she had two terminations before conceiving her daughter), reports that "many of the women I've interviewed are emphatically supportive of reproductive rights, and have had abortions in the past. When they were ready to have children, they chose to go ahead with pregnancies even after the Down syndrome was identified. And they're happy with that decision" ("Choosing"). She concludes, "All disabilities are not the same. If our culture assumes that across the board, a child with a disability is defective, and a problem best avoided, then we're encouraging people who want to be parents to make a decision based on bad information. And having an abortion because of bad information is a preventable tragedy" ("Choosing").[1]

While Piepmeier represents both proabortion and pro-disability perspectives, antiabortion groups have been quick to take up disability as a means for attacking abortion access. Karen Weingarten argues that neo-eugenics is the "logic that antiabortionists have latched onto in their arguments that abortion should not be allowed when a fetus has been diagnosed with a possible disability" ("It's" 157). The antiabortion movement accuses abortion advocates of

1. In *The Turnaway Study,* a sweeping investigation into the experiences of women who, after seeking abortions, either had them or were turned away, Foster notes that there is a lack of research on women who terminate wanted pregnancies (21).

discrimination against people with disabilities, claiming one "cannot be pro-choice and anti-discrimination" (Jarman) and has proposed bans and measures to stop therapeutic abortion. Beginning with North Dakota, seven additional states have banned abortion based on fetal anomaly ("Abortion Bans"). Additionally, other states are looking for antiabortion models of doctor–patient communication, such as Pennsylvania's Chloe Law—which requires physicians to provide information about life expectancy, developmental outcomes, treatment, and support services for people with Down syndrome to patients who receive a positive test for fetal anomalies. Some observers are alarmed, according to Giric, by how such policies may introduce bias into the private space of doctor–patient conversations:

> Although Chloe's Law and the eight other pieces of legislation that are modeled after it in other states strive for neutrality on their face, the state of Pennsylvania essentially seeks to upend the ethical norms of autonomy and patient centeredness in genetic counseling and prenatal diagnosis by mandating that certain information be provided regarding Down syndrome during the doctor–patient interaction. (740)

Additionally, the Guttmacher Institute reports that three states currently require "counseling on perinatal hospice services available before a patient can undergo an abortion if it may be based on a lethal fetal condition. Kansas requires counseling on perinatal hospice services before an abortion can be performed" ("Abortion Bans"). These policies favor continuing pregnancies even in cases of fatal fetal conditions. Abortion law expert, Mary Ziegler, predicts that at the least, proposed bans will reshape the abortion debate ("Disability").

Feminists and abortion advocates contend that antiabortion groups have disingenuously appropriated disability rights and misapplied the term *neo-eugenic* to selective abortion practices (Weingarten, "It's"). They point out that antiabortion support for fetuses with disabilities has not translated into meaningful support for people with disabilities. Giric notes, "Though pro-life advocates' hardline stance against abortion is at first glance couched in this social model of disability, such advocates often actively oppose funding for social service programs for the disabled" (741). Antiabortion groups also remain silent concerning other barriers facing women with disabilities, including lack of access to "strong disability services like education supports, employment, housing, robust healthcare, and public spaces" (Jarman 48). Laws prohibiting selective abortion will not alleviate threats posed by neoliberal governance. Giric argues that the real goal behind bans on selective abortion

> is to legislate extremely private individual and family decisions rather than to focus public policy where it may be more productive, ie by mandating access to services, education, and support for families and individuals caring for individuals with disabilities and embracing disability as a part of the human experience. (742)

In sum, antiabortion advocates do not voice support for expanding disability rights beyond banning abortion, leading Piepmeier to observe that "outlawing abortion won't help children with Down syndrome" ("Outlawing").

Furthermore, bans on abortion will negatively impact people with disabilities. As Giric points out, this is already the case for women with disabilities on Medicare who are prevented by the Hyde Amendment from using federal funds to pay for abortion. Katie O'Connell provides another example of the harm posed to disabled women by antiabortion policies in her discussion of living with a chronic pain condition for which she takes numerous, expensive medications daily that are contraindicated during pregnancy. She argues that "controlling my own reproductive future is absolutely vital to me as a disabled woman" (304), and she refutes the suggestion that her support for abortion access somehow contributes to neo-eugenics: "Choosing not to have children due to my disability does not mean that I think other people with disabilities should not have children" (305). Like Jarman, Giric, and Piepmeier, O'Connell redirects attention to problems with the social infrastructure: "Institutions are not set up to help parents raise high-needs children, particularly when those parents face other barriers like racism, immigration status, queerphobia, and socioeconomic oppression" (304). Indeed, abortion access is vital to families who choose to prioritize the care of a disabled child or children over expanding their families. O'Connell concludes that abortion advocates should not allow themselves to be muted by charges of neo-eugenics; instead she calls for a nuanced proabortion defense grounded in a pro-disability rights discourse to counteract the fact that "folks in the mainstream reproductive rights movement do not talk about disability enough" (302).

Silence and stigma have contributed to the absence of a nuanced discussion of abortion and disability. The responsibilization of women in this context has produced additional, unnecessary stress. Mothers can feel blamed for having therapeutic abortions *and* for not terminating pregnancies; in both cases, they stand accused of harming their child or causing their suffering. For example, on *Slate* Emily Rapp shared the story of her son, who was born with Tay-Sachs disease, which went undetected by testing ("I Would"). His disease caused distressing levels of suffering, and she recalls the sense that others assumed she chose to have her son—knowing his diagnosis—and that they judged her as "not loving" him. Rapp's experience of feeling condemned for not preventing her son's pain is echoed in Zhang's essay, in which Danish parents reported similar feelings of being judged for failing to prevent their children's suffering. Unlike the Danish parents of children with Down syndrome, Rapp remarks that, although she cherished her son, she was devastated by witnessing the effects of Tay-Sachs, and had she known his fate, she would have had an abortion. On the other hand, the sometimes fleeting promises of medicalized cures can pressure women and parents to continue pregnancies. These promises do not challenge the stigma on disability; rather, they offer the possibility of normalization. According to David Mitchell, the neoliberal state no longer conspicuously enacts punitive policies of race hygiene through "confinement and legal prohibitions" (9) but instead views "disabled people . . . in paradoxical terms as new commodification opportunities, evidence of the triumph of American exceptionalism, and/or as threats to the productive mandates of market capitalism" (11). This paradox can be seen in the market-based prenatal testing culture that simultaneously routinizes selective abortion and promises of normalcy through "cyborgian overcompensations" (36). These promises of cures frame selective abortion with the stigma of eugenics; however, giving birth to a child with impairments that cannot be cured, who occupies "peripheral embodiments" (Mitchell 7), is also stigmatized for creating suffering and demands on the state (for access and rights). Thus, parents who are given a prenatal diagnosis of chromosomal or genetic anomaly are faced with an impossible choice between actions weighted heavily with social stigma against simultaneously alleged eugenic abortions and high-needs children. These accounts point to the toll on women of responsibilization.

Any discussion of responsibilization must also consider how neoliberal privatization of care and the dismantling of social safety nets have placed enormous strains on women. Women who are disproportionately responsible for reproductive labor—the care of children, the elderly, disabled people, and dependents of any sorts—have experience of neoliberalism in terms of care–work balance (sometimes called life–work balance). Reproductive labor is not inherently oppressive, although as Martha Saxton rightly cautions, it must be understood in terms of the devaluation of women, their labor, and people with disabilities:

> Women can be overwhelmed and oppressed by their work of caring for disabled family members. But this is not caused by the disabilities per se. It is caused by lack of community services and inaccessibility, and greatly exacerbated by the sexism that isolates and overworks women caregivers.

> Almost any kind of work with people, if sufficiently shared and validated, can be meaningful, important, joyful, and productive. (112)

The neoliberal economic demand for women/mothers in the paid labor force conflicts with the increasing requirement for their unpaid (and devalued) reproductive labor at home. It's worth noting how this crisis, Laura Briggs correctly points out, has been deliberately misattributed to feminism. Feminism is assumed to have propelled women into the workforce, but now it becomes a woman's *choice* how she will negotiate an impossible conflict between career and family in the absence of universal childcare, eldercare, healthcare, and support for families of members with disabilities. According to Wendy Brown, the interpellation of individuals as "entrepreneurial" actors (*Undoing* 42) signals the transformation of political problems into personal ones that require market solutions, that is, work–life balance programs. So while feminism is blamed for creating a care–work balance problem for women, the focus on individual solutions banishes collective feminism from popular discourse.

In this work, I am arguing that abortion is ordinary, by which I mean that despite the drama of political debates, abortion has an undramatic place in women's reproductive healthcare. This healthcare now includes the regular use of fetal genetic testing during pregnancy and the normalized solution of abortion as a responsibilized answer to fetal genetic anomaly. The responsibilization of pregnant women has put abortion on the table in a way that has made it ordinary. To be clear, abortions due to genetic anomalies are not common: In a study including data from sixty countries between 1990 and 2014, of all the abortions that took place, one-tenth were due to genetic disease (Kivity and Barnoy). However, fetal testing is common, and the act of undergoing these screenings means that most pregnant people intending to carry their pregnancies ordinarily have a moment when they are required to bring their values regarding disability and abortion to bear, weighing their personal values and their social responsibilization. The mommy memoir, a genre that blossomed in the twenty-first century, illustrates the ordinariness of discussions about fetal testing, abortion, and responsibilization in pregnancy narratives.

## The Mommy Memoir

The mommy memoir arose in the context of the 1990s backlash against feminist advances for women in the workforce and the rise of what Susan Douglas and Meredith Michaels call "the new momism." In their work, Douglas and

Michaels describe a resurgence of essentialized motherhood, in which women (married and resourced) retreated from the paid workforce and devoted their attention wholly to having and raising children, claiming this was more fulfilling than paid labor. This ideology manifests most clearly in the practice of attachment parenting, a style that emphasizes forming bonds through hyper-responsiveness to children's needs. The new momism, according to Douglas and Michaels, reified this type of parenting for women in particular, while it enlisted all of American society in disciplining good and bad mothers.

Mommy memoirs reflect their authors' engagement with this ideology—ranging from wholehearted embrace to arm's-length rejection. The genre encompasses life-writing about all aspects of motherhood, loosely structured by a pronatalist description of the decision to become a mother. Mommy memoirs are first-person narratives, often epistolary in form, and address either the author's child or an implied readership of sympathetic fellow mommies. The epistolary form reflects how many texts began as blogs—serial publications in the form of diaries, journal entries, or letters. Topics and themes include conception, pregnancy, delivery, infancy, childhood, and adolescence, as well as conflicts between motherhood and careers, and conflicts between mothers and fathers. The tone of the mommy memoir can range from confessional to outraged to prescriptive. They frequently include lengthy discussions of the medicalization of fertility, pregnancy and childbirth, which sometimes include (unexpectedly) the experience of having an abortion. In this way, the mommy memoir genre does important work in illustrating the idea that abortion is ordinary. Numerous authors in this genre discuss having one or more abortions before and while creating their families. As Rebecca Walker observes in, *Baby Love,* her contribution to the genre, "Oh, that it were possible to write about having a baby in America without writing about not having a baby" (99). Texts like Walker's reveal that many women's stories of becoming and being mothers contain stories about abortions. References to previous abortions and/or the author's support for abortion rights is conventional in mommy memoirs. An early example of the genre is Anne Lamott's *Operating Instructions: A Journal of My Son's First Year.* Lamott's breathless account of her headlong dive into motherhood shares her lack of preparation (she was newly sober and was breaking up with the father of her son), her bad timing (her father had died recently and she was losing her childhood friend to cancer), her determination (she had terminated previous pregnancies), and her infectious wonder. Although her memoir is a celebration of the choice to become a mother, it directly refers to Lamott's previous abortions. She decides to keep her unplanned pregnancy, "having decided that I couldn't survive any more abortions, having decided that I did in fact want this baby, and at the same time feeling it was impossible to have a baby when the father (who is six-foot-four and two hundred pounds) was so frantically and maybe violently opposed" (31). Lamott's commitment to abortion rights is unwavering although she decides to continue the pregnancy: "I could have had an abortion—the pressure to do so was extraordinary—and if need be I would take to the streets, armed, to defend the right of any woman for any reason to terminate a pregnancy" (14).

In some ways, the mommy memoir appears to be transgressive. It critiques openly the demands of responsibilized new momism, and, as noted above, tells secondary stories about how women rely on abortion as they decide if, when, and how to mother. Despite these transgressive traits, the genre fails at a politically progressive message. The critique of new momism never evolves into a raised consciousness of systemic gender-based oppression. Instead, feminism is frequently identified as the enemy of mothers and women. In "The Motherhood Memoir and the 'New Momism,'" Andrea O'Reilly has pointed to a central contradiction in many mommy memoirs: On the one hand, the authors embody the hard-won benefits of feminism (education, careers, and reproductive control), yet they re-essentialize normative ideas about motherhood and explicitly reject feminism, a retreat into patriarchal ideology that O'Reilly likens to "biting the hand that feeds you" ("Motherhood" 479). The genre's politics are also limited by the perspectives of its authors, who are mostly white, middle-class, heterosexual women. The genre uses their relatively rare and privileged experiences to make generalized claims about a universal, essential motherhood. The genre also provides these women with a space for representing their neoliberal subjectivation as fit mothers.

Privileged young women and mothers, according to Angela McRobbie in *The Aftermath of Feminism: Gender, Culture and Social Change,* play an important role in an emergent, neoliberal sexual contract. Young women appear as emblematic beneficiaries of neoliberalism's economic, political, and social transformations, and their freedoms are understood to be measurements of Western progress and advancement. Young mothers—whom McRobbie names "yummy mummies"—command a space of attention or "luminosity" as new global subjects (54) in an economy that privileges self-reliance, individualism, and personal responsibility. This new female subject enacts her freedom through an ongoing performance of choice-making and self-monitoring, performing and embracing the identity of someone "who can make the right choices" (19). Women who cannot access educations, careers, and reproductive control, McRobbie points out, are perceived as failing to apprehend freedom rather than reflecting freedom's absence. Furthermore, the promise of subjectivation in the global market is extended on the condition that these women distance themselves from feminism: The new sexual contract "also encompasses the existence of feminism as at some level transformed into a form of Gramscian common sense, while also fiercely repudiated, indeed almost hated" (12). Catherine Rottenberg has named the new sexual contract "neoliberal feminism." Like McRobbie, she sees subjectivation—social recognition—extended to young women through a simultaneous embrace of neoliberal values and disavowal of feminist social critique. This soi-disant feminism of the twenty-first century, Rottenberg argues, is characteristically preoccupied with the choices pertaining to work–life balance and the avoidance of questions about why imbalance exists in the first place. The mommy memoir genre—in which women's reproductive decision-making serves as a site for the authors' subjectivation—has emerged as the perfect vehicle for the gender ideology of neoliberalism.

In what follows, I discuss how the mommy memoir reflects the neoliberal responsibilization of the author, which is secured through the trope of fit motherhood. In the pages of the mommy memoir, young, middle-class, educated-careerist, usually white women perform their identities as privileged choice-makers through their relationships to feminism and family-making decisions—including prenatal testing and selective abortions. They draw on the trope of the fit mother to justify their choices to have or not to have selective abortions.

## Beck's *Expecting Adam*

Martha Beck published *Expecting Adam,* her story of fetal testing and disability, in 1999. I'm opportunistically including Beck's memoir in my discussion of twenty-first-century texts because it is a fruitful introduction to not just the mommy memoir but also the interwoven themes of feminism, fetal testing, and abortion that span the late twentieth and early twenty-first centuries. Beck's memoir, along with Michael Bérubé's *Life as We Know It: A Father, a Family, and an Exceptional Child,* a memoir about forgoing genetic testing and raising a son with Down syndrome, are two of the first examples of life-writing about parenting children with disabilities. *Expecting Adam* reflects Beck's skepticism about the social benefit of prenatal screening technologies, which she describes as a type of eugenics, and feminism.

Beck received a PhD in sociology from Harvard before leaving academia to pursue a career as a life coach, writer, and speaker. She is the best-selling author of *Leaving the Saints: How I Lost the Mormons and Found My Faith* (2005), in addition to several other books, and was a monthly columnist for

*O, the Oprah Winfrey Magazine*. Beck met her husband, John Christen Beck, a fellow Mormon, at Harvard, and before divorcing in 2005, they had three children. Since their divorce, both Beck and her ex-husband have come out as gay. In *Expecting Adam* she recalls being married with an infant daughter, enrolled in graduate school, and pregnant with her second child, when, following a severe fever, she requests an amniocentesis. She discovers her fetus has a chromosomal mutation, a trisomy, meaning that her son, Adam, would be born with Down syndrome. The memoir recounts her experience making the decision to keep her pregnancy and facing the disapproval of feminists, her family, her peers, and society.

When Beck receives the results from her amniocentesis, her first thought is for how her feminist peers will view the impact that a disabled child would have on her education and career. The memoir previously describes her feminist cohort as narrowly focused on competing with male students without acknowledging gender or gender-based oppression, something Beck's pregnancies expose as impossible. She describes the feminist graduate students shaming her for being pregnant and for not planning her pregnancies better, and she recalls a feminist peer scolding her for having morning sickness: "Stop it! It does not look right. It makes us all look bad. You're a dead weight on every woman alive. Just stop it!" (82). She speculates that a "staunch feminist" would have an abortion following a diagnosis like hers because a child with disabilities threatens a mother's chances of having a professional life. She recalls,

> I had several friends who obtained abortions when accidental pregnancies threatened to scuttle their academic progress. One woman I knew decided, with her husband, to abort a planned pregnancy when a crucial three-day exam was scheduled near her due date. I don't know whether she even asked if the exam could be rescheduled. (11)

This anecdote of extreme behavior serves to distance Beck from her feminist peers. Believing herself already to be a failure at feminism for having started her family before finishing her education, Beck recalls fearing the feminist response to her having a disabled child. She identifies as "pro-choice" (26, 135), and her narrative is critical of doctors who would compel women to continue pregnancies (228, 250), but after her diagnosis and decision to continue her pregnancy, she fears and condemns her feminist peers as well as doctors who would mandate selective abortions based on their "medical authority" (228).

Rottenberg's discussion of neoliberal feminism suggests that Beck's fear of her feminist peers is misplaced and that her distress originates in the illusion of having meaningful choices in the first place. Rottenberg notes that the kind of female subject produced by neoliberal feminism must find a work–life balance through responsible choice-making, and while she is the beneficiary of feminism, she must reject it. Neoliberal feminism promises women they will enjoy the freedoms that men enjoy, but it fails to acknowledge—and actively denies—the reality of patriarchal systems. Rayna Rapp's analysis of fetal testing reveals a similar false promise being offered to women. Fetal testing promises educated, professional, middle-class women that they will be empowered by having a choice, but it does not allow for how those choices will be judged: "Medical technology transforms their 'choices' on an individual level, allowing them, like their male partners, to imagine voluntary limits to their commitments to their children," but unlike their male peers, these same women experience the double bind of being labeled "selfish" for not prioritizing their children and families (161). Beck uses the term "staunch feminists" (28) for careerist women and, by contrast, "wimpy feminists" (154)—including herself—for women who prioritize their families, but her memoir reveals how both types of women are feeling the pressure of responsibilization as they navigate education, professional careers, and family-making.

In addition to weathering the judgment of her feminist peers, Beck recalls the social pressure from doctors, peers, and academic mentors not to "burden" society, her husband, and her existing child with a disabled son. She claims this message was first transmitted when she scheduled the amniocentesis and learned that screenings normatively take place early enough in a pregnancy to allow for scheduling a therapeutic abortion if "there's something wrong" (133). Additionally, the normalization of therapeutic abortion as a way to avoid burdening society is voiced later in one of Beck's graduate seminars. In a discussion of new obstetric technologies, a fellow (male) student argues, "It is the duty of every woman to screen her pregnancies and eliminate fetuses that would be a detriment to society" (247). Beck also relates how, after learning about her diagnosis, her husband's advisor suggested that Beck and her husband should have an abortion so as not to interfere with his career (214). She is then told by her own doctor, "You realize that you are placing a very heavy burden on yourself and your entire family. Did you realize that eighty percent of couples who have a child with this condition end up divorcing?" (227). These messages suggest that, by giving birth to Adam, Beck will have chosen badly and will appear not fully responsibilized.

Even within her marriage, Beck experiences a conflict between fears that her son will be a burden and her own growing sense that an abortion would be wrong. Going into the amniocentesis, Beck's husband John thought that they would have an abortion if there were a fetal anomaly (134). They had, in the past, discussed such a situation and "both of us thought it a very good idea to abort fetuses with birth defects"; however, Beck at five months pregnant feels differently: "Now that the abortion in question concerned a baby I could already feel moving inside me, the very idea that anyone could say I 'had to' end my pregnancy filled me with an almost primeval rage" (135). In a discussion with her husband, Beck deconstructs the idea of burden by considering hypothetical scenarios for which abortion might be sought, such as a child being born without a hand, or with the gene for alcoholism or mental illness, or a gene for homosexuality, or being the wrong gender, or being ugly, weak, and so on. Beck pushes her husband on these scenarios until he objects, "This is not eugenics. We aren't talking about breeding a race of supermen. We're talking about taking some of the tragedy out of life" (137). Beck, however, suspects that they *are* talking about eugenics. When her husband observes that they might "have to have" an abortion, she rejects the suggestion: "It's not as though we're deciding whether or not to have a baby. We're deciding what kind of a baby we're willing to accept. If it's perfect in every way, we keep it. If it doesn't fit the right specifications, whoosh! Out it goes!" (135). While reaffirming her commitment to abortion "in general," she questions the trend of "designer babies" (135) and likens selective abortion to the termination of female babies in China as an example of how far the label "defective" could be stretched (136).

Beck's memoir asserts her fit motherhood and responsibilization in defense of her decision to have Adam and not an abortion. For example, Beck enlists her skeptical husband in continuing their pregnancy, but she assumes responsibility in doing so: "I was the one who had chosen to make our lives so hard" (238). Against the accusation that she has burdened society by having Adam, she emphatically asserts that he is a miracle of sorts. She recount various quasi-spiritual moments, mystical occurrences, and coincidences throughout his life in addition to his "miraculous" influence on her own life:

> This has been the second phase of my education, the one that followed all those years of school. In it, I have had to unlearn virtually everything Harvard taught me about what is precious and what is garbage. I have discovered that many of the things I thought were priceless are as cheap as costume jewelry, and much of what I labeled worthless was, all the time, filled with the kind of beauty that directly nourishes my soul. (331)

Beck continues to deconstruct the idea that Adam is a burden by identifying ableism as a social harm: "It hurts every time people look at Adam and see only the deformity of their own perceptions, instead of the beauty before their eyes. But more and more, I felt this pain not for my son but for the people who are too blind to see him" (332).

*Expecting Adam* questions the previously unquestioned benefits of amniocentesis and genetic testing—as well as prevailing medical authority—by asserting maternal agency: "My firm opinion is that women should be given all relevant medical information and then allowed to make up their own minds about whether or not to abort their fetuses" (228). The memoir stops short of demanding greater support and protections from the state for families, mothers, and people with disabilities. Instead, Beck defends her argument through acceptance of her responsibilization and subjectivation as a fit mother. Although Beck challenges the normalization of selective abortion following a diagnosis of Down syndrome, her mommy memoir reveals how abortion has become ordinary as a result of routine fetal genetic testing.

## Waldman's *Bad Mother*

Ayelet Waldman is a novelist and essayist who is perhaps best known as the author of the *Mommy-Track Mysteries* series. Her mommy memoir, *Bad Mother,* is a collection of essays on her family life, including a chapter in which she describes having a selective abortion. Like Beck, Waldman identifies adamantly as pro-choice but is skeptical of feminism, and like *Expecting Adam, Bad Mother* acknowledges that new reproductive technologies—in Waldman's case ultrasounds—have made pregnancy a fraught site of responsibilization for women.

In *Bad Mother,* Waldman observes—with considerable dismay—the expanding surveillance and judgment of mothers—what Michaels and Douglas named "the new momism." Waldman gives the title of "bad mother police" to those who most enthusiastically enact the scrutiny and judgment of mothers. Waldman argues that mothers should resist this surveillance by preemptively claiming the title of "bad mother"—beating their critics to the punch, so to speak—and openly embracing their deviance from the maternal ideal. Deviance for Waldman means resisting the subordination of mothers to the needs of their children (3), and her text offers anecdotal models. She confesses to loving her husband more than her children (7), to giving up on breastfeeding her son when it just wasn't working (64), to using disposable diapers because they're easier (69), to continuing to take an antidepressant while pregnant (160), and to having a selective abortion (122).

*Bad Mother* may seem to thumb its nose at the new momism, but it can only appear to reject the responsibilization of mothers. The memoir does not reflect a broader feminist critique of gender and maternal norms; instead, it aligns with a rejection of feminism that Rottenberg attributes to neoliberalism and that O'Reilly claims characterizes the mommy memoir genre ("Motherhood"). *Bad Mother* cites two feminists (Lynn Paltrow and Judith Warner) whose works critique the new momism, but in several places it rejects the argument that patriarchy is involved in the construction and regulation of motherhood. Waldman observes that the bad mother is "the primary victim of her own tragedy" (14), and she goes on to explain that

> something in me rebels at the notion that we can attribute our communal obsession [with maternal behavior] primarily to the patriarchy. . . . The blare of condemnation that drowns out so much of civil discourse on the subject of mothering and child rearing originates not from some patriarchal grand inquisitor's office but, in large part, from individual women. . . . We women are the primary authors of our own subjugation. The Bad Mother cops with the most aggressive arrest records are women. (8–9)

To prevent mothers from policing each other, Waldman advocates for "confessing" to maternal "sins" such as her own and developing compassion for fellow mothers, including "mothers on the BART" (5), or the "Andrea Yates and Susan Smiths" of the world (9), or Britney Spears—Waldman's personal whipping girl mom (6). Waldman's gesture of solidarity and plea for compassion, while welcome, is nevertheless an individual-level critique and solution to the problem of neoliberalism's rescripting of gender and maternal norms. The neoliberal reshaping of the economy and privatization of support services, which has resulted in unprecedented demands on women's labor, is obscured through a discourse of choices and freedoms. In this situation it becomes easier to claim that feminism lied than to contradict the dominant narrative telling women that they are free. Waldman's act of appropriating the label of "bad mother" does not succeed in disarming the neoliberal governance of mothers, and—while humorous—the strategy feels more like a defeat. If Waldman beats her critics to the self-deprecating punch, she still gets punched. She herself observes: "Despite the effectiveness of this technique, despite its power to inoculate you against attack, it allows you to define yourself only in negative terms," and she disappointingly admits, "There is no inherent nutritional value in the antidote to poison" (18).

*Bad Mother*'s analysis of maternal struggles and blaming of feminism as their source continues through a depiction of Waldman's mother. In a few references, Waldman's mother is depicted as out-of-date and clinging to the expectations and hopes of a earlier generation of feminism. She believes, for example, that her daughter should be capable of having a career and a family. In response, Waldman claims she "had been lied to" by her mother and by "professors of our women's studies courses" who promised she could "have it all" because feminism had won women the right to careers and families; Waldman counters that this older generation of optimistic feminists needs "a dose of realism" (40). As in most mommy memoirs, feminism is at best unrealistic and at worst the very thing making women unhappy. The commentary on feminism in *Bad Mother* uses similar rhetoric as the women interviewed by Lisa Belkin in her 2003 article in the *New York Times Magazine*, "The Opt-Out Revolution." Belkin's piece describes women who left the paid workforce to stay home with their children. These women—including Belkin herself and other Princeton graduates—left fast-track, high-salary careers to stay home full-time with children. Belkin casts their experiences as revealing the failed promise of feminism: When possible, women would rather stay home and raise children and leave the high-pressure world of paid labor to men. The downside is a lingering "angst" over having disappointed feminism's goals, which are revealed to be unrealistic. Similarly, Waldman, who is married to the novelist Michael Chabon, with whom she has four children, practiced law briefly, until her first child was born, after which she left her career to be a full-time mother, asserting, "This was my decision" (37). Waldman, too, experienced "angst," and found being a stay-at-home mother unsatisfying until she started writing.

The choice to opt out made by Waldman, Belkin, and the women she interviewed is unrelatable to women outside their economic class, making their critique of feminism less credible. Similarly, Waldman's complaint that her motherhood is subject to unreasonable amounts of scrutiny may seem inflated. The kind of private surveillance of her mothering that Waldman chafes against, for example, pales in comparison to that of mothers who are Temporary Assistance for Needy Families (TANF) recipients, whose income, living arrangements, homes, and children are monitored by the state. However, Waldman's account of the pressure she felt to balance her work and family, to redirect her energies to raising her children, and to fend off unwanted surveillance of her efforts captures the suffering of all women under neoliberal responsibilization. In her analysis of Belkin's article, Zarena Aslami argues, for example, that the "angst" in these privileged women's accounts of their struggles to balance career and families is a useful affective site for understanding the pressures experienced by women across the socioeconomic spectrum.

The pressure to perform responsibilized, fit motherhood is most clearly represented in the chapter "Rocketship," where Waldman narrates her experience terminating a pregnancy due to chromosomal mutations. While pregnant with her third child, she discovers through amniocentesis that the fetus has a trisomy, likely indicating Down syndrome (124). Waldman describes launching into action, including doing research into teratology and percentages and consulting genetic counselors and the Web, as well as mothers of children with disabilities. One mother of a child with severe "mental retardation" (127) tells Waldman that, although her son is "the light of [her] life," she would have had an abortion if she had to do it all again. In making her decision, Waldman uses rhetoric that equally reflects cost–benefit analysis and gambling: "roll of the dice," "never feel lucky," "my chances," "I did calculations" (125). Heartsick, Waldman concludes that she is unable to parent a child with "developmental delay" or "mental retardation" (127). Her husband reluctantly agrees, observing that a child with disabilities "would burden [our children] for the rest of their lives with the care of their brother, and burden us so much our relationship might be in danger" (128). Waldman is unwilling to continue the pregnancy, but her emotional response to this decision is one of devastation, using the language of judgment and guilt. In contrast to her husband, she describes herself as "not strong enough," "so inadequate," and the "worst of mothers" and the decision as a "crime." Although Waldman does not regret the decision to terminate the pregnancy, she confesses her abortion to her synagogue on Yom Kippur (133), where it may be tolerated or approved,[2] suggesting that she experiences it as a atonable transgression. Waldman's deliberating her choice, her grief over the supposed transgression, and her confession serve to frame her action as an example of fit motherhood in the text. Her account of personal failure transforms into an assertion of fit motherhood without questioning the social circumstances that make raising a child with disabilities untenable. Although *Bad Mother* reifies and celebrates personal responsibility as maternal heroism, it also exposes the process of responsibilization.

McKinney argues that Sherri Finkbine's public account of her "tragic" narrative of having a selective abortion successfully drew on the trope of fit motherhood even as it failed to safeguard abortion access for other women. Unlike Finkbine's story, Waldman's narrative makes a powerful defense of abortion access for all from her position as a fit mother. During the process of making

2. In their study of intentions to terminate pregnancies after a diagnosis of genetic disease in three countries, including Israel, Kivity and Barnoy suggest the following:

> The results show that the intention to terminate the pregnancy, regardless of the severity of the illness, was higher among Israelis than among either Cypriot or German women. This might be related to the impact of unique Israeli cultural features . . . [including] the social and medical emphasis on the importance of producing healthy, strong, and viable offspring. This is promoted by encouraging the performance of diagnostic tests and approval of pregnancy termination.

her decision and later healing from the loss of her pregnancy, Waldman joins A Heart-Breaking Choice, an online support group for women who have had selective abortions. Waldman recalls haranguing fellow members to stop relying on this euphemistic title:

> I made them uncomfortable—especially the many pro-life women among them—by insisting that we accept the term "abortion" for what we had done. . . . We cannot hide from the fact that when Congress or the courts restrict abortion, we are the women they are talking about. Our refusal to confront this truth will be the undoing of the women who come after us. If we allow the language of the debate to encompass only the experience of those women who abort for what others like to call "convenience," and they themselves know as necessity, then we risk losing this precious right altogether. How many of us, I asked, would want to have been forced to carry these babies to term? (132)

In this passage, Waldman recognizes that abortion access cannot be protected by continuing to make distinctions between good abortions and bad abortions, good choice-makers and bad choice-makers.

Both Waldman's and Beck's memoirs critique prenatal technologies for contributing to the burdensome weight of women's choice-making struggles. While Beck casts amniocentesis as a moral Pandora's box for women, Waldman criticizes the ascendent power of ultrasound technology and the images that it produces:

> When women of my mother's generation fought for the right to choose, they did not need to confront the ugly physical reality. But women of my generation, women who have strips of grainy ultrasound photographs on our fridges, women who watch on three-dimensional monitors first flickering heartbeats at six weeks, then babies who suck their thumbs and wiggle their toes at four months, cannot deny it. When we choose to have an abortion, we must do so understanding the full ramifications of what we are doing. (130)

While it may seem unfair of Waldman once again to make her mother's feminism the scapegoat for her distress when antiabortion interpretive frameworks have encouraged bonding with ultrasound images of the fetus in ways that are also distressing, this scene exposes the discomfort that women/mothers experience in response to new technologies that allegedly make their lives better. As new reproductive technologies are celebrated for expanding family-making choices, Beck's and Waldman's memoirs expose how these technologies encourage the responsibilization of women, a process that provides subjectivation while denying the freedom not to choose. Selective abortion has become an ordinary or common site where this process takes place.

## Yamanaka's *Father of the Four Passages*

As noted above, in the nonfiction memoirs by Beck and Waldman, the authors' status as privileged (married, heterosexual, adult, white, middle-class) women provides access to the trope of fit motherhood to authorize their decisions to have or not to have abortions. In what follows, I turn to a work of fiction for its representation of a mother perceived to not reflect fit motherhood, who fails at being responsibilized. In Lois-Anne Yamanaka's *Father of the Four Passages,* Sonia Kurisu, the protagonist, slowly gains acceptance of her son's disability after a literal and figurative homecoming to her working-class, Japanese American community in Hawai'i. Sonia's homecoming is a spiritual journey that involves honoring her previous abortions. The novel depicts a maternal subjectivity that rejects responsibilization, that grieves but does not regret abortion, and that embraces disability in the contexts of social oppression and trauma.

The narration of *Father of the Four Passages* is focalized through Sonia, a native of Hawai'i who is of Japanese descent, and the story moves between her time at college in Nevada, memories of her birth home in Hilo, and her childhood at her grandmother's home in Honolulu. The narrative begins in Nevada, where Sonia, in art school, is living with an abusive boyfriend and battling substance abuse. Additionally, she is struggling to care for her newborn, Sonny Boy. Sonia's decision to become a mother while in college was motivated by her belief that it would benefit her art, not because she wanted a baby. Sonia does not align with the characteristics of responsibilized, fit motherhood, as the following internal monologue reveals:

> Sonny Boy, I had fertility to prove. Proven. Now I need you out of my life. Gone away like a tiny casket. Grieving mother all in black. . . . Sonny Boy, a painter cannot paint, sculptor cannot sculpt, photographer photograph, musician compose, not without the experience; your birth was to enhance my art. Art enhanced. Now how do I get rid of you? All evidence of you? Everything. I should kill you. Artfully. I've done it before. What a requiem I would compose. (26)

As this passage reveals, Sonia had a particular idea of what an artist is and of herself when she was pregnant—"the single artist mother, breast-feeding lounge singer mother, earth righteous minority mother" (3)—but this image is fading in light of the reality of life with a newborn. Instead Sonia is fighting to survive, and this fight is against her infant son. In addition to benefitting her art, she had hoped that Sonny would redeem her reproductive history: "Sonny Boy, I had to birth you. I thought you were the blessing of a uterine lining, gone for what they all told me was forever. The possibility of redemption, a miracle from God, who found me at last" (26). This hope has also faded. Since childhood, Sonia has possessed the ability to see spirits, and as she struggles with the reality of motherhood, she begins seeing and conversing with the figures of her aborted children, who also have questions and demands for her.

Part of Sonia's struggle to identify as a mother arises from her own traumatic family history. Sonia is scarred by the repeated and prolonged absences of her artistic father, Joseph, the embodiment of freedom, artistic temperament, and masculine privilege: "My father, a man who knows about leaving. Lucky him. Never looked back. Never wanted to look back" (8). In contrast to Joseph's desirable freedom, Sonia learns to associate her gender with inferiority and abandonment: "Joseph left us for good in the time of blood. We all bled, Mama, Celeste, and I, the three house dogs, females in heat—stained panties, dog diapers, and sanitary napkin belts on the clothesline, bloody pads wrapped in newspaper in the trash" (10). Menstruation—the marker of feminine difference and inferiority—reduces the Kurisu women to animal corporeality in Joseph's eyes. In response to his abandonment, Sonia recalls her act of misogynistic self-harm: "I hit myself over and over until my vagina bruised and swelled" (10–11). Importantly, Joseph identified Sonia as his "surrogate" who shared his "solitary yearning for beauty" (85, 97), but her differences—marked by gender and symbolized by blood—repel him. These gendered messages that equate masculinity with artistry and freedom and femininity with being trapped or stuck inform Sonia's troubled sense of herself, her gender, and motherhood. She too wishes to escape.

Joseph's absences plunge Sonia's family—including her sister, Celeste, and her mother, Grace—into poverty and chaos. One of Sonia's earliest memories is of Grace attempting suicide after Joseph's first abandonment (5). His departure and Grace's instability lead to Sonia and Celeste being moved to live with their religious Granny Alma in Honolulu, where Sonia is thrown into the life of the church and the life of the bar where Alma works. Supervised primarily by her traumatized older sister, Sonia is marked by the signs of trauma that in turn become traumatizing: drug and alcohol abuse and unplanned pregnancy. She has her first abortion at sixteen, compelled by Celeste and Granny Alma (6). Her second abortion is during the summer between semesters of college (12). Her third abortion is performed on the kitchen floor by her roommate and best friend, Mark, after which they bury the fetus in a jar in the backyard (16–17). When Sonia gives birth to Sonny, the aborted children return to Sonia as reminders of how she, unlike her father, lacks the socially sanctioned, masculine privilege to leave. Sonny's birth and infant demands remind her again of her shameful differences from her father, the artist. She is truly stuck with Sonny Boy (although she fantasizes about giving him to Grace or Granny Alma).

Sonny's demands on Sonia are soon recognized as those of a child with disabilities, and he is diagnosed as having autism, paralyzing Sonia with despair after her boyfriend leaves her (119). At first, she believes the diagnosis is a sign of her failure to achieve forgiveness: "How I had hoped in his birth that God would forgive me everything I had done in this Life. God's grace, my own at last, abundant as air. I would not have to know more struggle" (119–20). She despairs further when she imagines the voices of others scornfully judging her situation: "What did you think it was all about, earth hippie mother?" (about her decision to have a child); "Seven years of school and no fine arts degree?" (about her education); and "Sonia acts like she's the only one eking out a living in the face of adversity. Always full of the same poor me, pity me complaints" (about her employment) (131). These messages reflect Sonia's awareness of the responsibilization of women and mothers: Her life with Sonny is perceived as a series of her (poor) choices and her failure to take personal responsibility (without complaint). These messages are voiced from within her community of working-class Japanese Americans specifically but reflect the values of the neoliberal state generally.

In despair, Sonia attempts suicide and is taken to the hospital in time to save her life. Her recovery comes with a new, empowering awareness: "I am to grieve, to cry, to accept, to move on" (121), and she begins to appreciate how Sonny Boy's needs require her to save her own life and to "seize love" (208). Home, memory, community, and family are transformed into a balm. Buoyed by the return of her friend Mark and the mystical support of neighbor Bob (who turns out to be another spiritual visitation), Sonia returns to Honolulu to care for Sonny (160), initiating a geographical and spiritual homecoming. During this journey, the figures of her would-be children continue to clammer for her attention, for information about their fathers, and for closure. These figures compel Sonia to confront her memories. She recalls how the father of her first pregnancy, her teenage Korean boyfriend Benjamin, had burns on his arms from his abusive mother's cigarettes. She recalls Grace's withering response to the news that Sonia was pregnant: "'Boys are lucky,' she would always say. 'They don't get stuck with the package.' Once in a while she called you, my Number One, the box, the bag, or simply it. 'Boys are lucky. They've got legs to run'" (77). Sonia recalls also Joseph's scornful response to his daughter's plea for help dealing with her unplanned but wanted pregnancy: "Whore. Stupid. Idiot. Baby. Bitch. Trap," and, crushingly, "I can't stand the sight of you" (78). These are the memories and words that need to be grieved so that Sonia may "move on." She recalls the father of her second pregnancy (also Sonny's father), Jacob, who is her drug-addicted cousin from the neighborhood, her sometimes boyfriend, and her sometimes dealer. Jacob also is in need of a homecoming of his own. Her third aborted child is buried in the backyard, restless and seeking release (154). He does not ask who his father is, and Sonia confesses that there were too many lovers at the time of his conception for her to know: "This is my sadness" (154).

Sonia's aborted children are never elevated to the level of regrets; instead, they seek peace from her, which in turn gives her the peace that she seeks in order to mother Sonny. As Sonia mothers Sonny Boy and these three figures of aborted children, she gains confidence—no longer letting her family push her around—and appreciation for her family and friends, including Jacob and especially Sonny. She realizes,

> I am the Hero of this Life. And fuck anybody and everybody who thinks otherwise. Because one morning when I wake, I look at my son asleep beside me. Face of the cherubim, Thorn of my side, Reason for being here, Reason for choosing me, all of my moments colliding into this one of sun through dirty curtains from Sears, the slow crowing of a neighbor's rooster, pit bulls barking and yanking on rusty chains, the screeching of the city bus around a hairpin turn. Perfect Imperfection. Complete Incompleteness: You and I are Home. Not in a house full of beds and chairs, dishes and toothbrushes, but in undeniable covenant. Home is the possibility of return. (173)

Sonny Boy compels Sonia's feminist awakening and homecoming, a return—the opposite of her father's perpetual leaving—that becomes grounding and empowering. As she claims her neighborhood ("dirty curtains," "pit bulls," and "bus"), she also reaffirms her body (again in contrast to Joseph's scorn for women's bodies) as the origin of Sonny: "I made you with my body. Your father is known to me. Until the Time of your knowing, understand this: You are mine. I will never Leave you. I will love this distance away" (157). Sonia is instructed by the autism specialist to listen to Sonny Boy, to mirror him (in action and sound), to know him, and to bridge the "distance" that autism creates. In so doing, as her second aborted son promises, Sonia is healed by Sonny (153), who teaches her to love and to forgive her family and herself (225).

Yamanaka's novel recounts the ordinary experience of multiple or repeat abortions. About half of women having abortions in the US have already had one (Cohen). The novel also depicts the ordinary way that abortions may demand closure, which is not the same thing as saying they are wrong or damaging to women. In this sense, the novel destigmatizes abortion, but it also seeks to destigmatize disability. What initially seems like tragic irony to Sonia—having a child with disabilities after having three abortions—becomes her story of healing and homecoming. The compassion that having a child with disabilities requires of Sonia is exactly the compassion that she needs for herself and her family.

## Conclusion

Despite their differences in genre, *Expecting Adam*, *Bad Mother*, and *Father of the Four Passages* all reflect the tensions created at the discursive intersection of motherhood with antiabortion and antidisability stigma. These three texts reveal the pressure of neoliberal responsibilization and the navigation of that pressure. In these texts, Beck, Waldman, and the character of Sonia resist this pressure by asserting their subjectivity as fit mothers, in the case of Beck and Waldman, and by asserting a sense of worth against the identity of unfit mother, in the case of Sonia.

These texts also point to an ongoing need for a feminist discourse that is both proabortion and pro-disability. The memoirs by Beck and Waldman demonstrate that neoliberalism's insistence on self-reliance and responsibility is a means to subjectivation and empowerment, but it also successfully divides and weakens resistance to its systems, as is the case when both authors doubt the need for feminism even as they battle to validate their reproductive labor and maternal decisions. This rejection of solidarity weakens both the defense of abortion access and disability rights. The stakes are real: In the decade(s) since the publication of Beck's and Waldman's texts, antiabortion groups have successfully introduced legislation banning abortion based on fetal anomaly as part of a larger strategy for constraining abortion access. At the same time, conservative groups have redoubled efforts at installing a philosophy of personal responsibility to replace state provisions and protections for the disability community and for women/mothers. These memoirs reveal the need for a nuanced feminism that is both proabortion and pro-disability. Yamanaka's novel offers a model of this feminism. Sonia's regret-free compassion for herself for having three abortions enables her to love herself, her disabled son, her family, and her community.

CHAPTER 5

# Choice Without Justice

## Reproductive Dystopias, Neoliberal Feminism, and Stratified Reproduction

In 2006 the Guttmacher Institute published *Abortion in Women's Lives,* which reported on three decades of legalized abortion access. The authors found that legalized abortion had enabled tens of millions of women to make better lives for themselves and their families, but since 1994, there has been a widening gap in reproductive healthcare between poor women and higher-income women (Boonstra et al.). The authors report that disadvantaged women are four times more likely to experience an unplanned pregnancy and require three weeks longer to obtain an abortion than higher-income women. In a press release announcing the findings, the Guttmacher Institute describes the reproductive health gap as reflecting "two Americas for women" ("Tale"). These gaps have expanded in the two decades since the Guttmacher report, revealing that not all women have enjoyed equal access to legalized abortion.

Simultaneously, over the two decades since the Guttmacher report, the genre of dystopian fiction has gained popularity. British, Canadian, and American examples of these narratives about alternative futures tell stories of reproductive horrors, in which women are denied access to abortion, or denied the right to have children, or compelled to surrender their children to more privileged groups. These stories reflect understandable alarm at the rise in violent extremism described by Miller-Idriss in *Man Up,* in which she argues that misogyny is fueling the violence that characterizes much of white Christian nationalist online discourse. This misogyny—informed by concerns over declining birth rates for white people—can be seen in online claims that women are naturally inferior to men and suited to childbearing and that the rejection of these roles merits harsh punishment. In dystopian fiction by women, reproductive control generally, and abortion specifically, are depicted as imperiled. The overwhelming majority of these novels, however, focus on the experiences of white protagonists confronted by "new" constraints on reproductive autonomy and lost abortion access, leading to the novels being criticized for an alleged blindness to ongoing reproductive injustices experienced by poor women and women of color. That is to say, these novels obscure the current dystopia of Guttmacher's "two Americas." Additionally, critics point out these novels lack the element of social satire that characterize many classic dystopias. Indeed, some critics call these novels "anti-utopian" because they depict violence against women without satirical critique or collective resistance; instead, the spectacle of suffering seems to be the point.

In this chapter, I consider a different type of literary dystopia by women writers, one that exposes the reproductive injustice of what the Guttmacher press release calls the "two Americas" of women's reproductive health ("Tale"). Unlike conventional dystopias, which are set in an unfamiliar future, these novels are *paratopias* set in the recognizable near present to critique instances of twenty-first-century reproductive injustice and expose components of stratified reproduction, including stigma, neoliberal responsibilized agency, and the disarticulation of resistance. This chapter examines how abortion is depicted in Celeste Ng's *Little Fires Everywhere* (2017), Joanne Ramos's *The Farm* (2019), and Leni Zumas's *Red Clocks* (2018). I argue that the paratopia setting of the novels, in addition to heterodiegetic narration, exposes and critiques stratified reproduction and defines reproductive freedom more broadly than abortion access.

The novels by Ng, Ramos, and Zumas depict abortion directly and indirectly but never in isolation from other reproductive issues. Ng's *Little Fires* explores the connections between adoption, surrogacy, and abortion to satirize the Clinton-era defense: "safe, legal, and rare." Ramos's *The Farm* reveals how the rapid expansion of the commercial surrogacy industry has appropriated the rhetoric of choice even as it conceals abortion. Zumas's *Red Clocks* narrates how a successful policy outlawing abortion becomes simultaneously a distraction from and a first step toward the related conservative goals to prohibit in vitro fertilization (IVF), surrogacy, and single-parent adoptions. By connecting abortion to a broad range of reproductive health needs, these novels portray women's reproductive health as ordinary. Abortion has been made extraordinary in the popular imagination (dramatic cases, exceptional stories) through the rhetoric of the abortion wars. The rhetorical polarization has distracted attention away from other reproductive freedoms that are equally threatened by conservative agendas and neoliberal regimes of gender and sexuality. Carole Joffe observes that the abortion wars have muted public discussions about "the full range of reproductive health needs of American women," leading her to challenge readers with solving the big picture problem: "What kind of America do we want?" (*Dispatches* 141). Joffe's question and the novels discussed in this chapter contain the seeds of utopian thinking. The America these novels implicitly seek is a country where ordinary abortion is part of a constellation of ethically just reproductive care that is accessible, legal, and destigmatized.

## Feminist Dystopian Fiction and Anti-Utopian Fiction

The claim that we live in dystopian times can be frequently heard in the twenty-first century. Certainly dystopian fiction—exemplified by Margaret Atwood's MaddAddam trilogy, Kazuo Ishiguro's *Never Let Me Go,* and Cormac McCarthy's *The Road*—occupies a prominent place in the popular culture. Instructors teaching dystopian texts in their literature courses, for example, told Lindsay McKenzie for an article in *The Chronicle of Higher Education* that "everyone is 'fixated on dystopia,'" an interest that McKenzie connects to the first Trump administration's rhetoric of doom and national collapse. Similarly, Cody Delistraty, in the online publication *Vulture,* ventured the explanation that the genre is an understandable response to the social moment: "We live in a world of wildly shifting norms, proliferating dangers, unstable systems and leaders—a world, in other words, in which the future's menace feels more or less imminent." Additionally, in the introduction to their edited volume, *The Postworld In-Between Utopia and Dystopia: Intersectional, Feminist, and Non-Binary Approaches in 21st-Century Speculative Literature and Culture,* Katarzyna Ostalska and Tomasz Fisiak contend that "people seem to be more inclined to believe in Dystopias rather than Utopias at the present time" (2).

Literary dystopia, according to Jean-Paul Engélibert in "Dystopian Fictions and Contemporary Fears," is a genre that "has a complex relationship with the fears and hopes of its readers, who are transported to imaginary worlds, different from their own, often worse, sometimes apocalyptic, in order to open up the distance of a critical view of their own world" (311). Conventionally, literary dystopian fiction is rooted in satire, in which the shared values of the author and reader are opposed to the defamiliarized society being critiqued:

> It, therefore, necessarily has an ethical and political significance: situated in history, it requires each reader to situate it in its original context and to

> recontextualize the reader's own world. It thus obliges a rational and critical reading, forbidding the escape into myth or fancy. Sometimes confused with forecasting or prophecy, because it is generally situated in the future, it has more the sense of a warning, warning against what might happen if the tendencies it brings to light are not effectively countered. (320–21)

In literary dystopias, the depicted society *seems* geographically or temporally distant, and it "flouts, fights against, or despises" (311) the values of the reader, but the reader's estrangement evolves into recognition. The process of defamiliarization and gradual recognition lead the reader to the warning "that reality could join the dystopian fiction if the dynamics at work in the present are not effectively combated" (311). The convention of a distant world (usually temporally) is important to Engélibert's understanding of how the genre provides social critique.

Engélibert goes on to observe that satire is balanced in dystopian fiction by the inclusion of utopian elements: "Dystopia . . . is not written against utopia, but preserves the desire for a better society and the belief in the possibility of its realization" (316). Similarly, the writer and Marxist thinker Kim Stanley Robinson shares this definition of dystopia as a blending of satire and utopian thinking. Building on this definition, Robinson critiques many of the contemporary dystopian texts that are popular today for being what he calls "anti-utopian." In his essay "Dystopias Now" in *Commune,* Robinson worries that contemporary dystopian fiction lacks a vision for how the future might be better. Using *The Hunger Games* trilogy as an example, he argues that dystopian fictions capture fear exaggerated to a kind of "surrealist" dream or nightmare, but they only distract audiences from the present moment with a sense of pity or "schadenfreude" for the future characters. Audiences are not moved to political action by these texts; instead, they foster an anti-utopian attitude and praxis, which contributes to the current social affect of hopelessness, detachment, and helplessness. Attacks on utopia (which, Robinson contends, many contemporary dystopias are) offer "reactionary statements on behalf of the currently powerful . . . who enjoy a poorly hidden utopia for the few alongside dystopia for the many." Robinson calls for texts that consciously resist this affective powerlessness, and that instead enact Gramsci's concept of anti-anti-utopianism:

> Maybe we should give up entirely on optimism and pessimism—we have to do this work no matter how we feel. So by force of will or the sheer default of emergency we make ourselves have utopian thoughts and ideas. This is the necessary next step following the dystopian moment, without

> which dystopia is stuck at a level of political quietism that can make it just another tool of control and of things-as-they-are. The situation is bad, yes, okay, enough of that; we know that already. Dystopia has done its job, it's old news now, perhaps it's self-indulgence to stay stuck in that place any more. Next thought: utopia. Realistic or not, and perhaps especially if not.

Robinson's reference to "this work" is a reminder that conventionally dystopian satire seeks to effect change by moving the reader to greater awareness of injustice and to action against it.

The gendered injustices of the first decades of the twenty-first century have inspired women writers to adopt the dystopian form. Novels like Naomi Alderman's *The Power,* Margaret Atwood's *The Testaments,* Hillary Jordan's *When She Woke,* Jane Rogers's *The Testament of Jessie Lamb,* Sophie Mackintosh's *The Water Cure* and *Blue Ticket,* and Jessamine Chan's *The School for Good Mothers* are some commonly cited examples. Sophie Gilbert observes in "The Remarkable Rise of the Feminist Dystopia" in *The Atlantic* that women's fictions are responding to new forms of misogyny that contradict hopes for feminist progress: "This feels like a particularly strange moment in history, but it's one that writers seem to have anticipated: The past two years have seen a spate of works delving into the discombobulation of the present." She goes on to describe the feeling of "discombobulation" she experienced while listening to Christine Blasey Ford's testimony against Brett Kavanaugh's confirmation hearings to the Supreme Court—and Trump's subsequent mocking of Ford: "Perhaps you felt, like I did, that something you'd previously felt safely taken for granted—that a man credibly accused of sexual assault might not be elevated to a position of profound power over women—was no longer something to trust." This sense that gender and reproductive politics are shifting, regressing, and that literature by women is reflecting these changes is echoed by Eir-Anne Edgar in "Re-Conceiving the World: Dystopia and Reproductive Justice." Edgar argues that the explosion of woman-authored dystopias in the twenty-first century reflects a "'discursive oscillation' or what we could call a 'shift in tides'" (201) brought about by the contrast between the almost simultaneous rise of the #MeToo movement and Trump's election.

The first decades of the twenty-first century have seen ongoing policy attacks against abortion access, and simultaneously many feminist dystopias imagine futures when human reproduction is more intensely surveilled and constrained by the state, rendering the bodies of the powerless vulnerable to the reproductive interests and needs of the elite. I refer to these texts as *reproductive dystopias* to distinguish them from dystopias that lack a specific focus on reproductive politics. Reproductive dystopias, such as many of the texts already mentioned and Megan McCafferty's *Bumped,* Amulya Malladi's *A House for Happy Mothers,* Carola Dibbell's *The Only Ones,* and Louise Erdrich's *The Future Home of the Living God,* build their plots and settings around biopolitical crises. Noting that this subgenre often depicts authoritarian regimes, Gilbert adds, "Of all the potential precipitating factors for totalitarian government, women writers have always found intriguing terrain in infertility." In "Biocolonial Pregnancies: Louise Erdrich's *Future Home of the Living God,*" Anna Kemball observes that neo-eugenic population control has become a popular trope in dystopian fiction, "a genre that frequently depicts fertility crises in order to question the survival of future populations." Edgar additionally calls attention to how these texts are concerned with the individual woman, noting how these novels pose "questions about the characters' abilities to choose, not just to choose abortion or motherhood but the freedom to make choices at all" (212).

Even as Gilbert welcomes these texts as important commentaries on gender politics, other cultural critics have questioned their intersectional and broader political awareness. Why, Sarah Dillon asks, are so many of these texts authored by white writers, and why do so many imagine horrific futures that look like the extant reality of racial minorities and people living in the Global South? Furthermore, in her essay "Who Rules the World?: Reimagining the Contemporary Feminist Dystopia," in *The New Feminist Literary Studies,* Dillon argues that many so-called feminist dystopian fictions fail to reflect resistance to gender-based oppression. The adaptation of Atwood's classic novel *The Handmaid's Tale* by Hulu, according to Dillon, is exemplary of the genre's shortcomings in this regard. These narratives present spectacles of female suffering without satire or meaningful critiques of heterosexist, racist, patriarchal capitalism. These critics echo Robinson's concern that the genre is increasingly embracing an anti-utopian stance. Dillon, for example, argues that feminist dystopias are failing at offering "cognitive estrangement" (173) and "new forms of oppositional agency" (171). In the absence of meaningful feminist analysis, resistance, and exploration of the question "What kind of America do we want?," these texts only sensationalize female victimization and suffering. Delistraty argues that these novels are so different from conventional dystopian fiction that they do not "qualify for the label" and might instead be better categorized as realist fiction. The absence (and in some cases rejection) of utopian imagination in these dystopias affirms Frederic Jameson's claim in "Future City" that "it is easier to imagine the end of the world than to imagine the end of capitalism" (76).

My contention in this chapter is that some twenty-first-century reproductive dystopias present not only satires of misogyny but also offer resistance and feminist imagination. The texts that are successful in this portrayal are ones that critique the gender politics of what Catherine Rottenberg has named "neoliberal feminism." As discussed in chapter 4, neoliberalism is the dominant political and economic philosophy of the early twenty-first century. It is perhaps easy to see how dystopian fiction has arisen in the context of neoliberalism's expanded and violent inequality and the state's abandonment of protections and social safety nets in favor of market growth. As described by Wendy Brown and Lisa Duggan, among others, the rise of neoliberalism has meant that the liberal values of egalitarianism are replaced by individualism, personal responsibility, entrepreneurialism, and self-reliance. The state commits to free markets instead of its duty to its citizens, and to lax regulation and the brutal extraction of resources—the mechanisms by which subjects are dispossessed and by which wealth is redistributed upward. Privatization transfers social services from public, accountable bodies to private, corporate entities and transforms the needs of citizens into personal responsibilities with market solutions (Duggin; Brown, *Edgework*). Neoliberal economies are dependent upon women's unpaid domestic care work even as women are simultaneously compelled or choose to enter into the paid workforce, according to Angela McRobbie, Catherine Rottenberg, and Laura Briggs. In the absence of childcare, eldercare, and healthcare, women must resolve the conflicts of work and family. It is their personal responsibility to make good reproductive choices that enable this resolution, which is often referred to as the work–life balance. In this context, family planning (including abortion) is an issue of personal responsibility, but choosing badly (in regard to whether, when, or not to have children) becomes a matter of enormous social scrutiny and struggle. These gendered inequalities call out for feminist analysis and protest.

Rottenberg defines neoliberal feminism as an ascendent response to neoliberal regimes of gender and sexuality that embraces the values of individualism and personal responsibility. Unlike liberal feminism, whose project was to resist the gendered exclusion of women from the promises of humanism, neoliberal feminism is "perfectly in sync with the evolving neoliberal order" (54). Rottenberg explains,

> Using key liberal terms, such as equality, opportunity, and free choice, while displacing and replacing their content, this recuperated feminism forges a feminist subject who is not only individualized but entrepreneurial in the sense that she is oriented toward optimizing her resources through incessant calculation, personal initiative, and innovation. . . . The question of social justice is recast in personal, individualized terms. (59)

The neoliberal feminist is disciplined to focus on her work–life balance to achieve the (future) promise of happiness, according to Rottenberg, because "this temporal/affect nexus produce[s] properly neoliberalized feminist subjects whose normative trajectory—striving to craft a work-family balance—helps to resolve the dilemma of reproduction for neoliberal rationality" (123). The desire for a better future for oneself, however, does not align with the traditional goals of the feminist movement, like coalition building and collective action; instead, "each woman is concerned with her own individual psychic well-being" (123).

To achieve this work–life balance, neoliberal feminism embraces "stratified reproduction," Shellee Cohen's term for how society assigns different value to the offspring and reproductive labor of different social groups (qtd. in Twine). In her study of migrant West Indian women serving as childcare workers for wealthy employers in New York City, Cohen describes this "splitting" of women into valued/worthy and devalued/unworthy subjects:

> By stratified reproduction, I mean that physical and social reproduction tasks are accomplished differentially according to inequalities that are based on hierarchies of class, race, ethnicity, gender, place in the global economy. . . . The reproductive labor of bearing, raising, and socializing children . . . is differentially experienced, valued and rewarded according to inequalities of access to material and social resources in particular historical and cultural contexts. (qtd. in Twine 3)

According to Rottenberg, high-potential women (those with economic, social, and symbolic capital) outsource reproductive labor to "a whole other class of women who are conceived as not wholly responsibilized and thus exploitable and disposable" (17). The result is an "unabashedly exclusionary feminism" (20) that "produces a splitting of female subjecthood: the worthy capital-enhancing feminist subject and the 'unworthy' disposable female 'other' who performs most of the reproductive and care work" (20). Rickie Solinger similarly notes the division and valuation of women through the labels of "good choice-makers" and "bad choice-makers," titles that reflect the social rewards, stigmas, and punishments of neoliberal biopolitics (*Beggars*). The extreme inequality of these divisions, according to Rottenberg, hinders women's abilities to recognize other women's suffering and their own roles in these oppressive systems. She argues that "neoliberal feminism must be understood as a key contemporary discourse that is overshadowing other forms of feminism, rendering it more difficult to pursue a vocabulary of social justice. Indeed, the notion of balance helps 'disarticulate' structural inequality by promoting individuation and responsibilization" (21). My point in this chapter is that some dystopian fictions by women embrace neoliberal feminism while other fictions, such as the novels by Ng, Ramos, and Zumas, satirize or resist the individuation of women.

The novels by Ng, Ramos, and Zumas combat disarticulation while promoting the utopian desire for a different world by introducing a reproductive justice viewpoint. Reproductive justice is an activist movement that originated in the twentieth century organizing of BIPOC reproductive healthcare providers who sought to redefine reproductive freedom to better reflect the experiences of poor women and women of color. The pro-choice movement focuses too narrowly on abortion access, these providers argue, as a result of its being the priority of white, middle-class women. They assert that in addition to being denied abortion access, women of color have experienced long racist histories of compelled surrogacy through enslavement; compelled sterilization through abusive state policies; coerced abortions; child removal as part of acculturation, immigration, or anti-poverty bias; and devalued motherhood in the popular imaginary, while poor women have served as the generalized reproductive Other that normalizes white middle-class family-making (Ross et al.; Ross and Solinger). This historical oppression requires a definition of reproductive freedom that includes not only the right to abortion, but also the right to have children and the right to raise children in safety and dignity. These tenets meet the needs of women facing ongoing racial discrimination against their mothering. The dominant US racist imaginary views poor women and women of color to be well suited to fulfilling the reproductive needs of the middle class (through surrogacy, nannying, baby nursing, and housekeeping), but it does not readily include women of color in ideas of good mothering (Ross et al.; Ross and Solinger). Thus, the reproductive justice movement foregrounds and resists the long history and ongoing reality of stratified reproduction, which, as discussed above, is a feature of neoliberal gender regimes. The novels by Ng, Ramos, and Zumas offer literary expressions of this viewpoint.

As I will show, these novels depict a reproductive justice viewpoint through heterodiegetic narration that allows for multiple, sometimes conflicted narrative perspectives across different ages, races, immigration statuses, and economic classes. Abortion, adoption, and surrogacy are represented through the perspectives of women seeking them, opposing them, or being otherwise impacted by them. By representing multiple viewpoints, the narratives reveal the stratification of reproductive labor. Additionally, these novels are not conventionally futuristic dystopias but are instead temporal paratopias set close to the present moment. Leni Zumas uses the term *paratopia*

(Crum) to describe settings that are less prophetic ("this may come to pass if we don't act") and more like warnings that "this is happening now with our permission." Rather than creating a temporal distance, the paratopias in Ng's, Ramos's, and Zumas's novels estrange readers by challenging a normative worldview that assumes reproductive freedom is secure and enjoyed broadly. Readers are confronted with present-moment narratives about uneven and eroding reproductive freedoms. These paratopias expose what Kennedy calls normative "white time," or "chrononormative regimes that regulate the social collective and thus the social imaginary" (5). By exposing the belief that reproductive freedom has been achieved to be a myth, these novels represent time more in alignment with the observation made by the novelist Louise Erdrich: "Indigenous people in the Americas are descended of relatives who survived the dystopia of genocide. To us, dystopia is recent history. (For many, it is the present)" (qtd. in Edgar 206). Erdrich's observation echoes Loretta Ross's response, when hearing laments suggesting that the current moment is somehow more threatening, calamitous, or misogynistic for (white) women: "It's *always* been these times" (see Thompson, "Resistance"). Ross's point is that emerging threats to middle-class white women's freedoms do not convey the same surprise to women of color. Through heterodiegetic narration and paratopic settings, the novels by Ng, Ramos, and Zumas represent experiences of stratified reproduction and its injustices.

## *Little Fires Everywhere*: Safe, Legal, and Rare

Celeste Ng's 2017 novel *Little Fires Everywhere* has not been critically recognized as a dystopia, but I include it in this discussion because it illustrates the characteristics of a reproductive paratopia. The novel is set in the 1990s in Shaker Heights, Ohio, and this temporal distance (in the past rather than the future) initially estranges readers from the narrative action. Ng's novel satirizes the biopolitical order of this historical moment through which characters come to recognize themselves as either properly or poorly responsibilized. The sanctimonious mistreatment of poor women, immigrant mothers, and single mothers and their access to reproductive healthcare—abortion, adoption, and surrogacy—exposes persistent inequalities in this order. Ng's work presents a dystopic satire of Shaker Heights and reveals how the rise of neoliberalism shaped reproductive politics from the 1990s onward.

By the start of the narrative's action in 1997, the ideological context of Shaker Heights is defined by the tenets of neoliberalism, which, following two terms of Reaganomics and one term of Clinton's deficit-cutting, had taken solid control of economic and political philosophy. This policy found expression in the Contract with/on America, a legislative agenda advocated by the Republican Party during the 1994 congressional election campaign, which leaned heavily on Reagan-era stereotypes of "welfare queens" to promote welfare reform, among other proposals to curb social services. This revision to the administration of life and population involved rescripting norms for gender and sexuality. Clinton oversaw, for example, the institution of the military's "Don't Ask, Don't Tell" policy requiring LGBTQ members of the armed services to stay in the closet. He also proclaimed that abortion should be "safe, legal, and rare," a phrase that Hillary Clinton later adopted. These "liberal" policies reflect the reassertion of heterosexism and stigmatization of LGBTQ identities as well as abortion access.

The novel satirizes the liberal values of the Clinton era through references to President Clinton's politically disastrous affair (implicitly compared through allusion to Hawthorne's *The Scarlet Letter*) that invoke the legacy of American puritanism, sexism, and sexual hypocrisy. It also satirizes the belief that these values and policies reflect progress. The narrative points out that this prosperous, solidly liberal, bedroom community of Cleveland is named for a community of nineteenth-century Shakers and the shared goal of creating intentional paradises. The suburb was "founded, if not on Shaker principles, with the same idea of creating a utopia. Order—regulation, the father of order—had been the Shaker's key to harmony" (22). The nineteenth-century celibate Shakers could only expand their communities through adoption, and eventually the community died out. Ng's Shaker Heights of the 1990s, contrary to its self-perception, does not regulate sexuality and reproduction any less than the original religious community did. The novel's paratopian satire of this community's self-perceived liberal attitudes toward sex and reproduction evolves into a recognition of ongoing twenty-first-century struggles for sexual and reproductive freedoms.

*Little Fires*' satire of Clinton-era neoliberal politics is expressed through the character of Lexie, the daughter of Elena Richardson, a longtime and prominent member of Shaker Heights. Lexie proudly identifies as a white, middle-class Shaker Heights progressive. She has an African American boyfriend from an upper-middle-class Shaker Heights family and naively describes her racial politics as "color-blind." As part of her liberal upbringing, she received comprehensive sexual education: "In Shaker Heights, every student had sex ed not just once, but five times: in the fifth and sixth grade, considered 'early intervention' by the school board; in the 'danger years' of seventh and eighth grade; and again in tenth grade, the last hurrah, in which sex ed was combined with nutrition basics, self-esteem discussions, and job-application advice" (172). Through this education, Lexie's character has been responsibilized to time her sexual and reproductive activities to align with social expectations, even as she is instructed to appreciate her "freedoms." Her character reflects neoliberal feminism's focus on personal responsibility and entrepreneurialism. For example, when she is given a writing assignment that asks her to retell a familiar narrative through the perspective of a noncentral character, she reconceives the fairy tale of Rumpelstiltskin from the perspective of the imp, imagining him as the wronged party in a contract dispute and the miller's daughter as an irresponsible trickster (55). Lexie's reading reveals that she views relationships—including motherhood—as transactional and the role of social institutions as protective of contracts rather than individuals.

When Lexie learns that she is pregnant after inconsistent use of birth control, she at first is charmed by the idea of having a biracial child and hopes to continue the pregnancy. When she hypothetically proposes having a baby to her boyfriend, Brian, his reaction challenges her awareness of racial politics: "You know what people would say? Everybody would say, oh look, another black kid, knocked a girl up before he even graduated high school. More teen parents. Probably going to drop out now. . . . No way I'm going to be that guy" (175–76). Like Lexie, Brian has been the recipient of neoliberal messages, but his responsibilizing has been racialized. Lexie decides to have an abortion, and asks Pearl, the daughter of Mia, an artist who rents from and works as a cleaner for Elena Richardson, to accompany her to the abortion clinic. Her explanation for this choice reveals her implicit, class-based assumption that Pearl is more experienced with and accepting of abortion. Lexie explains obliquely, "I thought you'd understand more. I thought you wouldn't judge" (178). When they arrive at the clinic, Lexie identifies herself using Pearl's name ("Quietly, as if she were ashamed, as if it were really her name" [180]) and uses Pearl's information on her intake form. By way of explanation, Lexie tells Pearl that she fears her prominent name will be recognized. She explains, "'It's just a name. . . . I'm the one in trouble here. Even if they don't know my real name.' She took a deep breath but seemed to deflate further. . . . 'You—you could be anyone'" (181). It is easier for Lexie—and her community—to imagine someone like Pearl, the daughter of a single mother, having an abortion than it is to imagine herself, a Shaker Heights good choice-maker. By shrouding herself in Pearl's low-income identity, Lexie protects her private and public images as a fully responsibilized member of Shaker Heights. Lexie's character is an indexical representation of Shaker Heights, which *Little Fires* satirizes for how its self-identification as progressive blinds it to racial and class-based biopolitics.

In addition to its paratopian setting in 1990s Shaker Heights, *Little Fires* uses the contrasting narrative perspectives of focal characters to expose neoliberalism's biopolitics and disarticulation of feminist solidarity. The narration shifts focus between the perspectives of two white mothers, Elena Richardson and Mia Warren, as they live out their own reproductive choices and those of their daughters. Elena is a native of Shaker Heights—with a "deep taproot"—who only left to attend college at Denison, down the road, where she met her husband Bill, a lawyer. Although she may at one time have had different ambitions—including fantasies of cross-country bohemian travel with a boyfriend—she is now a reporter for a lesser local newspaper, where she submits stories about PTA events that are "nice." Her carefully timed education, career, and family of four children embodies the Shaker Heights philosophy: "In Shaker Heights there was a plan for everything. In fact, the city's motto was . . . 'Most communities just happen; the best are planned': the underlying philosophy being that everything could—and should—be planned out, and that by doing so you could avoid the unseemly, the unpleasant, and the disastrous" (10). Elena, thoroughly responsibilized to plan and time her life meticulously, sees it as her duty to enforce her values through fostering and supporting good choice-making in others.

By contrast, Mia Warren is a "rootless" "vagabond" and a single mother, whose transiency hides a mystery. A successful artist, her arresting photography provides barely enough income to support her and Pearl, but it feeds her soul. Mia has moved dozens of times with her quiet, possibly brilliant, teenage daughter Pearl—named for that infant character in Hawthorne's novel about socially unacceptable sexual and reproductive behaviors. Mia promises Pearl she will settle down, which leads them to Shaker Heights and to renting a house owned by the Richardsons. In addition to holding menial jobs to support herself and Pearl, Mia agrees to become the Richardsons' housekeeper in return for a break on the rent. Compared to Elena Richardson, Mia is a poorly responsibilized mother who nevertheless provides the moral center of the novel's satire.

The contrast between perspectives is heightened when the McCulloughs, friends of the Richardsons, adopt an infant after trying for many years to have children. Mia realizes the infant's mother is her coworker, Bebe, a recent immigrant from China who suffered from postpartum depression and financial ruin after being abandoned by the baby's father. Bebe left her infant daughter in a moment of desperation but has been looking for her ever since, and with the help of Mia, she begins a media and legal campaign to reclaim her child from the McCulloughs. Meanwhile, Mr. Richardson, a lawyer, agrees to represent the interests of the McCulloughs. The story of competing custody claims distracts the Shaker Heights community from coverage of the Clinton-Lewinski scandal and plunges it into a debate over mothers, mothering, and motherhood. Elena Richardson, betrayed by Mia's helping Bebe, seeks revenge against her. She discovers that many years earlier, Mia contracted to be a traditional surrogate for a wealthy couple, and that she reneged on the agreement. Elena does not know that after a promising year in art school, Mia's student loans were cut due to state budget constrictions and becoming a surrogate paid for her education. When Mia realizes she wants the child she is carrying and to whom she is biologically related, she flees to California, where she gives birth to Pearl after telling the intended couple that she miscarried. About Mia's desperate situation as a surrogate gone rogue, Elena reassures herself, "I would never have let myself get into that situation. . . . I would have made better choices" (239). Finally, Elena mistakenly discovers "Pearl's" abortion (really Lexie's) and feels vindicated in her sense that Mia and Pearl do not share the values of Shaker Heights, which are pro-choice but qualified by the belief that abortion should be "safe, legal, and rare." Elena tells Mia to clear out—threatening to expose the secret of Pearl's father if she does not.

The three reproductive storylines about adoption, surrogacy, and abortion, which are narrated by focalization through characters who occupy different social positions, deepen the critique of neoliberal biopolitics by further exposing the prejudices and ignorance of Elena Richardson and Shaker Heights that blind them to stratified reproduction. The reproductive labor of disadvantaged women supports the family-making choices of the privileged class in Shaker Heights and beyond: Mia is a surrogate and housekeeper to the wealthy class, while her daughter Pearl provides indirect cover for Lexie's abortion and Bebe is dispossessed of her daughter to serve the interests of the McCulloughs. While Shaker Heights' dependency on reproductive stratification is satirized in the novel, Mia, Bebe, and even Lexie, whose reproductive lives reflect failed responsibilization, simultaneously invite compassion.

Jessica Norledge argues in her work on ethics and dystopian fictions that a didactic lesson in compassion characterizes many contemporary feminist dystopias, in which, she argues,

> It is by considering the indifference, inaction and disbelief of each of these characters that the reader is invited to check their own apathetic responses to socio-political happenings, and in identifying with the characters, position themselves in relation to textworld events and respond ethically to the worlds of dystopia. (148)

Norledge's assessment of feminist dystopian realism echoes the hopeful observations made by Delistraty about the genre's ability to affect readers. He notes, "Whereas classic dystopian fiction trafficked in the faceless villainy of Big Brother, the best of its modern descendants are able to implicate us in the future so nearly at hand—humanizing antagonists as people making selfish choices in the face of dilemmas at once fantastical and painfully realistic." Additionally, Edgar is optimistic that feminist dystopias present readers with important, hopeful lessons. In the feminist dystopian novels, she claims, "we see self-determination, alliance building, interconnectivity between humans and the environment, and much more" (202–3). These critics express hope about the possibility of feminist dystopias exposing readers to their own inaction and lack of compassion.

While the novel's condemnation of Shaker Heights' self-identification as a utopia may suggest that the novel is anti-utopian, Mia's compassion in the face of Elena's and Lexie's hypocrisy asserts a utopian element. After her abortion, Lexie goes home with Pearl to Mia, who welcomes her with understanding: "She felt nothing but a flood of deep sympathy for Lexie, for the bind she had found herself in, for the pain—both physical and emotional" (241). Mia tells Lexie, "You'll always be sad about this. . . . But it doesn't mean you made the wrong choice. It's just something that you'll have to carry" (245). Readers witness Mia's sense of connection with Lexie's reproductive struggle as arising from her experience as a surrogate; Lexie, subsequently, turns against her family and begins to sympathize with Bebe's struggle to reclaim her daughter. She asks her mother (who was unaware of Lexie's pregnancy and abortion), "If I got pregnant, you'd make me give it up, too?" (267), and Elena replies, "That would never happen. We raised you to have more sense than that" (268).

The novel's dystopic satire of suburban hypocrisy is balanced with the utopian imagery of fire from which the novel takes it name. On the same evening that Mia and Pearl leave town, Bebe, denied custody of May Ling, also returns to China after secretly taking her daughter from the McCulloughs' house. Izzy, Elena's other daughter, who is loyal to Mia and dismayed by her family's values, runs away, but not before symbolically setting fires in each family member's bed, which build to a conflagration that consumes the entire structure. Izzy's action is motivated by her memory of Mia's speech when a devastated Bebe was denied custody of her daughter:

> Like after a prairie fire. I saw one, years ago, when we were in Nebraska. It seems like the end of the world. The earth is all scorched and black and everything green is gone. But after the burning the soil is richer, and new

> things can grow. . . . People are like that, too, you know. They start over. They find a way. (295)

Mia makes this pronouncement at what seems like the darkest moment in the book, without knowing it will inspire a different character in a different situation, implicitly suggesting the text's own allegorical aims. The real utopia of Ng's novel lies not in Shaker Heights but in the "spark" of life that resists neoliberal responsibilization, neoliberal feminism, and their injustices. In the place of neoliberal feminism's self-interest and self-reliance, Ng's novel raises awareness of what Rottenberg calls a politics of "redistribute[ed] vulnerability" (21) based in the knowledge that everyone is vulnerable at different times. Like Rottenberg, *Little Fires* combats the disarticulation of women by rejecting the false security of independence and self-reliance in favor of recognizing vulnerability, mutual dependence, and mutual reliance. Finally, an additional way that Ng's novel combats stratified reproduction lies in its connection of abortion to surrogacy and adoption to equalize its importance with other issues of reproductive freedom that it has overshadowed.

## *The Farm*: Suffering Agency

*The Farm* by Joanne Ramos is a paratopian novel about commercial surrogacy, set in what was, in 2019, the near future. In the US, surrogacy law is unregulated and varies by state, and the debate about whether and how to allow this new technology has not been widely explored. As Sophie Lewis and other scholars have noted, surrogacy has made favorable gains in the popular imagination due to pronatalist ideology, the rhetoric of altruism, and a lack of critical discourse about reproductive labor. Lewis defends surrogates as laborers who merit legal protection by contracts that reflect their interests. She dismisses arguments that surrogacy violates essential motherhood, at the same time as she rejects proponents' arguments that surrogacy should be an unregulated expression of bodily autonomy, like abortion ("my body, my choice"). Lewis contends that these rhetorical positions all fail to identify surrogacy as work and surrogates as workers with rights. Ramos's text offers a fictional exploration of this discussion.

Ramos published *The Farm* during a period when commercial surrogacy was not legal in New York and when the burgeoning international industry was forcing lawmakers to create policy and regulations on the fly. Following the novel's publication, surrogacy for hire became legal in New York in 2021 through the Child-Parent Security Act (CPSA). According to the state Health Department website, "the CPSA establishes protections for gestational surrogates and a simple path to establish legal parental rights for parents who rely on assisted reproductive technology (ART) to have children" ("New York State"). As this statement suggests, surrogacy regulations, policies, and contracts must balance the needs of commissioning parents and surrogates whose rights, health, and interests have not always been well guarded in the wildcat expansion of the global surrogacy market. Ramos's novel is a paratopian warning set just as these policies were being debated.

*The Farm* tells the story of Golden Oaks, a gestational retreat set in upstate New York, which serves the family-making needs of the global elite, whose other reproductive labor needs—baby nursing, childcare, eldercare, and domestic work—are already serviced by an underclass of poor, mostly immigrant and mostly nonwhite women. The novel satirizes how the concept of choice has been taken up by neoliberal discourse as a way of responsibilizing women without protecting their reproductive freedom.

The narration is focalized through the perspectives of four women characters who are part of the surrogacy industry and who occupy different social locations based on race, immigration status, age, and economic class. Evelyn "Ate" Arroyo is a longtime Filipina immigrant and expert baby nurse to Upper West Side families and has numerous side hustles—including being a scout for potential surrogates at Golden Oaks. For forty years, she has sent money home to Bulacan to support her disabled son and other adult children. Ate's younger cousin, Jane Reyes, is Filipina and a more recent immigrant. She is a single mother who becomes a host (surrogate) at Golden Oaks to earn money to support her daughter after leaving her abusive boyfriend. The tragic irony of her situation is that she must leave her daughter with her cousin for the duration of her surrogate pregnancy and stay at Golden Oaks. Mae Yu is the Chinese American director of Golden Oaks. She works for Holloway Clubs—connecting clients, who are members of the global elite, with hosts—and has an MBA from Harvard. She is climbing the corporate ladder while simultaneously planning her lavish wedding and perfectly timed family. Finally, Reagan McCarthy is the daughter of a wealthy but disapproving father who refuses to support her pursuit of a degree in studio art, and so she decides to become a host with the dual goals of becoming financially independent from her father and helping someone make a family. She becomes one of the few and highly coveted white surrogates at Golden Oaks.

As in *Little Fires*, *The Farm*'s dystopian outlook is achieved through heterodiegetic narration that exposes stratified reproduction. The shifts in narration between desperate Ate Arroyo and Jane Reyes, privileged Reagan McCarthy, and savvy, neoliberal Mae Yu allow readers to ascertain the desperation of women who become hosts, the impunity and power of desperate clients, and the industry's sensitivity to markets rather than to human rights. On the surface, Golden Oaks sounds like a luxury vacation for surrogates; however, it becomes clear that the women are prisoners to the contracts they have signed, which reflect the interests of their powerful clients. Lisa, another host, bursts the myth of altruistic surrogacy when she tells Jane that she is a surrogate "only because of the money" and that she is "over the romance of being pregnant" (71). It is Lisa who sneeringly names Golden Oaks "the Farm," observing, "Some Clients don't give a shit about their Host. But most do, because they're obsessed with everything related to their babies. It's the new narcissism. That's the Farm's gig: feeding it, fanning it" (72). Vulnerable hosts are the recipients of elite care not because of their own worth but because of the value placed on their pregnancies. The novel satirizes the clients who are interested in the well-being of hosts only as a reflection of their own virtue or, more importantly, as a concern for their investments. In a memo to her executive team, for example, Mae Yu acknowledges the indifference of clients toward hosts' well-being: "Another agenda item for Monday. Please review attached studies. We discussed this trend at last month's 'big picture' powwow: wealth and empathy inversely correlated, ie: the richer you are, the less empathetic" (242). The clients are absent figures, rarely part of the action, rendering them unsympathetic to the reader.

Other instances of satire are reflected in portrayals of the clients' troubling neo-eugenic values. Commissioning parents have the ability to select the biological material (sperm, eggs) that make a baby and the gestational womb for that baby, creating racialized markets of eggs, sperm, and carriers. In musing about clients' preferences for hosts, for example, Mae notes that conventionally unattractive (including darker-skinned) women are not selected: "The Clients would never say this [that a potential Host is ugly], of course, at least not the American ones. But when paging through the dozens of online Host profiles in Mae's sleek office, Clients would almost invariably skip past someone who looked like Divina and settle on a prettier Filipina with paler skin, or a Polish girl with a fresh-scrubbed face and freckles across her nose, or a slender Trinidadian with glossy eyes and dimples" (41). As paying consumers, clients expect to have their family-making desires satisfied—and not just the desire for a healthy baby but also their preferences for race, gender, abilities, and appearance. These preferences also tend to deselect disability.

The novel further satirizes how the clients, who are able to pay for high-end services, see their family-making investments at Golden Oaks in terms of consumer logic, causing them to perceive the ensuing babies as commodities and the hosts as something less than human. For example, the hosts sign surrogacy contracts that may grant fetal life precedence over their own, which is seen when Jane leaves Golden Oaks without permission to see her infant daughter and is charged with kidnapping the fetus she carries. Hosts must wear tracking devices, agree to be under constant video surveillance, follow scripted diets and disciplined workouts, and limit their outside communication and contact with family and friends—including visits to hospitals, funerals, and their own children. They are trapped by contracts and contexts that have been crafted to privilege the needs of powerful clients over the health, rights, and interests of surrogates. Often, hosts like Jane are in desperate circumstances when they sign. Not only do these characters not negotiate their contracts, they do not even read them (211).

Although the novel is an exploration of the issue of surrogacy, it reveals the not uncommon role of abortion in surrogacy and satirizes how the interests of clients usurp the hosts' bodily sovereignty in these cases. In commercial surrogacy, not only may commissioning parents require the host to abort following prenatal testing, but selective pregnancy reduction following the insertion of multiple embryos is a normal part of the IVF/surrogacy process.[1] In *The Farm,* abortion becomes an issue when the character of Anya, a Polish host, is found to be carrying a pregnancy with a trisomy—a genetic condition that commonly results in Down syndrome. Anya undergoes an amniocentesis and learns the results from the Golden Oaks staff, but whether or not to continue the pregnancy is not her decision to make due to the surrogacy contract she signed. While the discovery about Anya's pregnancy sends Mae into a frenzy of risk–cost analysis and careful communication with a potentially litigious, powerful client, Anya is not consulted about the fate of the pregnancy she carries. The other hosts are told that she miscarries, but they subsequently learn that she was compelled to have an abortion, even though, as another host reports, "she is Catholic"; she explains, "They made her sleep. With gas. Maybe they worry she might get hysterical" (129), suggesting her unwillingness to terminate the pregnancy. Ramos's inclusion of Anya's character is interesting to the discussion of abortion because of the client's decision to terminate but also because of Anya's choicelessness in the matter. Anya and the other hosts may perceive themselves to be neoliberal feminist entrepreneurial actors who choose to become surrogates ("my body, my choice") even as they are contractually denied the ability to abort or not abort the pregnancies they carry.

Ramos's novel satirizes the neoliberal experience of being required to choose when the freedom not to choose is unavailable. Jane and Ate, for example, must provide for their own families, and the surrogacy industry is one of only a few viable opportunities for a living. Twenty-first-century fiction

1. The documentary *Made in Boise* (2019), about commercial surrogacy, reveals how contracts can require surrogates to have abortions at the request of commissioning parents, and conversely, surrogates can be obligated to continue nonviable pregnancies at the behest of clients who are opposed to abortion.

is particularly interested in capturing forms of desperate decision-making, a trope that Jane Elliott calls "suffering agency" in her analysis of "survival tales" by Cormac McCarthy, Kazuo Ishiguro, and Yann Martel. In texts by these authors, characters have had "the necessity for action . . . foisted upon them" in contexts of simultaneous life-and-death decision-making and extreme precarity (Elliott 85). Their choices, she notes, challenge our understanding of agency as always an "index of the political good" (87), as they must endure "the peculiar experience of domination that constitutes suffering agency, in which choice is experienced as a curse without simultaneously becoming a farce" (84). In contrast to prevailing humanist ideas of agency that attribute bad choices to false consciousness, suffering agency instead describes how under neoliberal governance, "choices made for oneself and according to one's interests can still feel both imposed and appalling" (84). Proving the lie of neoliberal feminism, suffering agency reflects how "neoliberal governance is obviously not the neutral framework for free choice it purports to be, but the unacceptability of the choices it offers does not render them illusory or without import—quite the opposite: the choices between gas or childcare, illegal immigration or destitution, prostitution or starvation, are so significant and so painful precisely because they are so unjust" (87). Lacking Reagan's economic and racial privilege, most of the host characters in *The Farm* are in desperate straits and cannot be described as making free choices.

The concept of choice is fundamental to neoliberal feminism's understanding of women's freedom. *The Farm* exposes how the responsibilized choice-making of neoliberal feminism disarticulates feminist solidarity. Mae Yu's character, for example, is alternately sympathetic and the target of the novel's satire of neoliberal feminism. A disciple of Ayn Rand's work and a seeming embodiment of *Lean In* author Sheryl Sandberg, Yu believes that commercial surrogacy reflects and extends the choices and therefore the power of privileged women like herself who rely on it for their family-making and career plans. Mae tells her boss Leon, "If women could outsource their pregnancies, they'd be the ones running the show" (169). When she pitched Golden Oaks to Leon, the executive for Holloway Clubs, a global, luxury hotel enterprise, Mae argued, "What woman do you know who'd trust some random in the middle of nowhere to carry her baby? . . . What you'd want, Leon, if you were a juggernaut—like, say, me—is a Holloway Baby Farm. You know, to make sure your baby got the Holloway treatment while you were off conquering the world" (170). Mae believes that surrogacy also benefits the disadvantaged women who are paid to be surrogates. Her awareness of women's subordination reveals another aspect of neoliberal feminism that acknowledges gender-based inequality but believes this inequality is a personal obstacle to overcome. Rottenberg describes the neoliberal feminist subject as aware of "particular inequalities between men and women," but

> she disavows the social, cultural, and economic forces producing this inequality . . . because she accepts full responsibility for her own well-being and self-care, which is increasingly predicated on crafting a felicitous work-family balance based on a cost-benefit calculus. The neoliberal feminist subject is thus mobilized to convert continued gender inequality from a structural problem into an individual affair. (55)

Arguably, Mae Yu's character is a site of satire in *The Farm*. There is no justice in her belief that women's subordination can be resolved through privileged women's exploitation of the low-paid reproductive labor of disadvantaged women.

Rather than focusing on individual women, however, the novel satirizes the cooptation of the once-feminist concept of choice to responsibilize all women to engage in the invisible and largely unpaid reproductive labor that is required by the neoliberal economy. In *How All Politics Became Reproductive Politics: From Welfare Reform to Foreclosure to Trump*, Laura Briggs defines reproductive labor (also called social reproduction) as the work that is "necessary to the reproduction of human life—not only having and raising children but also feeding people; caring for the sick, the elderly, and those who cannot work; creating safety and shelter; building community and kin relationships; and attending to people's psychic and spiritual well-being" (2). This type of labor has historically been performed by women, unpaid, and associated with the private sphere. It is, Briggs observes, "critical to the production and maintenance of a labor force but outside the formal system of work, wages, and production—. . . the opposite of the public, where politics and economics live" (2). Briggs observes that reproductive labor has intensified in the twenty-first century as a result of neoliberal policies, and women in particular are bearing the brunt of this work: Increasingly, government policies ban or limit access to abortion and birth control; penalize single mothers, incarcerated mothers, mothers with disabilities, and mothers of children with disabilities; delegitimize the motherhood of nonwhite women and immigrant mothers; and hinder queer family-making. These reproductive politics have intimate bearing on how women navigate the politics of reproductive labor. Supporting a family in the twenty-first century—and sometimes simply surviving—make family planning an urgent necessity, but increasingly decisions about whether, when, and how to have and raise children do not always feel like free choices. The situation of constrained choice-making, which is a product of neoliberalism—its philosophy and its effects—is creating a hellish contemporary moment of gross inequity, exploitation, and suffering, which Ramos effectively satirizes in *The Farm.*

## *Red Clocks*: Disarticulation

Leni Zumas's paratopia *Red Clocks* is set in what was a not-so-distant future in the fictional fishing village of Newville, Oregon. In the novel, the federal government has outlawed abortion as well as IVF, established a Pink Wall between the US and Canada to prevent women from seeking reproductive healthcare internationally, and is about to require that adoptions only be permitted to married couples. In 2018, when Zumas's novel was published, many of these policies seemed unlikely if not unthinkable, but this paratopian narrative seems prescient after the *Dobbs* decision in 2022, the Alabama Supreme Court defense of extrauterine personhood rights in 2024, and the Southern Baptist Convention vote to outlaw IVF in 2024. The physical setting for the novel is similarly threatening: dark forests, a powerfully menacing sea, and vertiginous views and dangerous plummets that alternately inspire and jeopardize the characters. The inhabitants of Newville are isolated, insular, and fearful: The villagers suspect a witch has cursed the waters and damaged the fishing industry. One character observes that Newville is "where humans are less, nature is more" (20). If humans generally are diminished in this novel, women are doubly reduced.

Similar to the other novels discussed in this chapter, *Red Clocks* uses third-person, removed, heterodiegetic narration. The narration is focalized through four women characters, who are unnamed and identified instead by title: the biographer, the wife, the mender, the daughter. The replacement of proper names with roles reminds readers that women are often dehumanized and generalized through their socially defined roles. Gin, identified by the narrator as "the mender," is shunned by the community as the witch, and lives and forages in the forest while providing clandestine herbal remedies and abortions to the village's women. Antisocial and arrogant, Gin reflects a timeless resistance to the laws of men as she practices her version of female healthcare. The direct descendent of a colonial-era witch, Gin is the daughter of a negligent mother and was abandoned years before to live with her aunt, who teaches Gin how to use herbs and traditional medicine. Gin provides aid to the women of Newville, but this does not earn her their gratitude (65, 70–72). Mattie, "the daughter," is a recently transferred high school student and is infatuated with her first sexual partner (a boy who dumps her after a month of sex, dismissing her as his "September girl"). She is reeling, additionally, because her best friend, Yasmine, who is coded African American (196) and who repeatedly challenges Mattie to reflect on her racial privilege, has been removed to a youth correctional facility for having an abortion (74). When Mattie learns that she herself is pregnant, she struggles to find an abortion without telling her adoptive parents, who are politically opposed to abortion (50). In addition to her plans to attend college for marine biology (122), Mattie's reasons for not having a baby include not wanting to put a child up for adoption who may wonder about their mother's decision the way Mattie wonders about her biological mother (123).

Two additional characters are paired as foils: Ro and Susan. Ro(berta), "the biographer," is a recent transplant to the area, recovering from the tragic loss of her beloved brother to heroin addiction. She supplements her job as a high school history teacher with her passion project: writing a biography of a nineteenth-century female polar explorer. Desperate to have a baby, although not uncritical of this desire, Ro pursues intrauterine insemination, only to learn that she has polycystic ovarian syndrome (PCOS) and is unlikely to conceive. Legally blocked from pursuing IVF as well as adoption, her chances of becoming a mother are dwindling, causing her to resent Susan, for whom family-making appears to have been easy. Susan, "the wife," is a former lawyer who has opted to be a stay-at-home wife and mother to her two beloved young children, but she is dissatisfied with her immature husband and the dull routines of housekeeping and childcare (25). In the face of her husband's refusal to attend marriage counseling and her inability to ask for a divorce, she alternates between fantasies of driving over a cliff (58) or having an affair (140). Symbolically, she sympathizes with an injured animal she imagines seeing in the road that seems doomed (55). Initially in the novel, all four focal characters are locked into their own worlds and problems and are fearful and resentful of other women.

Like *Little Fires* and *The Farm, Red Clocks* offers a portrait of the disarticulation of women by class, age, and race. The women are not only isolated, but initially in the narrative they are turned against each other. Gin is a loner outcast who holds the townspeople in contempt for their misunderstandings of her. Mattie fears that Yasmine's fate—meted out by punitive adults—will be her own (106). Ro and Susan circle each other warily, each suspecting the other's contempt for her life and family-making choices. When Susan attempts to support Ro during her sessions of hormone injections in preparation for artificial insemination, for example, Ro remarks to herself, "Susan has a knack for commiserating with suffering she hasn't suffered. Which doesn't feel like compassion or empathy, but why not? Here is a friend trying to connect over a trouble. But the effort itself is insulting, the biographer decides" (67). Later Ro reflects about the women like herself who are impacted by the reproductive policies: "If not for her comparing mind and covetous heart, the biographer would feel compassion for her fellow criminals" (267). Gender-based oppression simmers below and alongside the appearance that women have choices about education, career, and family, but the women are disconnected from each other as they struggle to make choices in circumstances that are increasingly punitive and dangerous. It becomes clear how the anti-woman policies in the novel reflect the disarticulation of neoliberal feminism: Women are facing their own challenges and are preoccupied with their choices, but there is no solidarity. Ro admits to herself, "While she hid out in Newville, they closed the clinics and defunded Planned Parenthood and amended the Constitution. She watched on her computer screen" (268), while Mattie, in a different context, reflects on how injustices occur daily in broad daylight: "The Bystander effect. Nobody helping a crime victim when other people are around because everyone thinks someone else is going to do it" (286).

Each woman in *Red Clocks* knows and fears judgment by other women, which keeps them isolated from each other, and yet they are all connected. These connections are made visible to the reader but are ironically obscured from the characters. Years before Gin surrendered a child for adoption, who, it turns out, is Mattie, although she does not know this (232). In her search for an abortion, Mattie visits Gin, but before she can return to the mender for the necessary herbs, Gin is arrested for medical malpractice and put in jail (153, 163). Mattie turns to her favorite teacher for help in traveling to an underground abortion service (301), not knowing that Ro desperately wants to ask Mattie to give her the baby (218). Ro has also sought reproductive care from Gin, who accurately detects Ro's PCOS, which was overlooked by her swaggering male doctor who instead prescribed her a series of doomed and expensive fertility treatments (47). Ro's antagonist, Susan, who has employed Mattie as a babysitter (27), recognizes during her failed seduction of the high school soccer coach that his cousin—a woman in an abusive marriage—is the principal's wife, Dolores, who is also Gin's lover/accuser (293). In addition to these connections, the novel suggests alliances between the women in their struggles with the biopolitical regime of the novel. Gin, Ro, and Mattie challenge the expectation that sex and reproduction take place within the institution of marriage, and Gin's lesbianism further challenges heteronormative reproductive politics. Susan challenges the idea that women might be happy in the normative arrangement, and Gin helps a woman in an abusive marriage (307). Gin helps women all along, and Ro takes Mattie to have an abortion, while Susan is roused into practicing law again by the arrest of and false accusations against Gin.

As the narrative focus shifts between these four women, readers come to appreciate how their stories are intricately intertwined and the role that secrecy and silence has played in their disarticulation. This theme is reenforced by the absent presence of the characters of Jasmine (imprisoned for having an abortion); Ro's biographical subject, Eivor Minervurdottir (whose lifework is misattributed to a male author); Gin's formidable female ancestors (a tradition of healers maligned as witches); and Dolores Fivey (a domestic abuse survivor). In addition to the silence of absent characters, the narrative style of withholding the connections between the characters provides an allegory about the political damage of keeping seemingly private experiences of oppression a secret. *Red Clocks* reveals that not only is silence damaging to individual women's integrity, but it also contributes to women's oppression. In *On Lies, Secrets, and Silence: Selected Prose 1966–1978,* Adrienne Rich observes that "lying is done with words, and also with silence" (186), suggesting that staying silent in the face of injustice is a dishonorable offense to the self and to others. In the foreword to the collection, Rich similarly explains that "the entire history of women's struggle for self-determination has been muffled in silence over and over. . . . This is one of the ways in which women's work has been made to seem sporadic, errant, orphaned of any tradition of its own" (11). Silence is coerced through threats of violence and through shame, two weapons that have served to keep women in line under heteronormative patriarchy. In response to a culture of heterosexist misogyny, Rich argues for the radical potential of women's honesty about forms of violence and about their love for each other:

> It is also crucial that we understand lesbian/feminism in the deepest, most radical sense: as that love for ourselves and other women, that commitment to the freedom of all of us, which transcends the category of "sexual preference" and the issue of civil rights, to become a politics of asking women's questions, demanding a world in which the integrity of all women—not a chosen few—shall be honored and validated in every aspect of culture. (17)

Rich calls for women to value their integrity and honesty to confront heteronormative social distortion: "I want to reiterate that when we talk about women and honor, or women and lying, we speak within the context of male lying, the lies of the powerful, the lie as false source of power" (190). *Red Clocks* similarly makes a utopian call for women to value each other and to be honest.

As with the other two novels discussed in this chapter, *Red Clocks* offers utopian hope to its readers. This hope is communicated in the final chapters through overcoming secrecy and isolation as it pertains to abortion. Abortion is a subtheme that touches each woman: Mattie wants one, Gin provides them, Ro takes Mattie to have one, Susan helps to free the woman who provides them. Hope is represented through Ro's taking Mattie to a *term[ination] house* called the Polyphonte Collective, in Portland. Seemingly alluding to the pre-*Roe* underground abortion service Jane, Polyphonte provides clandestine but safe illegal abortions (314–19). After their shared experience, Mattie is freed to plan for her education (310) and Ro resolves to finish her biography and engage in more activism (318). Additionally, hope is reflected in the freeing of Gin, who returns to providing herbal abortions to the village women and to watching over Mattie from a distance (338), and by Susan, who decides to separate from her husband (328).

Significantly, the final chapter, focalized through Mattie's perspective, is just her letter to Yasmine (343), responding with new awareness to her friend's chastising comment, "You are a very ignorant white girl" (311). Mattie now recognizes by comparison to her own difficult but successful abortion experience how Yasmine's racial identity shaped her experience. Yasmine, despite being the daughter of a state legislator, knew that her teenage pregnancy would be viewed socially as the fulfillment of a racial stereotype: "I'm not giving them another reason to think I'm not smart" (311). Similarly, Mattie now recognizes that racial politics played a role not only in her inability to obtain an abortion and her subsequent self-abortion but also in the disproportionately punitive sentence she received when her illegal action was discovered. Mattie recognizes that her ability to receive an (illegal) abortion is facilitated by her racial privilege, exemplified through the support of Ro, who is also white. In the letter Mattie apologizes to Yasmine for calling for help when Yasmine began to hemorrhage, thereby exposing her friend's secret, explaining her fear that her friend was going to die. She concludes the letter by confessing, "Also: I had a procedure something happened" (343), and concludes by asking, "Can we be friends again?" *Red Clocks* concludes with the hopeful message that disarticulation—between women of different ages, classes, and races—can be overcome.

## Conclusion

Rather than being interpreted as failed examples of the dystopian genre, the novels by Ng, Ramos, and Zumas reflect revisions to the genre that enable the exploration of abortion and biopolitics in the twenty-first century. The paratopian settings of these novels, which are temporally located in the near past and near future, accomplish an estrangement of the reader that is not temporal. Instead, an estranging distance is created by the use of heterodiegetic narration that reveals the simultaneous and varied perspectives of characters who occupy different social locations. The use of heterodiegetic narration in these novels has two important effects. First, it reveals the threat to feminist solidarity posed by neoliberal feminism's embrace of self-reliance and independence as values. The women characters who uncritically adopt these values in *Little Fires Everywhere, The Farm,* and *Red Clocks* are revealed through the narration to be self-interested and isolated, to their detriment and sometimes endangerment. These novels explore and resist their disarticulation. Secondly, the heterodiegetic narration raises awareness of women's intersectional identities and experiences of stratified reproduction. Through this narrative technique, women characters are revealed in their social location and subsequently show how one woman's choices can depend upon another woman's choicelessness.

These paratopian novels contribute to an understanding of ordinary abortion—the commonplace, undramatic access to abortion and its permeation of the US imaginary—in three ways. They reveal how abortion has become so ordinary in US society that its outlawing seems nightmarish. Additionally, they expose how the ubiquitous rhetoric of choice has been co-opted by the responsibilization of women. It no longer serves the purpose of defending abortion access. Finally, these novels emphasize that abortion cannot be thought about in isolation from other issues of reproductive freedom. Abortion is no more or less extraordinary than other reproductive healthcare. For too long it has distracted attention from or transferred polarization to other sites of reproductive injustice. These novels deftly weave abortion into a reproductive healthcare web.

Finally, the paratopias discussed in this chapter reject the anti-utopian impulse that has dismayed critics of many contemporary feminist dystopias. Through the satirization of neoliberal feminism, as well as allegorical lessons in gaining compassion to resist stratified reproduction and neoliberal disarticulation, these novels offer hope and fuel for answering Joffe's question about "what kind of America" is desired.

CONCLUSION

# Picking Each Other Up

Abortion is ordinary. Early twenty-first-century writing by women depicts terminating a pregnancy as an undramatic, even normal, part of reproductive healthcare and family-making. While individual decisions to control fertility and reproduction are momentous, abortions themselves are common, safe, widely supported, and widely beneficial. The Supreme Court decision in *Dobbs v. Jackson*, however, intensifies the politicization and stigmatization that redramatizes legal access. The literature examined in this book counters antiabortion rhetoric and ideology by normalizing abortion, centering the perspectives of women, framing the fetus in terms of loss rather than rights, condemning violence against patients and providers, and elucidating the relationship between abortion and mothering, mothers, and motherhood.

How do we resist the backlash against women, feminism, and reproductive freedom that *Dobbs* represents? How do we pick ourselves up from this loss? These are the questions on the minds of people who support reproductive freedom—the majority of Americans. Trying to answer this question is daunting as additional assaults on reproductive freedom are announced regularly in the media, including congressional blocks to support for IVF access (Walsh); legal decisions favoring fetal personhood (Sussman); proposals to redirect Title X funding away from birth control and toward incentivizing childbearing (Kitchener and Stolberg); proposals to incinerate contraceptives no longer headed to West African countries after the defunding of the US Agency for International Development, or USAID (Smialek and Nolen); threats against providers sending abortion medication across state lines (Belluk and Cochrane); and the Trump administration's sympathetic reception of rhetoric extending the dehumanizing rollback of women's rights (French). How do we resist the fallout from *Dobbs* and recuperate lost ground?

Alongside providing abortion, the work of defending abortion continues on numerous fronts (legal, medical, and popular). Writing—reporting, literature, and scholarship—plays a role in this advocacy. Activist writer Jessica Valenti, for example, in her Substack newsletter, *Abortion, Every Day,* provides reliable, up-to-the-minute reporting on reproductive health policy news. Krystale Littlejohn and Rickie Solinger's timely edited volume, *Fighting Mad,* provides inspiring, boots-on-the-ground accounts by providers and activists. Marlene Fried and Loretta Ross's *Abortion and Reproductive Justice: An Essential Guide for Resistance* articulates how a reproductive justice lens can reframe understandings of abortion and promote new forms of advocacy. These texts respond to the need to stay informed about the dizzying array of attacks on reproductive freedoms, and they reveal the community of legal, medical, and religious representatives and organizations that are fighting for reproductive freedom.

Twenty-first-century literature by women has a role in this fight. For the past two and a half decades, writers have been taking the temperature of antiabortion political and religious discourse, and they have responded in their poetry, fiction, memoirs, and other writings with depictions of ordinary abortion. Literature is not more or less important than other forms of advocacy, but it is often overlooked in the rush to present statistical data for public debates. In her well-known work "Poetry Is Not a Luxury," Audre Lorde describes the subtle and vital role that literature plays in social movements. In this essay, Lorde addresses fellow activists to dispute the idea that literature's only purpose is to divert or entertain readers; instead, she argues, poetry expresses the fears and hopes that underpin social change. Art is where we express socially muted perspectives, articulate critique, and imagine justice. This emotional language is the foundation for action and the guiding star of activism. Above all, art is where community is found, reflected, and made. Sara Ahmed echoes Lorde's celebration of literary expression when she points out that "books make communities" (17). The communities that are built through literature are how we affirm experience, dispute misinformation, and lessen stigma. Community is how we connect, educate each other, and raise consciousness. Community is how "the two Americas" that Guttmacher identified ("Tale") come together.

Communities are needed to protect reproductive freedom. Carole Joffe argues that in order for a brick-and-mortar abortion clinic to survive, "you need a community with you" (*Dispatches* 21), a directive that is true of abortion defense more broadly. Joffe recounts her experience observing patients in abortion clinic recovery rooms, and her disappointment at "the palpable sense of isolation and corresponding lack of solidarity with other abortion patients" (116). She uses this scene to illustrate the Guttmacher Institute's report observing that privileged women experience declining rates of unplanned pregnancy at the same time as disadvantaged women's rates are increasing ("Tale"). The divisions between women who have abortions and women who do not, as well as the divisions between women having abortions, need to be bridged.

The fight for reproductive freedom can no longer be about abortion alone. As Joffe notes, "abortion serves as a 'brilliant distraction' from a serious confrontation with the full range of reproductive health needs of American women" (*Dispatches* 141). Some of the issues calling out for nuanced discussion, according to Joffe, include incarcerated women's rights to abortion and dignity during childbirth, the failure of the private market to meet the demand for child- and eldercare, the need for universal preventative healthcare, issues of teen sexuality and sexual education, and the right of poor women to have children. Much feminist work on behalf of these issues gets "derailed" (144) by a focus on defending abortion. Katie Watson similarly observes that public debates have used abortion to obscure other discussions. She groups these debates into two categories: "Trojan horses" are policy debates that pretend to be about "women's welfare" but are really disguised assertions of fetal rights, and "Russian dolls" are debates about abortion that mask conversations about the desired social role of women (175). The literature examined in this book reflects how abortion is not isolated from other issues of reproductive justice or from the struggle for gender-based equality. When the issues facing a broader community are included, the fight for reproductive freedom is strengthened.

Twenty-first-century literature also tells the cultural and collective histories of struggle that provide models and inspiration for speaking out against injustice and defending reproductive freedom, including abortion. Many twenty-first-century African American women writers, for example, use historical poetry and fiction to look to the past to comment on today's reproductive landscape. This literature has been fostered by the research of medical historians like Linda Villarosa and Harriet Washington, whose *Medical Apartheid* revised received knowledge about Marion Sims, the so-called father of gynecology who experimented on enslaved women. The poetry of Bettina Judd (*Patient: Poems*, 2014), Dominique Chistina (*Anarcha Speaks*, 2018), and Kwoya Fagin Maples (*Mend*, 2018) gives voice to these women and reflects historical research, imagination, and social commentary on the present crisis in black maternal health (Dudley; Vrana). Similarly, some works of twenty-first-century fiction by African American women writers use historical settings to raise awareness of reproductive health concerns. For example, Morgan Jerkins's *Caul Baby* (set in 1990s Harlem), Dolen Perkins-Valdez's *Take My Hand* (set in the 1970s), and Sadeqa Johnson's *The House of Eve* (set in the 1950s) listen to the archives for voices that have been omitted and are motivated by concern for present reproductive injustices. Although futuristic, reproductive dystopias by and about white women have received perhaps undue popular attention in the media, historical literature by African American women recounting past and present reproductive injustices enriches the communal conversation in defense of reproductive freedom.

As this book has argued, literature offers space for new forms, language, and rhetoric for exploring and expressing the epistemology of abortion. Of course, to accurately depict ordinary abortion, there is a need for more depictions of mothers having abortions and of medication abortions, but it seems reasonable to expect that these will come. Equally important is the way that literature has identified and raised awareness of what Katie Watson calls the "web of beneficiaries" of legal abortion. Literature is one way of connecting this web or community of people who have not had abortions themselves but who have benefited from someone else having one. To recognize oneself in a work of literature about ordinary abortion is to join a community defending reproductive freedom. It is, as Sara Ahmed says about books and community, "how we pick each other up" (1).

# ACKNOWLEDGMENTS

This book is dedicated to the memory of Mary Helen Spaulding Thompson (1897–1930), my paternal grandmother, who died from sepsis following an abortion. My father was only four years old, and he grew up without his mother, moving between the homes of different relatives. Her story was an open secret in my family and has served as a reminder for me of why abortion needs to be safe, accessible, and destigmatized. The ripples of this loss wash against the shores of this book.

I am indebted to numerous people who made this book possible, and as is customary, I start with apologies to anyone whose support, labor, and encouragement I overlook here. I would like to express my gratitude, even if I am unable to name everyone.

My gratitude and appreciation to The Ohio State University Press, and to my editor, Kristen Elias Rowley, and assistant editor, Rebecca Bostock, whose guidance and support have been invaluable. My sincere thanks to them for seeing this book through the process to completion. I am truly grateful to Rebecca S. Bender for her work copyediting the manuscript and to Elizabeth Zaleski for her assistance in the final stages of the book's preparation. I also wish to thank the anonymous reviewers for their generous feedback and enthusiasm. Words cannot adequately convey my gratitude for their expertise, patience, and insight. Special thanks to Carmen Winant for permission to use her compelling work for the cover and in the introduction for this book. The cover image is taken from *The Last Safe Abortion* when it was on exhibit at the Bemis Center for Contemporary Arts in 2025 (used with permission from Carmen Winant and Bemis Center; photography by Colin Conces). My thanks to Susan Zucker for designing the cover.

A part of chapter 4 was originally published as "Bad Mothers and Staunch Feminists: Selective Abortion in Mommy-Memoirs by Ayelet Waldman and Martha Beck" in *Mothering and Abortion,* which was edited by Heather Jackson and Jessica Shaw and published by Demeter Press in 2022.

I would like to thank the staff and patients at the clinics where I've worked: Planned Parenthood, Woman Care, and the Center for Choice. This book would not have been possible without the experiences I had in these spaces and the people I met there. I learned so much about feminism, patient care, and activism from them.

Numerous colleagues and friends have made this book possible. I wish to thank my feminist collaborators, Jeannie Ludlow and Modhumita Roy, for countless papers, panels, and conversations over meals and coffees. I thank my James Madison University accountability writing group: Becca Howes-Mischel, Danielle Price, Melinda Adams, Heidi Pennington, and Holly Yanacek—how wonderful it has been to share time if not space with you regularly. I also thank my JMU friends for game night, a welcome weekly respite: Dawn Goode, Debali Mookerjea-Leonard, Spencer Leonard, Laura Henigman, and Bill Lawton. My thanks also to the pickleball group (Betty, Elaine, Eileen, Ronda, Sandy, and Mary Helen); your gracious sportsmanship, encouragement on and off the court, and good humor provided me with a much-needed outlet. I am grateful to Carol Yoder—once my running partner, now my coffee partner—thanks for keeping pace with me. Thank you, thank you, to Antonia for keeping house and making writing possible. Thanks also to Karl and my brothers, Jay and Darrell, for their support during the writing of this book and the loss of our (step)mother.

I wish to acknowledge the generous support of the JMU College of Arts and Letters for a Summer Research Grant and the JMU English Department for providing funding for manuscript preparation. In the English Department office, I thank Rose Gray for her kindness and assistance with all things bureaucratic.

# WORKS CITED

"Abortion Bans in Cases of Sex or Race Selection or Genetic Anomaly." The Guttmacher Institute, https://www.guttmacher.org/state-policy/explore/abortion-bans-cases-sex-or-race-selection-or-genetic-anomaly. Accessed 13 Jan. 2024.

"Abortion in the United States." The Guttmacher Institute, Apr. 2025, https://www.guttmacher.org/fact-sheet/induced-abortion-united-states.

"Abortion Onscreen." Advancing New Studies in Reproductive Health, University of California San Francisco, https://www.ansirh.org/research/ongoing/abortion-onscreen. Accessed 30 Aug. 2024.

Ahmed, Sara. *Living a Feminist Life*. Duke UP, 2017.

Alderman, Naomi. *The Power*. Back Bay Books, 2019.

Allison, Dorothy. *Bastard out of Carolina*. Dutton, 1992.

Andrews, Becca. *No Choice: The Destruction of Roe v. Wade and the Fight to Protect a Fundamental American Right*. PublicAffairs, 2022.

Apter, Emily. "'Women's Time' in Theory." *Differences: A Journal of Feminist Cultural Studies*, vol. 21, no. 1, 2010, pp. 1–18, https://doi.org/10.1215/10407391-2009-013.

Arcana, Judith. "What If Your Mother." *What If Your Mother*, Chicory Blue Press, 2005, p. 7.

Arey, Whitney. "Real Men Love Babies: Protest Speech and Masculinity at Abortion Clinics in the Southern United States." *Norma: International Journal for Masculinity Studies*, vol. 15, nos. 3–4, 2020, pp. 205–20.

"As Many As 16% of People Having Abortions Do Not Identify as Heterosexual Women: LGBTQ+ Patients Face Overlapping Barriers to Care." The Guttmacher Institute, June 2023, https://www.guttmacher.org/2023/06/many-16-people-having-abortions-do-not-identify-heterosexual-women.

Aslami, Zarena. "The Work/Life Equation: Notes Toward De-Privatizing the Maternal." *The Politics of Reproduction: Adoption, Abortion, and Surrogacy in the Age of Neoliberalism*, edited by Modhumita Roy and Mary Thompson, Ohio State UP, 2019, pp. 101–18.

Atwood, Margaret. *The Testaments*. Nan A. Talese / Doubleday, 2019.

Balsamo, Anne. *Technologies of the Gendered Body: Reading Cyborg Women*. Duke UP, 1996.

Bechdel, Alison. *Are You My Mother? A Comic Drama*. Houghton, Mifflin, Harcourt, 2012.

Bechdel, Alison. *Fun Home: A Family Tragicomic.* Houghton, Mifflin, Harcourt, 2006.

Beck, Martha. *Expecting Adam: A True Story of Birth, Rebirth, and Everyday Magic.* Three Rivers Books, 1999.

Beizer, Janet. *Thinking Through the Mothers: Reimagining Women's Biographies.* Cornell UP, 2008.

Belkin, Lisa. "The Opt-Out Revolution." *The New York Times Magazine,* 26 Oct. 2003, https://www.nytimes.com/2003/10/26/magazine/the-opt-out-revolution.html.

Bell, Virginia, Christine Maul Rice, and Ignatius Valentine Aloysius, editors. *The Overturning Anthology: Writers Respond.* Independently published, 2025.

Belluk, Pam, and Emily Cochrane. "New York Doctor Indicted in Louisiana for Sending Abortion Pills There." *The New York Times,* 31 Jan. 2025.

Bérubé, Michael. *Life as We Know It: A Father, a Family, and an Exceptional Child.* Knopf, 1998.

Boonstra, Heather D., Rachel Benson Gold, Cory L. Richards, and Lawrence B. Finer. *Abortion in Women's Lives.* The Guttmacher Institute, 2006.

Bordo, Susan. *Unbearable Weight: Feminism, Western Culture, and the Body.* U of California P, 1993.

Boss, Pauline. *Ambiguous Loss: Learning to Live with Unresolved Grief.* Harvard UP, 2000.

Boudreau, Brenda, and Kelli Maloy. *Abortion in Popular Culture: A Call to Action.* Bloomsbury, 2023.

Briggs, Laura. *How All Politics Became Reproductive Politics: From Welfare Reform to Foreclosure to Trump.* U of California P, 2017.

Brooks, Gwendolyn. "The Mother." *Selected Poems,* Harper and Row, 1963, pp. 4–5.

Brown, Karen McCarthy. "Fundamentalism and the Control of Women." *Fundamentalism and Gender,* edited by John Stratton Hawley, Oxford Academic, 1994, pp. 175–201, https://doi.org/10.1093/oso/9780195082616.003.0007.

Brown, Wendy. *Edgework: Critical Essays on Knowledge and Politics.* Princeton UP, 2005.

Brown, Wendy. *Undoing the Demos: Neoliberalism's Stealth Revolution.* Zone Books, 2015.

Butler, Judith. *Frames of War: When Is Life Grievable?* Verso, 2009.

Capo, Beth Widmaier, and Laura Lazzari, editors. *The Palgrave Handbook of Reproductive Justice and Literature.* Palgrave Macmillan, 2022.

Castle, Terry. *The Apparitional Lesbian: Female Homosexuality and Modern Culture.* Columbia UP, 1993.

Chan, Jessamine. *The School for Good Mothers.* 37 Ink, 2022.

Christina, Dominique. *Anarcha Speaks: A History in Poems.* Beacon Press, 2018.

Cockrill, Kate, U. D. Upadhyay, J. Turan, and D. Greene Foster. "The Stigma of Having an Abortion: Development of a Scale and Characteristics of Women Experiencing Abortion Stigma." *Perspectives on Sexual and Reproductive Health,* vol. 45, no. 2, June 2013, pp. 79–88.

Coleman, Christian A. "Interview: Louise Erdrich." *Lightspeed Magazine,* no. 91, Dec. 2017, https://www.lightspeedmagazine.com/nonfiction/interview-louise-erdrich/.

Cooke, Jennifer. *Contemporary Feminist Life-Writing: The New Audacity.* Cambridge UP, 2020.

Cowan, Sarah K. "Enacted Abortion Stigma in the United States." *Social Science and Medicine,* vol. 177, Mar. 2017, pp. 259–68.

Crum, Maddie. "When Your Feminist Dystopia Becomes a Work of Realism: Speaking with Leni Zumas About Her New Novel, *Red Clocks.*" *Literary Hub,* 18 Jan. 2018, https://lithub.com/when-your-feminist-dystopia-becomes-a-work-of-realism/.

de Beauvoir, Simone. "The Manifesto of the 343 Sluts." *Le Nouvel Observateur,* 5 Apr. 1971, https://web.archive.org/web/20160611012314/https://manifesto343.wordpress.com/.

Delistraty, Cody. "Welcome to Dystopian Realist Fiction." *Vulture,* 8 Jan. 2019, https://www.vulture.com/2019/01/modern-feminist-dystopia-is-basically-realism.html.

Deutscher, Penelope. *Foucault's Futures: A Critique of Reproductive Reason,* Columbia UP, 2017.

Diaz, Jaclyn, Koko Nakajima, and Nick Underwood. "Seven Persistent Claims About Abortion, Fact-Checked." *NPR,* 24 June 2022, https://www.npr.org/2022/05/06/1096676197/7-persistent-claims-about-abortion-fact-checked.

Dillon, Sarah. "Who Rules the World?: Reimagining the Contemporary Feminist Dystopia." *The New Feminist Literary Studies,* edited by Jennifer Cooke, Cambridge UP, 2020, pp. 169–81.

Doan, Alesha. *Opposition and Intimidation: The Abortion Wars and Strategies of Political Harassment.* U of Michigan P, 2007.

Doan, Alesha, and Shoshana Erlich. "'Reimagining What Might Have Been': A Comparative Analysis of Abortion and Maternal Regret." *Maternal Regret: Resistances, Renunciations, and Reflections,* edited by Andrea O'Reilly, Demeter Press, 2022, pp. 57–74.

"Dobbs Got It Wrong." The Center for Reproductive Rights, 23 June 2025, https://reproductiverights.org/resources/analysis-dobbs-got-it-wrong/.

Donnar, Glen. "Remasculinizing American Cinema Post-9/11." *Troubling Masculinities: Terror, Gender, and Monstrous Others in American Film Post-9/11.* UP of Mississippi, 2020.

Douglas, Susan J., and Meredith W. Michaels. *The Mommy Myth: The Idealization of Motherhood and How It Has Undermined All Women.* Free Press, 2004.

Doyle, Jennifer. "Blind Spots and Failed Performance: Abortion, Feminism, and Queer Theory." *Qui Parle,* vol. 18, no. 1, fall/winter 2009, pp. 25–52, https://doi.org/10.5250/quiparle.18.1.25.

Dreweke, Joerg. "Promiscuity Propaganda: Access to Information and Services Does Not Lead to Increases in Sexual Activity." *Guttmacher Policy Review,* vol. 22, 11 June 2019, https://www.guttmacher.org/gpr/2019/06/promiscuity-propaganda-access-information-and-services-does-not-lead-increases-sexual.

Dubow, Sara. *Ourselves Unborn: A History of the Fetus in Modern America.* Oxford UP, 2011.

Dudley, Rachel. "The Role of Feminist Health Humanities Scholarship and Black Women's Artistry in Re-Shaping the Origin Narrative of Modern, U.S. Gynecology." *Humanities,* vol. 10, no. 58, 23 Mar. 2021, https://doi.org/10.3390/h10010058.

Duggan, Lisa. *The Twilight of Equality? Neoliberalism, Cultural Politics, and the Attack on Democracy.* Beacon Press, 2004.

Edelman, Lee. *No Future: Queer Theory and the Death Drive.* Duke UP, 2004.

Edgar, Eir-Anne E. "Re-Conceiving the World: Dystopia and Reproductive Justice." *The Palgrave Handbook of Reproductive Justice and Literature,* edited by Beth Widmaier Capo and Laura Lazzari, Palgrave Macmillan, 2022, pp. 199–217.

Elliott, Jane. "Suffering Agency: Imagining Neoliberal Personhood in North America and Britain." *Social Text,* vol. 31, no. 2, summer 2013, pp. 83–101.

Engélibert, Jean-Paul. "Dystopian Fictions and Contemporary Fears." *The Routledge Handbook of Fiction and Belief,* edited by Alison James, Akihiro Kubo, and Francoise Lavocat, Routledge, 2024, pp. 311–22.

Erdrich, Louise. *The Future Home of the Living God.* Harper, 2017.

Ernaux, Annie. *Happening.* Seven Stories Press, 2000.

Felski, Rita. "Telling Time in Feminist Theory." *Tulsa Studies in Women's Literature,* vol. 21, no. 1, 2002, pp. 21–28.

Finch, Annie, editor. *Choice Words: Writers on Abortion.* Haymarket Books, 2022.

Fissell, Mary. *Pushback: The 2,500-Year Fight to Thwart Women by Restricting Abortion.* Seal Press, 2025.

Flanagan, Caitlin. "Losing the 'Rare' in 'Safe, Legal, and Rare.'" *The Atlantic,* 12 Dec. 2019, https://www.theatlantic.com/ideas/archive/2019/12/the-brilliance-of-safe-legal-and-rare/603151/.

Foster, Diana Greene. *The Turnaway Study: Ten Years, a Thousand Women, and the Consequences of Having—or Being Denied—an Abortion.* Scribner, 2021.

Fraser, Nancy. "From Progressive Neoliberalism to Trump—and Beyond." *American Affairs,* vol. 1, no. 4, winter 2017, https://americanaffairsjournal.org/2017/11/progressive-neoliberalism-trump-beyond/.

French, David. "This Evangelical Pastor Wants to Replace Women's Right to Vote." *The New York Times,* 14 Aug. 2025.

Fried, Marlene Gerber. *From Abortion to Reproductive Freedom: Transforming a Movement.* South End Press, 1990.

Fried, Marlene, and Loretta Ross. *Abortion and Reproductive Justice: An Essential Guide for Resistance.* U of California P, 2025.

Gallagher, Katie, Davina Porock, and Alison Edgley. "The Concept of 'Nursing' in the Abortion Services." *Journal of Advanced Nursing,* vol. 66, no. 4, Apr. 2010, pp. 849–57. *National Library of Medicine,* https://pubmed.ncbi.nlm.nih.gov/20423372/.

Garland Thomson, Rosemarie. *Extraordinary Bodies: Figuring Physical Disability in American Culture and Literature.* Columbia UP, 1996.

Gerdts, Caitlin, Anna Rupani, Kamyon Conner, and Sachiko Ragosta. "Collapse of the Abortion Care Infrastructure: There Aren't Enough Hands to Fill the Gaps." *American Journal of Public Health,* vol. 112, no. 9, Sept. 2022, pp. 1278–79.

Gilbert, Sophie. "The Remarkable Rise of the Feminist Dystopia." *The Atlantic,* 4 Oct. 2018, https://www.theatlantic.com/entertainment/archive/2018/10/feminist-speculative-fiction-2018/571822/.

Gilligan, Carol. *In a Different Voice: Psychological Theory and Women's Development.* Harvard UP, 1993.

Ginsburg, Faye D. *Contested Lives: The Abortion Debate in an American Community.* U of California P, 1989.

Giric, Stefanija. "Strange Bedfellows: Anti-Abortion and Disability Rights Advocacy." *Journal of Law and the Biosciences,* vol. 3, no. 3, 7 Dec. 2016, pp. 736–42. *National Library of Medicine,* https://pubmed.ncbi.nlm.nih.gov/28852553/.

Gordon, Avery. *Ghostly Matters: Haunting and the Sociological Imagination.* U of Minnesota P, 1997.

Haigh, Jennifer. *Mercy Street.* Ecco, 2022.

Hartouni, Valerie. "Fetal Exposures: Abortion Politics and the Optics of Allusion." *Camera Obscura,* vol. 10, no. 2(29), 1 May 1992, pp. 130–49, https://doi.org/10.1215/02705346-10-2_29-130.

Hess, Amanda. "When an Abortion Story Is Told as a Caper, Thriller, or Farce." *The New York Times,* 27 June 2022.

Hirsch, Marianne. *The Mother/Daughter Plot: Narrative, Psychoanalysis, Feminism.* Indiana UP, 1989.

Holland, Jennifer. *Tiny You: A Western History of the Antiabortion Movement.* U of California P, 2020.

"How the Issue of Abortion Touches Americans Personally." Pew Research Center, 6 May 2022, https://www.pewresearch.org/religion/2022/05/06/how-the-issue-of-abortion-touches-americans-personally/.

Hubbard, Ruth. "Abortion and Disability: Who Should and Who Should Not Inhabit the World?" *The Disability Studies Reader,* edited by Lennard Davis, 2nd ed., Routledge, 2006, pp. 93–103.

Huet de Guerville, Diana. "Birth Is Not Always Best: Confessions of an Unwanted Child." *Abortion Under Attack: Women on the Challenges Facing Choice,* edited by Krista Jacob, Seal Press, 2006, pp. 111–18.

Hume, Angela. *Deep Care: The Radical Activists Who Provided Abortions, Defied the Law, and Fought to Keep Clinics Open.* AK Press, 2023.

Hurst, Rachel Alpha Johnston, editor. *Representing Abortion.* Routledge, 2021.

Hyde, Elisabeth. *The Abortionist's Daughter.* Vintage, 2006.

"Induced Abortion in the United States." The Guttmacher Institute, Sept. 2019, https://www.guttmacher.org/sites/default/files/factsheet/fb_induced_abortion.pdf.

Jackson, Heather, and Jessica Shaw, editors. *Abortion and Mothering: Research, Stories, and Artistic Expressions.* Demeter Press, 2021.

Jacob, Krista, editor. *Abortion Under Attack: Women on the Challenges Facing Choice.* Seal Press, 2006.

Jacobson, Mireille, and Heather Royer. "Aftershocks: The Impact of Clinic Violence on Abortion Services." *American Economic Journal: Applied Economics,* vol. 3, no. 1, Jan. 2011, pp. 189–223, https://pubs.aeaweb.org/doi/10.1257/app.3.1.189.

Jameson, Frederic. "Future City." *New Left Review,* vol. 21, May 2003, pp. 65–79.

Jarman, Michelle. "Relations of Abortion: Crip Approaches to Reproductive Justice." *Feminist Formations,* vol. 27, no. 1, spring 2015, pp. 46–66.

Jerkins, Morgan. *Caul Baby.* Harper, 2021.

Joffe, Carole. *Dispatches from the Abortion Wars: The Cost of Fanaticism to Doctors, Patients, and the Rest of Us.* Beacon Press, 2009.

Joffe, Carole. "The Politicization of Abortion and the Evolution of Abortion Counseling." *American Journal of Public Health,* vol. 103, no. 1, 2013, pp. 57–65.

Johnson, Barbara. *A World of Difference.* Johns Hopkins UP, 1987.

Johnson, Sadeqa. *The House of Eve.* Simon and Schuster Paperbacks, 2023.

Johnston, Margaret (Peg). "We Have Met the Enemy, and She/He Is Us." *Abortion Under Attack: Women on the Challenges Facing Choice,* edited by Krista Jacob, Seal Press, 2006, pp. 75–86.

Jones, Rachel K., Candace Gibson, and Jesse Philbin. "The Number of Brick-and-Mortar Abortion Clinics Drops, as US Abortion Rate Rises: New Data Underscore the Need for Policies that Support Providers." The Guttmacher Institute, June 2024, https://www.guttmacher.org/report/abortion-clinics-united-states-2020-2024.

Jordan, Hillary. *When She Woke.* Algonquin Books, 2011.

Judd, Bettina. *Patient: Poems.* Black Lawrence Press, 2014.

Kann, Claudia, Daniel Ebanks, Jacob Morrier, and R. Michael Alvarez. "Persuadable Voters Decided the 2022 Midterm: Abortion Rights and Issues-Based Frameworks for Studying Election Outcomes." *PloS One,* vol. 19, no. 1, e0294047, 19 Jan. 2024, https://doi.org/10.1371/journal.pone.0294047.

Kaplan, Carla. "Reading Feminist Readings: Recuperative Reading and the Silent Heroine of Feminist Criticism." *Listening to Silences: New Essays in Feminist Criticism,* edited by Elaine Hedges and Shelley Fisher Fishkin, Oxford UP, 1994, pp. 168–94.

Kemball, Anna. "Biocolonial Pregnancies: Louise Erdrich's *Future Home of the Living God.*" *Medical Humanities,* vol. 48, no. 2, June 2022, pp. 159–68.

Kennedy, Tanya Ann. *Reclaiming Time: The Transformative Politics of Feminist Temporalities.* SUNY Press, 2023.

Kimmel, Michael. *Angry White Men: American Masculinity at the End of an Era.* Nation Books, 2013.

Kimmel, Michael S., Jeff Hearn, and Robert W. Connell, editors. *Handbook of Studies on Men and Masculinities.* Thousand Oaks, 2005.

Kingston, Maxine Hong. *The Woman Warrior: Memoirs of a Girlhood Among Ghosts.* Vintage International, 1975.

Kirsch, Adam. *The Modern Element: Essays on Contemporary Poetry.* W. W. Norton, 2008.

Kitchener, Caroline, and Sheryl Gay Stolberg. "Under Trump, a New Focus for a Birth Control Program: Helping Women Get Pregnant." *The New York Times,* 18 July 2025.

Kivity, Sara, and Sivia Barnoy. "Women's Intention to Abort a Fetus Diagnosed with a Genetic Disease: Results from Israel, Cyprus, and Germany." *Sage Open,* 3 July 2023, https://doi.org/10.1177/21582440231184974.

Kristeva, Julia. "Women's Time." Translated by Alice Jardine and Harry Blake. *Signs,* vol. 7, no. 1, autumn, 1979, pp. 13–35.

Kumeh, Titania. "Mother Sues Anti-Choice Groups Behind Billboards." *Mother Jones,* 29 Apr. 2011, https://www.motherjones.com/politics/2011/04/mother-sues-anti-abortion-groups-billboards/.

Lamott, Anne. *Operating Instructions: A Journal of My Son's First Year.* 1993. Anchor, 2005.

Latimer, Heather. *Reproductive Acts: Sexual Politics in North American Fiction and Film.* McGill-Queen's UP, 2013.

Lewis, Sophie. *Full Surrogacy Now: Feminism Against Family.* Verso Books, 2021.

Lindo, Jason M., Caitlin Knowles Myers, Andrea Schlosser, and Scott Cunningham. "How Far Is Too Far? New Evidence on Abortion Clinic Closures, Access, and Abortions." *Journal of Human Resources,* vol. 55, no. 4, pp. 1137–60.

Littlejohn, Krystale, and Rickie Solinger, editors. *Fighting Mad: Resisting the End of "Roe v. Wade."* U of California P, 2024.

Lorde, Audre. "Poetry Is Not a Luxury." *Sister, Outsider: Essays and Speeches by Audre Lorde,* Crossing Press, 1984, pp. 36–39.

Ludlow, Jeannie. "It's A~~-Boy!-~~Borted: Fetal Bodies, Graphic Abortion, and the Option to Look." In *Representing Abortion,* edited by Rachel Alpha Johnston Hurst, Routledge, 2021, pp. 49–60.

Ludlow, Jeannie. "Love and Goodness: Toward a New Abortion Politics." *Feminist Studies,* vol. 38, no. 2, 2012, pp. 474–83.

Ludlow, Jeannie. "Sometimes, It's a Child *and* a Choice: Toward an Embodied Abortion Praxis." *Feminist Formations,* vol. 20, no. 1, spring 2008, pp. 26–50.

Luker, Kristin. *Abortion and the Politics of Motherhood.* U of California P, 1984.

Luker, Kristin. *Dubious Conceptions.* Harvard UP, 1996.

Mackintosh, Sophie. *Blue Ticket.* Doubleday, 2020.

Mackintosh, Sophie. *The Water Cure.* Anchor, 2019.

Malin, Jo. *The Voice of the Mother: Embedded Maternal Narratives in Twentieth-Century Women's Autobiographies.* Southern Illinois UP, 2000.

Maples, Kwoya Fagin. *Mend.* UP of Kentucky, 2018.

McGowan, Michelle L., Alison H. Norris, and Danielle Bessett. "Care Churn—Why Keeping Clinic Doors Open Isn't Enough to Ensure Access to Abortion." *The New England Journal of Medicine,* vol. 383, no. 6, 5 Aug. 2020, pp. 508–10.

McIntosh, Peggy. "White Privilege: Unpacking the Invisible Knapsack." *White Privilege: Essential Readings on the Other Side of Racism,* edited by Paula Rothenberg, Worth Publishers, 2002, pp. 97–102.

McKenzie, Lindsay. "In Courses on Dystopian Literature, Everybody Wants to Talk About Trump." *The Chronicle of Higher Education,* 7 Feb. 2017, https://www.chronicle.com/article/In-Courses-on-Dystopian/239125.

McKinney, Claire. "A Good Abortion Is a Tragic Abortion: Fit Motherhood and Disability Stigma." *Hypatia,* vol. 34, no. 2, 2019, pp. 266–85, https://doi.org/10.1111/hypa.12461.

McRobbie, Angela. *The Aftermath of Feminism: Gender, Culture and Social Change.* Sage Publications, 2008.

"Medication Abortions Accounted for 63% of All US Abortions in 2023, an Increase from 53% in 2020." The Guttmacher Institute, 19 Mar. 2024. https://www.guttmacher.org/news-release/2024/medication-abortions-accounted-63-all-us-abortions-2023-increase-53-2020.

Melendez, Tanya. "How TV Lied About Abortion." *Vox,* 14 Oct. 2021, https://www.vox.com/culture/22715333/tv-abortion-plot-storyline-lies.

Messud, Claire. "'The Woman Upstairs': A Saga of Anger and Thwarted Ambition." Interview by Terry Gross. *Fresh Air,* NPR, 9 May 2013.

Miller-Idriss, Cynthia. *Man Up: The New Misogyny & the Rise of Violent Extremism.* Princeton UP, 2025.

Mitchell, Kaye. "This Is Not a Memoir: Feminist Writings from Life." *The New Feminist Literary Studies,* edited by Jennifer Cooke, Cambridge UP, 2020, pp. 208–21.

Mitchell, David. *The Biopolitics of Disability: Neoliberalism, Ablenationalism, and Peripheral Embodiment.* U of Michigan P, 2015.

Moore, Honor. *A Termination.* A Public Space Books, 2024.

Morgan, Lynn M., and Meredith Wilson Michaels. *Fetal Subjects, Feminist Positions.* U of Pennsylvania P, 1999.

Mottley, Leila. *The Girls Who Grew Big.* Knopf, 2025.

*Ms.* editors. "From the Vault: We Have Had Abortions (Spring 1972)." *Ms.* magazine, 1 Mar. 2024, https://msmagazine.com/2024/03/01/we-have-had-abortions-petition-spring-1972/.

Muñoz, José Esteban. *Cruising Utopia: The Then and There of Queer Futurity.* NYU P, 2009.

"The New York State Child-Parent Security Act: Gestational Surrogacy." New York State Department of Health, May 2025, https://health.ny.gov/community/pregnancy/surrogacy/.

Ng, Celeste. *Little Fires Everywhere.* Penguin Press, 2017.

Nixon, Rob. *Slow Violence and the Environmentalism of the Poor.* Harvard UP, 2013.

Norledge, Jessica. "Dystopian Ethics." *The Language of Dystopia,* Springer, 2022, pp. 125–55.

Oaks, Laurie. *Giving Up Baby: Safe Haven Laws, Motherhood, and Reproductive Justice.* NYU P, 2015.

Oates, Joyce Carol. *A Book of American Martyrs.* Ecco, 2017.

O'Connell, Katie. "We Need to Talk About Disability as a Reproductive Justice Issue." *Radical Reproductive Justice: Foundations, Theory, Practice, Critique,* edited by Loretta Ross, Lynn Roberts, Erika Derkas, Whitney Peoples, and Pamela Bridgewater, Feminist Press, 2017, pp. 302–5.

*October Baby.* Directed by Andrew Erwin and Jon Erwin, Gravitas Ventures, Providence Films, 2011.

Office of Justice Programs. "Statistical Briefing Book." *Office of Juvenile Justice and Delinquency Prevention Programs,* https://www.ojjdp.gov/ojstatbb//population/qa01303.asp?qaDate=2020.

Olds, Sharon. "The End." 1984. *The Dead and the Living,* Knopf, 1992, p. 26.

Olds, Sharon. "I Go Back to May 1937." *Strike Sparks: Selected Poems, 1980–2002,* Knopf, 2004, p. 44.

Olds, Sharon. "The Unborn." *Satan Says,* U of Pittsburgh P, 1980, p. 54.

Olds, Sharon. *The Unswept Room,* Knopf, 2002.

Olsen, Tillie. *Silences.* Delacorte Press, 1978.

O'Reilly, Andrea, editor. *Maternal Regret: Resistances, Renunciations, and Reflections.* Demeter Press, 2022.

O'Reilly, Andrea. "The Motherhood Memoir and the 'New Momism': Biting the Hand That Feeds You." *In (M)other Words: Writings on Mothering and Motherhood, 2009–2024,* Demeter Press, 2024, pp. 479–90.

O'Reilly, Andrea. "'Out of Bounds': Maternal Regret and the Reframing of Normative Motherhood." *Maternal Regret: Resistances, Renunciations, and Reflections,* edited by Andrea O'Reilly, Demeter Press, 2022, pp. 21–35.

Ostalska, Katarzyna, and Tomasz Fisiak. *The Postworld In-Between Utopia and Dystopia: Intersectional, Feminist, and Non-Binary Approaches in 21st-Century Speculative Literature and Culture.* Routledge, 2021.

"Our History." Abortion Conversation Projects. https://www.abortionconversationprojects.org/our-history. Accessed 20 Aug. 2025.

Parvulescu, Anca. "Reproduction and Queer Theory: Between Lee Edelman's *No Future* and J. M. Coetzee's *Slow Man.*" *PMLA,* no. 132, no. 1, Jan. 2017, pp. 86–100.

Perkins-Valdez, Dolen. *Take My Hand.* Berkeley, 2022.

Petchesky, Rosalind. *Abortion and Woman's Choice: The State, Sexuality, and Reproductive Freedom.* Northeastern UP, 1990.

Phelan, Peggy. "White Men and Pregnancy: Discovering the Body to Be Rescued." *Acting Out: Feminist Performances,* edited by Lynda Hart and Peggy Phelan, U of Michigan P, 1993, pp. 383–401.

Piazza, Alessandro, and Grace L. Augustine. "Nevertheless, They Persisted: How Patterns of Opposition and Support Shaped the Survival of U.S. Abortion Clinics." *The Journal of Management Studies,* vol. 59, no. 8, Dec. 2022, pp. 2124–53, https://doi.org/10.1111/joms.12865.

Picoult, Jodi. *A Spark of Light: A Novel.* Ballantine Books, 2018.

Piepmeier, Alison. "Choosing to Have a Child with Down Syndrome." *Motherlode* blog, *The New York Times,* 2 Mar. 2022, https://archive.nytimes.com/parenting.blogs.nytimes.com/2012/03/02/choosing-to-have-a-child-with-down-syndrome/.

Piepmeier, Alison. "Outlawing Abortion Won't Help Children with Down Syndrome." *Motherlode* blog, *The New York Times,* 1 Apr. 2013, https://archive.nytimes.com/parenting.blogs.nytimes.com/2013/04/01/outlawing-abortion-wont-help-children-with-down-syndrome/.

Pinto, Samantha. "After Choice, After Justice? Race, Reproduction, and the Uncertain Futures of Feminist Political Desire." *The International Journal of Human Rights,* vol. 28, nos. 8–9, 2024, 1526–46, https://doi.org/10.1080/13642987.2023.2241018.

Pollitt, Katha. *Pro: Reclaiming Abortion Rights.* Picador, 2014.

Poovey, Mary. "The Abortion Question and the Death of Man." *Feminists Theorize the Political,* edited by Judith Butler and Joan Wallach Scott, Routledge, 1992, pp. 252–61.

Pridemore, William Alex, and Joshua D. Freilich. "The Impact of State Laws Protecting Abortion Clinics and Reproductive Rights on Crimes Against Abortion Providers: Deterrence, Backlash, or Neither?" *Law and Human Behavior,* vol. 31, no. 6, Dec. 2007, pp. 611–27, https://psycnet.apa.org/doi/10.1007/s10979-006-9078-0.

"Protecting Access to Clinics." The Guttmacher Institute, 14 Mar. 2016, https://www.guttmacher.org/state-laws-and-policies-status.

"Public Opinion on Abortion." Pew Research Center, 12 June 2025, https://www.pewresearch.org/religion/fact-sheet/public-opinion-on-abortion/.

Ramos, Joanne. *The Farm.* Random House, 2019.

Randall, D'Arcy. "Adrienne Rich's 'Clearing in the Imagination': *Of Woman Born* as Literary Criticism." *From Motherhood to Mothering: The Legacy of Adrienne Rich's "Of Woman Born,"* edited by Andrea O'Reilly, State U of New York P, 2004, pp. 195–208.

Rankin, Lauren. *Bodies on the Line: At the Front Lines of the Fight to Protect Abortion in America.* Counterpoint, 2022.

Rapp, Emily. "I Would Have Saved My Son from His Suffering." *Slate,* 27 Feb. 2012, https://slate.com/human-interest/2012/02/rick-santorum-and-prenatal-testing-i-would-have-saved-my-son-from-his-suffering.html.

Rapp, Rayna. *Testing Women, Testing the Fetus: The Social Impact of Amniocentesis in America.* Routledge, 1999.

Reagan, Leslie. *When Abortion Was a Crime: Women, Medicine, and Law in the United States, 1867–1973.* U of California P, 2022.

Rich, Adrienne. *Of Woman Born: Motherhood as Experience and Institution.* 1976. W. W. Norton, 1995.

Rich, Adrienne. *On Lies, Secrets, and Silence: Selected Prose 1966–1978.* 1979. Norton, 1995.

Rich, Adrienne. "To A Poet." *The Dream of a Common Language: Poems 1974–1977,* W. W. Norton, 1978, p. 15.

Robinson, Kim Stanley. "Dystopias Now." *Commune,* no. 5, winter 2020, https://communemag.com/dystopias-now/.

Rochlin, Martin[?]. "The Heterosexual Questionnaire." Jan. 1972. Unpublished.

Rogers, Jane. *The Testament of Jessie Lamb.* Harper Perennial, 2012.

Ross, Loretta, Lynn Roberts, Erika Derkas, Whitney Peoples, and Pamela Bridgewater, editors. *Radical Reproductive Justice: Foundations, Theory, Practice, Critique.* Feminist Press, 2017.

Ross, Loretta J., and Rickie Solinger. *Reproductive Justice: An Introduction.* U of California P, 2017.

Rottenberg, Catherine. *The Rise of Neoliberal Feminism.* Oxford UP, 2018.

Roy, Modhumita, and Mary Thompson. *The Politics of Reproduction: Adoption, Abortion, and Surrogacy in the Age of Neoliberalism.* Ohio State UP, 2019.

Saletan, William. *Bearing Right: How Conservatives Won the Abortion War.* U of California P, 2004.

Saloman, Randi. "'Unsolved Problems': Essayism, Counterfactuals, and the Futures of *A Room of One's Own.*" *Tulsa Studies in Women's Literature,* vol. 32, no. 1, spring 2013, pp. 53–73.

Saxton, Martha. "Disability Rights and Selective Abortion." *The Disability Studies Reader,* edited by Lennard Davis, 2nd ed., Routledge, 2006, pp. 105–16.

Schechtman, Arielle. "Abortion Protesting." *The Georgetown Journal of Gender and the Law,* vol. 24, no. 22, 2023, pp. 253–64.

Scheidler, Joseph. *Closed: 99 Ways to Stop Abortion.* Tan Books & Pub, 1985.

Schoen, Johanna, editor. *Abortion Care as Moral Work: Ethical Considerations of Maternal and Fetal Bodies.* Rutgers UP, 2022, https://doi.org/10.2307/j.ctv2vr9dmn.

Sherman, Renee Bracey. "Dear Politicians, Put 'Safe, Legal, and Rare' in the Dustbin." *Rewire,* 5 Apr. 2021, https://rewirenewsgroup.com/2021/04/05/dear-politicians-put-safe-legal-and-rare-in-the-dustbin/.

*Shout Your Abortion.* https://shoutyourabortion.com/.

*The Silent Scream.* Directed by Bernard Nathanson, American Portrait Films, 1984.

Silliman, Jael, Marlene Gerber Fried, Loretta Ross, and Elena R. Gutiérrez. *Undivided Rights: Women of Color Organize for Reproductive Justice.* Haymarket Books, 2004.

Simonds, Wendy. *Abortion at Work: Ideology and Practice at a Feminist Clinic.* Rutgers UP, 1996.

Smialek, Jeanna, and Stephanie Nolen. "As Trump Administration Plans to Burn Contraceptives, Europeans Are Alarmed." *The New York Times,* 7 Aug. 2025.

Solinger, Rickie. *Abortion Wars: A Half Century of Struggle, 1950–2000.* U of California P, 1998.

Solinger, Rickie. *Beggars and Choosers: How the Politics of Choice Shapes Adoption, Abortion, and Welfare in the United States.* Hill and Wang, 2001.

Solinger, Rickie. *Pregnancy and Power: A Short History of Reproductive Politics in America.* New York UP, 2005.

Solinger, Rickie. *Wake Up Little Susie: Single Pregnancy and Race Before "Roe v. Wade."* Routledge, 2000.

Stabile, Carol. "Shooting the Mother: Fetal Photography and the Politics of Disappearance." *Camera Obscura,* vol. 10, no. 1, 1992, pp. 178–205.

Steinem, Gloria. "If Men Could Menstruate." *Ms.* magazine, Oct. 1978. Rpt. In *Women's Reproductive Health,* vol. 6, no. 3, 2019, pp. 151–52, https://doi.org/10.1080/23293691.2019.1619050.

Strayed, Cheryl. *Wild: From Lost to Found on the Pacific Crest Trail.* Vintage, 2012.

Sullivan, Mairead. "Kill Daddy: Reproduction, Futurity, and the Survival of the Radical Feminist." *WSQ: Women's Studies Quarterly,* vol. 44, nos. 1–2, 2016, pp. 268–82.

Sussman, Anna Louie. "Are Embryos Property? Human Life? Neither?" *The New York Times,* 8 Apr. 2025.

Swernoff, Arielle. "Knowing Someone Who Has Had an Abortion Correlates with Increased Support for Abortion Rights." Data for Progress, 8 Sept. 2022, https://www.dataforprogress.org/memos/knowing-someone-who-has-had-an-abortion-correlates-with-increased-support-for-abortion-rights.

"A Tale of Two Americas." The Guttmacher Institute, 4 May 2006, https://www.guttmacher.org/news-release/2006/tale-two-americas-women.

Thompson, Mary. "Believing Is Seeing Is Believing: Elective Abortion and Visual Closure." *Interrogating Reproductive Loss: Feminist Writings on Abortion, Miscarriage, and Stillbirth,* edited by Emily R. M. Lind and Angie Deveau, Demeter Press, 2017, pp. 61–74.

Thompson, Mary. "Impossible Motherhood: Irene Vilar's Misconceived Metaphors." *Frontiers: A Journal of Women's Studies,* vol. 35, no. 1, 2014, pp. 132–59.

Thompson, Mary. "Resistance and Reproductive Justice Post-*Dobbs*: An Interview with Rickie Solinger." *Modern Language Studies,* 2025, https://www.mlsjrnl.com/resistance.

Thompson, Mary. "The Mommy Memoir." *The Microgenre: A Quick Look at Small Culture,* edited by Molly O'Donnell and Anne Stevens, Bloomsbury, 2020, pp. 147–53.

Tierce, Merritt. "The Abortion I Didn't Have." *The New York Times Magazine,* 5 Dec. 2021.

Todd, Sarah, Andrew Parnaby, and Todd MacCullum. "Secrecy and Safety: Healthcare Workers in Abortion Clinics." *Labour/Travail,* vol. 50, 2002, pp. 401–6.

Twine, France Winddance. *Outsourcing the Womb: Race, Class, and Gestational Surrogacy in a Gestational Market.* Routledge, 2011.

"Unintended Pregnancy and Abortion in North America." Global and Regional Estimates of Unintended Pregnancy and Abortion series, The Guttmacher Institute, Mar. 2022, https://www.guttmacher.org/fact-sheet/unintended-pregnancy-and-abortion-northern-america.

"Updated Methodology to Estimate Overall and Unintended Pregnancy Rates in the United States Data Evaluation and Methods Research." Centers for Disease Control and Prevention National Center for Health Statistics. Series 2, no. 201, Apr. 2023, https://www.cdc.gov/nchs/data/series/sr_02/sr02-201.pdf.

Valenti, Jessica. *Abortion: Our Bodies, Their Lies, and the Truths We Use to Win.* Crown, 2024.

Vilar, Irene. *Impossible Motherhood: Testimony of an Abortion Addict.* Other Press, 2009.

"Violence Against Providers Continues to Rise Following Roe Reversal, New Report Finds." National Abortion Federation, 11 May 2023, https://prochoice.org/violence-against-abortion-providers-continues-to-rise-following-roe-reversal-new-report-finds/.

Vrana, Laura. "Monuments and Moral Memory: Contemporary Black Women's Experimental Poetics of Reproductive Justice." *Tulsa Studies in Women's Literature,* vol. 43, no. 1, 2024, pp. 91–116.

Waldman, Ayelet. *Bad Mother: A Chronicle of Maternal Crimes, Minor Calamities, and Occasional Moments of Grace.* Anchor Books, 2006.

Walker, Alice. *In Search of Our Mother's Gardens: Womanist Prose.* Harcourt, Brace and Jovanovich, 1983.

Walker, Rebecca. *Baby Love: Choosing Motherhood After a Lifetime of Ambivalence.* Riverhead Books, 2007.

Walsh, Deirdre. "Senate Republicans Block IVF Bill, As Democrats Elevate Issue Ahead of November Elections." *NPR,* 17 Sept. 2024, https://www.npr.org/2024/09/17/g-s1-23414/senate-republicans-block-ivf-legislation.

Watson, Katie. *Scarlet A: The Ethics, Law, and Politics of Ordinary Abortion.* Oxford UP, 2018.

Weingarten, Karen. *Abortion in the American Imagination: Before Life and Choice, 1880–1940.* Rutgers UP, 2014.

Weingarten, Karen. "It's All Biopolitics: A Feminist Response to the Disability Rights Critique of Prenatal Testing." *The Politics of Reproduction: Adoption, Abortion, and Surrogacy in the Age of Neoliberalism,* edited by Modhumita Roy and Mary Thompson, Ohio State UP, 2019, pp. 155–71.

Weinstock, Jeffrey. "Introduction: The Spectral Turn." *The Spectralities Reader: Ghosts and Haunting in Contemporary Cultural Theory,* edited by Maria del Pilar Blanco and Esther Peeren, Bloomsbury, 2013, pp. 61–68.

Weitz, Tracey Ann. "Rethinking the Mantra that Abortion Should Be 'Safe, Legal, and Rare.'" *Journal of Women's History,* vol. 22, no. 3, fall 2010, pp. 161–72.

Weitz, Tracey Ann, and Kate Cockrill. "Abortion Clinic Patients' Opinions About Obtaining Abortions from General Women's Health Care Providers." *Patient Education and Counseling,* vol. 81, no. 3, 2010, pp. 409–14.

Williams, Raymond. "Culture Is Ordinary (1958)." *Raymond Williams on Culture & Society: Essential Writings,* edited by Jim McGuigan, SAGE, 2014, pp. 1–18, https://doi.org/10.4135/9781473914766.n1.

Williams, Terry Tempest. *Refuge: An Unnatural History of Family and Place.* Vintage, 1991.

Williams, Terry Tempest. *When Women Were Birds: Fifty-Four Meditations on Voice.* Picador, 2012.

Wilt, Judith. *Abortion, Choice, and Contemporary Fiction: The Armageddon of the Maternal Instinct.* U of Chicago P, 1990.

Wirken, Bart, Dennis G. Barten, Harald De Cauwer, Luc Mortelmans, Derrick Tin, and Gregory Ciottone. "Terrorist Attacks Against Health Care Targets That Provide Abortion Services." *Prehospital and Disaster Medicine,* vol. 38, no. 3, 2023, pp. 409–14, https://doi.org/10.1017/S1049023X23000341.

Wolkomir, Michelle, and Jennifer Powers. "Helping Women and Protecting the Self: The Challenge of Emotional Labor in an Abortion Clinic." *Qualitative Sociology,* vol. 30, 2007, pp. 153–69, https://link.springer.com/article/10.1007/s11133-006-9056-3.

Woolf, Virginia. *A Room of One's Own.* Hogarth Press, 1929.

Yamanaka, Lois-Ann. *Father of the Four Passages.* Farrar, Straus and Giroux, 2001.

Zhang, Sarah. "The Last Children of Down Syndrome." *The Atlantic,* Dec. 2020, pp. 43–55.

Ziegler, Mary. *Abortion and the Law in America.* Cambridge UP, 2020.

Ziegler, Mary. "The Disability Politics of Abortion." *Utah Law Review,* no. 3, article 4, 2017, pp. 587–631, https://dc.law.utah.edu/ulr/vol2017/iss3/4/.

Zumas, Leni. *Red Clocks.* Back Bay Books, 2018.

# INDEX

www.ingramcontent.com/pod-product-compliance
Lightning Source LLC
LaVergne TN
LVHW100921110826
845155LV00035B/41

* 9 7 8 0 8 1 4 2 5 9 8 7 0 *